KU-720-859

RUSSIAN TANKS
OF WORLD WAR II
STALIN'S ARMOURED MIGHT

RUSSIAN TANKS
OF WORLD WAR II
STALIN'S ARMOURED MIGHT

TIM BEAN AND WILL FOWLER

Ian Allan

60th
ANNIVERSARY

First published 2002

ISBN 0-7110-2898-2

All rights reserved. No part of this book may be reproduced or transmitted
in any form or by any means, electronic or mechanical, including photocopying, recording or by any
information storage and retrieval system, without permission from the the Publisher in writing.

Copyright © 2002 Amber Books Ltd

Published by Ian Allan Publishing
an imprint of Ian Allan Publishing Ltd, Hersham, Surrey KT12 4RG.

Code: 0204/B

Editorial and design by
Amber Books Ltd
Bradley's Close
74–77 White Lion Street
London N1 9PF

Project Editor: Charles Catton
Editor: Vanessa Unwin
Design: Brian Rust
Picture Research: Lisa Wren and TRH Pictures

Printed and bound in Italy by: Eurolitho S.p.A., Cesano Boscone (MI)

20085881
MORAY COUNCIL
LIBRARIES &
INFORMATION SERVICES
940.54217

CONTENTS

1. THE BIRTH OF THE TANK ARM   6

2. DEEP BATTLE   22

3. LIGHT TANKS   40

4. MEDIUM AND FAST TANKS   60

5. THE T-34   74

6. HEAVY TANKS   106

7. LATE WAR TANKS   126

8. FOREIGN TANKS IN SOVIET SERVICE   144

9. STALIN'S LEGACY   156

APPENDIX   169

INDEX   174

CHAPTER ONE

THE BIRTH OF THE TANK ARM

The Soviet tank arm was based on British and French built tanks captured from White Russian forces and technology from secret overseas purchases. However many of those responsible for creating this new force disappeared during Stalin's purge of the army in the 1930s.

On 25 April 1945 the powerful First, Second, Third and Fourth Guards tank armies of the Red Army consolidated the iron grip they had thrown around Berlin, capital of Adolf Hitler's Thousand Year Reich. Ten days previously, these Soviet armoured forces, totalling 4000 tanks and self-propelled guns (out of a total 6250 available for the assault on Berlin), had broken out of their bridgeheads across the River Oder, 80–144km (50–90 miles) east of the German capital. The First and Second Guards tank armies of Marshal G.K. Zhukov's 1st Byelorussian Front battered their way slowly forwards, at great cost, towards the outskirts of Berlin through the prepared German defence lines. In stark contrast, the Third Guards and Fourth tank armies of

LEFT: The French Renault FT-17 was the first tank to have a centrally mounted turret armed with a 37mm (1.46in) gun or machine gun. Large numbers were built for service in World War I and those sent to Russia to assist the White Russians were eventually captured by the Red Army.

RUSSIAN TANKS

ABOVE: A British Royal Artillery sergeant passes a French Renault FT-17 on the Western Front near the close of World War I. Over 3000 were built during the war, and the FT-17 was still in use in the French Army in World War II – captured tanks were used by the German garrison in the street- fighting in Paris in 1944. The tank was built to be used *en masse*, and little thought had gone into repair and maintenance of the vehicle, a feature that would serve to make them very unreliable in action.

Marshal I.V. Konev's 1st Ukrainian Front, striking from further south, encountered less resistance and rapidly sliced through German positions racing their rivals to Berlin. However, despite the desire to beat each other into Berlin by 26 April, all four élite tank armies – supported by 464,000 troops and 12,700 artillery pieces – were actually in position for the final assault into the heart of Berlin.

VICTORY OF THE ARMOURED GUARDS

Under the cover of the massed fires of the Soviet artillery corps ringing Berlin, the forces of the 1st Byelorussian and 2nd Ukrainian fronts moved against the last lines of German resistance in a gruelling battle of attrition among the shattered buildings. Operating in narrow streets where close-quarters battle dominated the style of fighting, Soviet tanks could move forwards only with infantry and engineer support. The Red Army utilized a variety of tanks in the Battle of Berlin. Most prominent in the Soviet inventory was the T-34/85 medium tanks designed for high-speed mobile operations in open terrain, but still flexible enough to

adapt to the requirements of urban warfare. Direct support for the infantry generally came from the well-armoured and well-gunned KV-1-s and IS-2 heavy tanks as well as a range of self-propelled guns. The most powerful of the SP guns was the ISU-152, whose large 152mm (5.9in) gun proved devastating in clearing houses at short range, quite often by simply blowing whole floors out with a single shell.

As Soviet armour pushed into the centre of Berlin, Red Army officers demonstrated their ability to adapt their forces and tactics to the peculiarities of fighting in built-up areas. The most serious threat came not from German armour, but from the hand-held infantry antitank weapon, the *Panzerfaust*. To counter this threat, Soviet tank officers broke down their large combat units, such as brigades, into small combat groups of three tanks. As one tank moved along the left-hand side of the street, another secured the right, whilst the third, slightly to the rear, moved down the centre. The tank on the left fired at targets – or suspected targets – to its right, whilst that on the right engaged the left-hand side of the street: both were covered by the centre tank. Behind this advance guard were usually 10 other vehicles acting as a reserve to replace losses amongst the front three vehicles.

Supported by tanks operating in this manner, by 5 May forward infantry elements of General V.I. Chuikov's Eighth Guards Army successfully assaulted the Reichstag, the German Parliament. Although the fighting in Berlin continued for several more days, and the war did not officially end until 9 May 1945, hoisting the Red Flag over the Reichstag on the Communist May Day holiday symbolized the Red Army's defeat of Nazi Germany and its finest hour. At the forefront of victory were the tanks, officers and men of the Armoured and Mechanized Forces of the Red Army.

In explaining the Red Army's victory over Germany in what the Russians call their Great Patriotic War, it is insufficient to simply consider the number, type and capabilities of Soviet tanks. Wars on the scale of World War II are waged by the mobilization of a state's entire human, economic, technical and financial resources in order to create massive armies, equipped with high-quality weapons, and trained to fight effectively. It is the careful blending of these various factors that bring victory in war. As the Battle for Berlin clearly demonstrates, Soviet forces in 1945 possessed not just the numbers to win, but the blend of weapons and tactics required.

It is arguable that by the end of the war, the Red Army had proved to be the most proficient amongst all the combatants at conducting large-scale armoured operations. Understanding the process by which the Soviet Union developed the technical and economic base necessary for the creation of powerful armoured formations, and the methods by which they were employed to achieve success in combat (what is termed doctrine by professional soldiers), will form the focus of the first two chapters of this book.

ORIGINS OF THE ARMOURED FORCES

The Red Army and its armoured forces were born out of the chaos and confusion of the Russian Revolution. In November 1917 the Bolshevik Party, under the iron leadership of Vladimir Ilyich Ulyanov

(Lenin), mounted a successful *coup d'état* to seize power in the Russian capital Petrograd. The Bolsheviks were aided by a number of disaffected army regiments and their own crudely armed and trained workers militia, which was rather grandly called the Red Guards. On 28 January 1918 these forces were re-named the Workers' and Peasants' Red Army and tasked with the role of defending the revolution from the right-wing anti-Bolshevik forces, which were now known generally as the Whites.

During the course of the Civil War (1919–21) on 4 July 1920 the Red Army fought its first tank action. This was a combined action involving the 2nd Tank Squadron, Armoured Train number 8 and Armoured Car Squadron number 14. The infant Soviet tank park was comprised of a modest number of British

ABOVE: Vladimir Ilyich Ulyanov (Lenin), who was smuggled by the intelligence services of Imperial Germany from Switzerland to St Petersburg during World War I to ensure that revolution would neutralize Russia. From 1919 to 1921, his Bolshevik Red Army fought the White Army, a force which was backed by the USA, France and Britain, all of which had supplied it with tanks, the new technology which had emerged during the last years of World War I.

Mark V and Medium B Whippet and French Renault FT tanks. These vehicles had originally been supplied to the Whites by the Western powers to aid them against the Bolsheviks, who had managed to capture a number and turn them against their former owners.

In the Civil War, tanks played only a minor role on both sides. The most obvious reason for this was lack of numbers. The British and French are estimated to have supplied the Whites with no more than 130 tanks, although it seems that a far larger number of armoured cars were sent. The tanks themselves were slow, mechanically unreliable, and lacked spares and fuel. Consequently, they were unsuitable for extensive use alongside the more rapid cavalry units employed in the deep mobile operations that were a characteristic of much of the fighting in the Civil War. Armoured trains had a greater impact than tanks, possessing high mobility coupled with substantial firepower, in a conflict in which securing railheads was often a key feature of engagements.

At the same time, the Red Army did devote much time and attention to its punitive armoured forces. The Bolsheviks had formed a Provisional Armoured Board as early as November 1917, with orders to oversee the Second All-Russian Armoured Car Conference, which was to discuss matters relating to the establishment of armoured forces for the new

Soviet state. These organizations were replaced in 1918 by the Revolutionary Military Council (RSVR) which took practical steps to establish tank detachments. The first dedicated tank units were formed in May 1920. Each consisted of three British-made Mk V tanks, with six lorries and three motorcycles.

As more types of vehicle were improvised or captured, the armoured forces were re-organized into three main groupings, according to the size of the tank. The Mark Vs constituted Type B *bolishie* (large) units; Whippets were placed in Type S *srednie* (Medium) units; and the FT tanks in Type M *malie* (light) units. This organization was more concerned with logistic matters and ease of coordinating the tanks, rather than any sophisticated ideas concerning the tactical role of different tank types. Yet, it is worth noting that the division of armoured forces into groupings based on the size and capabilities of tank types did become a characteristic feature of Soviet organization during the interwar years and World War II, and was strongly related to their use in combat.

In the immediate aftermath of Bolshevik victory in the Russian Civil War, the Red Army continued to show interest in armoured warfare, especially the creation of native means of production to replace captured western vehicles. War Commissar Leon Trotsky, the man often accredited with laying the foundations of the Red Army, wrote that tank factories should be created to supply the Soviet Union's requirements. In fact, as early as 1919, a team of technicians under N. Kruhlev had set about reverse-engineering the French Renault FT tank at the AMO (*Avtomobilnoye Moskovskoye Obshchestvo*) Factory, which had been newly nationalized. The decision to try and reproduce the FT tank was taken on the grounds that it was smaller and simpler than the other types of vehicle that had been captured. Although one vehicle was produced, Soviet claims of 14 vehicles seem extreme, considering the run-down state of Russian industry in the immediate aftermath of the Civil War: it is more likely that these tanks were refurbished FTs, not new vehicles.

Lack of industrial resources and technical skills also prevented the large number of original Soviet tank designs

---

RENAULT FT-17

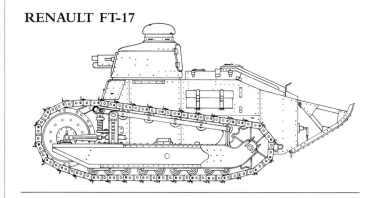

SPEED: 8km/h (5mph)

DIMENSIONS: Length: 5.02m (16ft 5in); Width 1.74m (5ft 9in); Height 2.14m (6ft 7in); Weight 7000kg (6.88 tons)

ARMOUR: 22mm (0.86in)

WEAPONRY: One 37mm (1.46in) gun or one MG

EFFECTIVE RANGE: 35km (22 miles)

CREW: 2

produced between 1919 and 1924 from progressing beyond paper concepts. Tank development was also inhibited by the designers' often fanciful and over-ambitious aims. A Red Army competition to design an armoured fighting vehicle in 1919 was won by a team from the Izhorskiy Factory whose *Tyeplokhod Tipa AM* (Motor Vessel Type AM) was a 10.1 tonne (10 ton) amphibious tank mounting a 76.2mm (3in) gun. The over-complication of the design and insurmountable technical problems forced work to be suspended in 1923.

Despite these setbacks, the Soviets continued to set up organizations to consider the design, organization and use of armoured forces. In 1923 the War Industry Main Directorate undertook the first systematic study of tank design in relation to the Red Army's requirements in war. This analysis contained a survey of tank actions from 1916 to 1918, and drew up outline proposals for training a cadre of tank men. The push towards acquiring a tank arm was furthered in 1925 with the establishment of a Technical Bureau for Tank Study. This body was largely responsible for directing the efforts of a recovering Soviet industrial base with the aim towards designing

the first large-scale production tank of the Red Army in 1926, called the MS-1 and subsequently known as the T-16/18.

THE MS-1/T-18 SOVIET TANK

The MS-1 or T-18 had its origins in a three-year plan drawn up in 1926 to produce a number of tanks to provide close support to infantry whilst breaking through enemy defences. A number of foreign designs were considered by the Red Army in order to speed design and production. Initial studies favoured the adoption of the Italian FIAT-3000 over the French Renault FT, or its Soviet modified variant the KS-1, because of its lower weight and relatively high speed. The accuracy and weight of the FTKS tanks was considered inadequate, and so too was the overall poor quality of the workmanship.

The first prototype was built by the Bolshevik Factory and was ready for trials in March 1927. Designated T-16, it performed adequately, but a number of improvements were recommended, including the addition of another road wheel and alterations to the transmission. Final tests on the new model were conducted in mid–1927, with the vehicle re-designated as Small Support Tank

ABOVE: A Medium Tank Mk A, widely known by the British as the Whippet, and a Mk V that appears to have its gun sponson removed at a depot in France. Both types of tank were sent to Russia to assist in the fighting against the Reds, and examples of both were captured. The drive to industrialize the newly-formed USSR allowed Soviet engineers to retro-engineer captured tanks in the new factories that were being built, which encouraged the development of a Soviet tank industry.

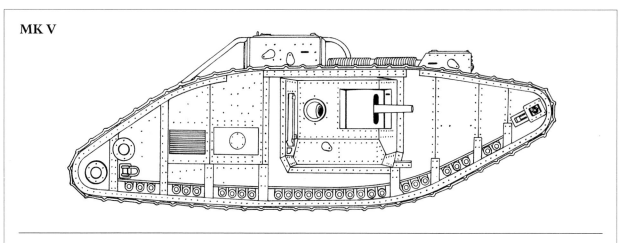

MK V

SPEED: 8km/h (5mph)

DIMENSIONS: Length: 8.04m (26ft 5in); Width 4.11m (13ft 6in);
Height 2.64m (8ft 8in); Weight 29,465kg (29 tons)

ARMOUR: 15mm (0.59in)

WEAPONRY: Two 6pdr (57mm (2.24in)); four 7.7mm (0.303in)
MG; or six 7.7mm (0.303in) MG

EFFECTIVE RANGE: 40km (25 miles)

CREW: 8

Model 1927, or T-18. Lack of a gun led to concentration on road tests, during which the T-18 was judged to have performed effectively and it was afterwards recommended for service. The Red Army ordered 108 vehicles to be built between 1928 and 1929, and the first 30 were available to take place in the 7 November 1929 Moscow and Leningrad parades celebrating the revolution.

However, production of the tanks had been difficult because of lack of facilities at the Bolshevik Factory to manufacture certain components, such as ball-bearings and carburettors. Eventually the required parts had to be imported, but even then the tanks delivered to the army were plagued with technical difficulties. Later field tests in 1929 revealed that the T-18 had problems in crossing trenches. This was rectified when the commander of the Leningrad Region Armoured Force ordered the fitting of a second tail at the front. The appearance of the tank with its iron struts at the front earned it the nickname *Nosorog* (Rhinoceros).

Although the T-18 remained in production until the end of 1931, as early as July 1927 the Revolutionary Military Council had stated that it was unsuitable for the conditions of modern combat, and consequently it was to remain in service only until a successor was available. In line with this, several modifications were undertaken to the T-18 as a stop-gap. There was some discussion about

replacing the copied French Hotchkiss 37mm (1.46in) gun with a new, high-velocity version, but nothing was done. The turret was extensively re-designed in order to create space for a radio, although not all tanks received radio.

The most important changes involved measures to increase the T-18's speed and mobility. The engine's power was increased to 29kW (40bhp) and a new gearbox and cast wheel drive were introduced. However, these measures failed to significantly increase the tank's overall performance, and later programmes to update the T-18's running gear in 1933 and in 1938 also failed to achieve any improvement in performance.

MS-1/T-18 IN ACTION

Despite the unfavourable opinion expressed about the T-18 soon after its acceptance by the Red Army, over 989 were produced between 1928 and 1931, and they saw successful, if limited, combat service, fulfilling their role of direct support to the infantry. In 1929, nine T-18 tanks saw action in the Far East in border clashes with Chinese forces. In one engagement, eight T-18s supported the attack of the 106th and 108th rifle regiments against Chinese forces dug in around Dzhalaynor Station. In one attack, the infantry advanced behind the cover of the T-18s against Chinese positions. The tank crews operated with skill, providing fire support with their guns as well. A later attack was less successful because the tanks initially couldn't cross an antitank ditch. Later several vehicles managed to get into the enemy lines, sweeping them with concentrated fire.

By the time of the outbreak of war with Germany in June 1941, few T-18s were left in running order. In 1938 over 700 were ordered to be re-armed and used as mobile firing points in the fortified regions along the borders with Poland and Romania. Some T-18s did see action during the opening days of the war with IX Mechanized Corps during the large tank battle in the Rovno-Broda-Lutsk area. However, these had been deployed almost randomly in a desperate attempt to replace the massive losses suffered amongst the corps' more modern BT and T-26 tanks during the previous weeks' fighting.

WAR SCARE AND INDUSTRIALIZATION

The initially small numbers of the T-18 produced and the reliance on imported parts and designs was a reflection of the critical problems facing the Red Army in the early- and mid–1920s. Prior to World War I, Russia had possessed only a limited industrial base for developing and building modern, sophisticated weapons. This had been reflected during World War I by the fact that although the Russians tried to develop numerous designs of armoured vehicles, they failed

to manufacture any type on a significant scale. The only tank factory in Russia had been set up during World War I by an industrialist who had bought the rights to build Fiat light tanks, essentially a copy of the French FT. Little had come of this venture: the factory was ill-equipped and the Revolution and Civil War soon plunged Russian industry into chaos, with disastrous effects for the long term.

The evolution of the first generation of Soviet tanks and the organization of the Red Army's Armoured and Mechanized forces was reliant on more than just the direction which was afforded by the government departments who were in charge of industry. Three other factors played an important role in establishing the nature of Soviet tank design and production: the development of the Red Army; its ideas on the conduct of war; and international relations coupled with internal Soviet political struggles. Developments in each of these individual areas eventually combined in the late 1920s to create a Soviet industrial-military organization which was capable of equipping the Red Army with the largest armoured forces in the world by the mid–1930s.

The first factor to play a role in establishing the nature of Soviet tank design was the development of the Red Army. The organization of the Red Army and its ideas on future war were largely

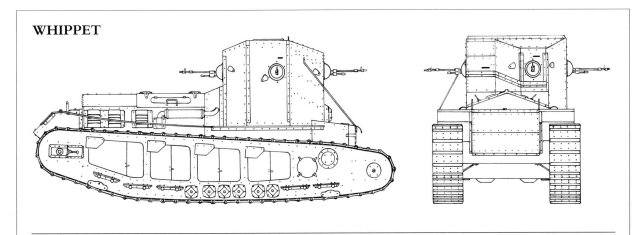

WHIPPET

SPEED: 12km/h (8mph)

DIMENSIONS: Length 6.10m (20ft 0in); Width 2.62m (8ft 7in); Height 2.74m (9ft 0in); Weight 14,225kg (14 tons)

ARMOUR: 14mm (0.55in)

WEAPONRY: Three or four 7.7mm (0.303in) MG

EFFECTIVE RANGE: 64km (40 miles)

CREW: 3

shaped between 1918 and 1927. The most immediate problem for the Bolsheviks on assuming power in 1917 had been the need to protect themselves from immediate internal and external threats. The creation of the Red Army on 28 January 1918 was critical to achieving this aim by 1921. However, although the Civil War had shown the value of a large standing Red Army, it did not guarantee the retention of such a force in the aftermath of the Civil War, for economic and ideological reasons.

For much of the 1920s, a significant portion of the Bolshevik Party, led by Trotsky, argued that the Soviet Union's lack of economic resources meant that it could neither afford nor equip a regular army with the advanced weapons needed to oppose the technically superior capitalist forces. Coupled with this was the belief that any invading force would be crippled by partisan warfare and uprisings by pro-Soviet workers in their own countries. The Trotskyite faction argued for the creation of a militia, rather than a standing army.

Trotsky's defeat by his political and military rivals at the Tenth Party Congress ensured that despite undergoing a dramatic demobilization – from five million to 562,000 troops by the middle of the decade – the Red Army remained a standing professional force, not a militia. This was vital to the ability of the Soviet State and its armed forces to develop a centralized and effective method of weapons design and procurement, and to train troops who were capable of using these new, complex weapons effectively in battle.

The second factor affecting the nature of Soviet tank design was the Red Army's ideas on the conduct of war. By the mid–1920s the Red Army had developed the outline of a sophisticated tactical doctrine called 'Deep Battle'. From studying the lessons of World War I and the Russian Civil War, Soviet military theorists argued that the key to breaking through strong enemy front-line defences was the infliction of shock, through the use of combined forces of infantry, artillery, engineers, tanks and aircraft.

By attacking the enemy defences throughout their depth with both fire and assault troops, it would prove possible to breach the Front and then carry out a decisive manoeuvre in the enemy's rear. The strong emphasis on the all-arms tactical deep battle convinced a number of radical and increasingly influential thinkers in the Red Army, such as Marshal M. Frunze, and generals V.K. Triandafillov and M.N. Tukachevsky, of the need to equip the Red Army with the most sophisticated new weapons, especially including tanks, to assist in breaking the front and then proceeding to drive rapidly in to the enemy's rear.

The third factor which affected Soviet tank design was international relations, coupled with internal Soviet political struggles. During the Russian Civil War,

RIGHT: The Russkiy-Reno, *legkiy* tank M (Light Tank M: *maliy* – small) was originally known more dramatically as the Freedom Fighter Lenin. These tanks were re-builds of the captured former French Renault FT- 17 light tanks. Fifteen of these vehicles were used to form the 7th Tank Unit in Moscow, which was used for all the military parades in Red Square. Some of these tanks were also used in armoured manoeuvres around the Moscow area.

the Whites had received support in the form of arms and direct intervention with punitive military forces from Britain, France, Japan, and the USA, whilst in 1920 Poland had embarked upon a brief and unsuccessful invasion of the Ukraine. Ultimately, these actions had not saved the Whites from defeat, but in the long term they had a profound impact on the Bolshevik régime's interpretation of international politics. To many in the Bolshevik Party and the military, it became clear that there could never be permanent peace between the Soviet Union and the capitalist powers.

At first sight, this appears to be something of a paradox, considering events in the early 1920s. The signing of the 1922 Anglo–Soviet Trade Treaty and military and economic agreements with Germany enshrined in the 1924 Treaty of Rappallo would appear to show the USSR as living in harmony with its neighbours. Yet to many Bolsheviks, including Lenin, peace was simply another phase in the struggle between them and their enemies, in which a variety of weapons available to a state – diplomacy, economic sabotage – would be used against the Soviet Union whilst the preparations for

full-scale war were undertaken. It was this belief that had played a key role in rejecting a militia and the assistance of external Communist movements in favour of a standing Red Army which would defend the Soviet Union.

Consequently, it was increasingly argued in the 1920s that the Soviet military had to become as well equipped and organized as its opponents if it was to win. This position was stated in the 1925 Provisional Field Regulations that stressed the role of new artillery guns, tanks and other advanced weapons in future combat. This position, however, created a paradox between the reality of a backward Soviet industrial base – especially short of technical personnel and a large, trained workforce – and the ability to create the large, modern army which had previously been envisaged.

This position, which seemed to justify some of Trotsky's views, spurred Soviet political and military leaders to recognize the need to develop internal resources if the Soviet Union was to be defended from hostile powers. It became axiomatic to many leading political and military figures that the only way to turn the Red Army into such an effective and modern

ABOVE: Amidst a cloud of exhaust fumes T-18 (also known as MS-1 *Maliy Soprovozhdyeniya-Pierviy*: First Small Support Vehicle) light tanks move through Red Square during a May Day Parade. Production of this vehicle was plagued with technical problems, but between 1928 and 1931 some 960 T-18s were built. This was an altogether incredible achievement considering that this total was churned out even though production was halted to rectify serious design flaws, including adding a turret bustle and a more powerful engine.

MS-3

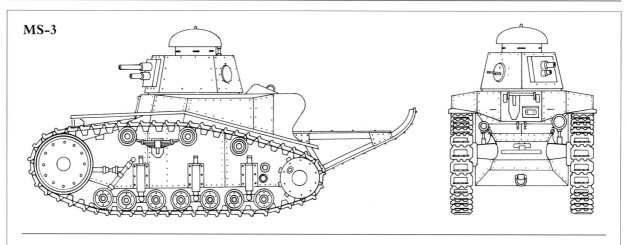

SPEED: 16km/h (10mph)

DIMENSIONS: Length 3.50m (11ft 6in); Width 1.76m (5ft 9in);
Height 2.12m (6ft 11in); Weight 5500kg (5.41tons)

ARMOUR: 16mm (0.62in)

WEAPONRY: One 37mm (1.46in), one MG

EFFECTIVE RANGE: 50km (31 miles)

CREW: 2

fighting force was through a radical policy of industrialization. The creation of a strong domestic advanced industrial base would overcome shortcomings in Soviet weapons design and production, as well as enabling the military to begin the implementation of their increasingly advanced combat methods.

The impetus for the creation of the Soviet warfare state demanded by the political and military decisions of the mid–1920s came spectacularly in 1926 and into 1927 in a series of apparently threatening international political incidents that became known as the 'War Scare'. In 1926 relations between the Soviet Union and Poland underwent a downturn when the right-wing Marshal Pilsudski gathered power into his own hands, establishing a strong military régime which was unfavourable to the Soviet Union. The situation was exacerbated when a Soviet minister was assassinated in Poland. This chain of events was viewed with concern by Moscow, where Poland was seen by the Red Army High Command as the most immediate and direct threat to the security of the Soviet Union. Security concerns increased further in 1927 when the Soviet Embassy in China was sacked and diplomatic relations with Great Britain were broken off after British police raids on Soviet offices in London. Panic gripped many Russians as war seemed imminent.

Yet the reality is more difficult to substantiate, since at that point no widespread mobilization of the Red Army took place. The War Scare may have been more concerned with the internal political aims of Josef Stalin, who used it to discredit the last main rivals to his hold on power. Trotsky was expelled from the party and later went into exile. It is, however, worth noting that substantial changes were made to the military share of the new, ambitious Five Year Plan begun in 1929, to transform the Soviet Union into a first-rate power. During the course of the First- and following the Second Five Year Plan, the Red Army would be allocated a sizeable portion of Soviet industrial output and planning.

THE FIRST FIVE YEAR PLAN

Soviet plans for the creation of a vast industrial base were ambitious. The government issued orders for the creation of the enormous Gorki and Moscow *Zavods* (factories), with an intended combined annual production of 125,000 vehicles. Tractor and tank production was concentrated at the Leningrad Putilov Works and the Stalingrad Tractor factory. At the start of this titanic process, military production targets were set at modest levels in accordance with the limited resources available. The Red Army's production priorities were artillery, aircraft, tanks and other motorized vehicles. In the earliest proposals of 1926–28, a total of 1025 tanks were ordered, but the rapid strides made in the creation of automotive and other heavy industries led to this total being increased to 3500 in May 1929. Soviet confidence reached new heights with the great tank programme of 1931, which called for the manufacture of 10,000 tanks in 1932 alone. This overly optimistic total, like so many during the plan, was not achieved, but it was still an outstanding feat on the part of Soviet industry to turn out just under 3000 tanks. This gave the Soviet Union the largest tank fleet in the world at this time, a position it would not lose until the catastrophic defeats suffered at the hands of the Germans in 1941.

The ability of the Soviet Union to expand her industrial, and consequently military, forces at such speed was the result of pragmatic, though at the time harsh, policies. The creation of a large workforce with rudimentary technical skills was accomplished through a series of policies introduced by Stalin. Agricultural reform termed collectivization – involving the creation of large state-run farms by dispossessing many peasants of their land – created a surplus of labour that could be used in the new, expanding industries. In the factories, ineffective management was brutally repressed and harsh punishments were carried out on those who failed to meet production targets. Enthusiastic for its new weapons, the Red Army was not averse to using its soldiers to enforce the new policies in rural areas. Several of the new military plants were in effect run as slave-labour camps.

Vital to the process of industrialization was foreign expertise. Stalin and the Revolutionary Military Council spent the Soviet Union's gold reserves on acquiring American and German technical experts and machine tools in order to circumvent existing deficiencies in Soviet industry and, at the same time, hasten its own build-up. American involvement in the Five Year Plan was notable for the fact that at this time the US Government did not officially recognize the Soviet Union. Yet only limited – and easily circumvented – measures were taken to prevent technical cooperation and the purchase of US equipment. The first deal was made in 1929 with the Ford Motor Company, which helped design and build

BELOW: A Red Army soldier guards an MS-3 bogged during a training exercise. The Renault 'tail' has failed to enable the crew to clear the ditch. The MS had a new transverse engine and transmission and sprung suspension on seven small coil sprung roadwheels. Numbers of the MS-3 had survived up to 1941 and were hurriedly fitted with a 45mm (1.77in) antitank gun, but proved useless against more modern German tanks.

ABOVE: A single British soldier of the Royal Tank Regiment mans a Vickers Carden-Loyd (otherwise known as VCL) Tankette during trials which were carried out in Britain. Developed between 1925 and 1929, these two- or three man vehicles – which were both light and open-topped – were the brainchild of Sir John Carden. They would influence international armour design during the 1920s and 1930s and were the basis of the Bren Gun Carrier developed by the British before World War II. Among the many armoured vehicles which were supplied to the USSR by the United Kingdom during World War II were large numbers of British- and Canadian-built Bren Gun Carriers.

the vast Gorki automobile plant, licensed to build Ford trucks. This factory would become one of the largest and most important production centres for the mechanization of the Red Army prior to and during the World War II. The sheer scale of equipment purchases from the United States is illustrated by the Soviet Union spending $79 million alone in 1932, which included 64 per cent of all machine tool exports for that year.

One area in which the Soviets became particularly adept and where they had notable success – with long-term implications – was the purchase of actual foreign military vehicles as a basis for developing native models. Tanks in particular were purchased from a wide variety of countries such as France, Italy and Czechoslovakia. The most important foreign designs, however, came from Britain, the USA and Germany.

CARDEN-LOYD MK VI TANKETTE

The acquisition of British and American designs was undertaken in 1929 by a special commission of the Directorate for Mechanization and Motorization (UMM), led by the head of the Military Technical Board, General I.A. Khalepsky. As the British were at this time seen as the leaders in tank design, Khalepsky paid particular attention to acquiring vehicles from the country's only tank manufacturer, Vickers-Armstrong Ltd, in 1931. In

particular the Vickers Carden-Loyd Mk VI tankette and Vickers-Armstrong E Tank provided the basis for several key early Red Army tanks.

One of the first designs to arrive was the Vickers Carden-Loyd (VCL) Mk VI tankette. This had been purchased because Red Army Armoured Regulations specified the need for a light reconnaissance tank. Soviet design teams had experimented with a number of their own ideas between 1927 and 1930. Based on the chassis of the T-16, they evolved the T-17 and T-25, but these had remained mere paper projects. Only the T-23 experimental tankette was built. The extensive time needed to correct defects in the T-23 led to the decision to buy the proven British design.

Soviet engineers weren't fully satisfied with the Mk VI, and a team led by N. Korzyrev at Zavod Nr 37 in Moscow made a number of changes to the hull. Performance was improved with a more powerful engine, new clutch and larger drive sprockets. The T-27 was armed with a 7.62mm (0.3in) machine gun, but lacked a radio, which meant that communication with other vehicles had to be conducted with flags, a standard Soviet procedure at this time because of the primitive state of the electrical industry. Several attempts were made to up-gun the T-27 by fitting 37mm (1.46in) Hotchkiss and 76.2mm (3in) Kt guns on the chassis, but these attempts proved to be largely abortive because of the inability of the chassis to cope with the extra weight, lack of stowage room for ammunition, and the instability and danger inherent in firing a large-calibre gun from such a small frame.

In the field, the T-27 proved of mixed value. Its simple construction required low maintenance, but it struggled to traverse swamps and snow-covered terrain because of its narrow tracks. Lack of a traversable turret and an amphibious capability was also acknowledged and led to the creation of the T-37 amphibious light tank. Even so, the T-27 was used extensively by the Red Army, which had 65 battalions each with 50 tankettes by the end of 1932. They were successfully used in operations in Central Asia to suppress the Basmachi uprising in the 1930s. When war came with Germany in 1941, the T-27 had long been classed as obsolete and removed from front-line service. Some are reported to have seen active service during 1941, but this was more an expression of the desperation of Soviet armoured forces for replacement vehicles than reflective of the T-27's combat value

Yet the decision to mass-produce the Mk VI tankette as the T-27 in 1931 marked the real start of the creation of the large armoured forces envisaged by Red Army commanders in the late 1920s When production ceased in 1941, over 12,000 vehicles had been built.

It was, however, in America that Khalepsky, after long and complex negotiations with the eccentric and irascible designer John Christie, was to make his most important purchase. Christie had developed a unique tank suspension system, called the M1928. The Christie suspensions system of long, individual helicoil springs allowed for large road wheels, reducing the overall weight and enabling a tank to traverse uneven ground with minimum vibrations. The design was far from perfect, but unlike the US Army, Khalepsky, along with the British, saw its potential. In the end, Christie's modified design became the basis for the T-34 medium tank which is considered one of the finest tanks ever designed and was a bedrock of Soviet victory between 1941 and 1945.

SOVIET–GERMAN COOPERATION

The most direct influences on the creation of Soviet armaments came from Germany. After World War I Germany, like the Soviet Union, was something of an international pariah. Cooperation between these two isolated nations germinated from the peculiarities of each other's predicaments that closely intertwined. In short, under the terms of the Treaty of Versailles the 100,000-man Reichswehr was permitted no planes or tanks. To the German High Command, the Soviet Union, with its vast space and closed borders, was the ideal place to

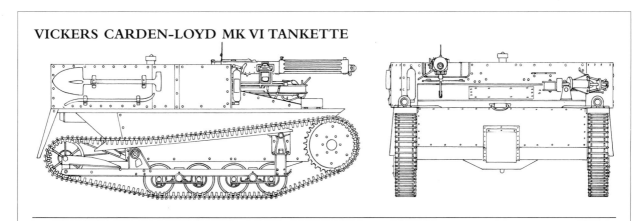

VICKERS CARDEN-LOYD MK VI TANKETTE

SPEED: 45km/h (28mph)

DIMENSIONS: Length 2.46m (8ft 1in); Width 1.70m (5ft 7in); Height 1.22mm (4ft); Weight 1525kg (1.5 tons)

ARMOUR: 9mm (0.35in)

WEAPONRY: One 7.7mm (0.303in) Vickers MG

EFFECTIVE RANGE: 96km (60 miles)

CREW: 2

secretly develop tanks and aircraft. To the Soviets, the benefit of access to German technical and military personnel and ideas was obvious. This mutually beneficial relationship began briefly in 1924, before several internal German political problems terminated the agreement. The attractions for the armed forces of both sides proved too great, however, and in the late 1920s cooperation resumed, which was to last until Hitler came to power in January 1933.

In 1927 the Germans established a tank development school in the Soviet Union at Kazan, referred to as the Heavy Vehicle Experimental and Test Station. Despite the obvious advantages to both sides, agreement was not achieved without some internal wranglings. Elements of the Soviet General Staff were opposed for military and ideological reasons. In 1928 the Kazan school was made operational with the arrival of 10 German prototypes, weighing 18.28 tonnes (18 tons) each, designed by Krupps and Rheinmetall. German aircraft were also tested at Lipetsk, near Moscow. Equally as important as military cooperation was the assistance received from German designers and technicians in many areas of the Soviet armaments industry. The exchange of ideas and acquiring of techniques were, at times, quite close. In 1932 a Soviet team which was headed by the German engineer Grotte, developed the TG-1 Heavy Breakthrough tank as part of the wider mechanization of the Red Army, and the Soviets also purchased and built under licence the Rheinmetall 37mm (1.46in) antitank gun.

The relationship between the Reichswehr and Red Army was also one of distrust. Some senior Soviet officers such as I.P. Uborevich studied at the German War College, and a small number of more junior officers did attend German training courses at Kazan. In general, Defence Commissar K.V. Voroshilov preferred to train Soviet tank officers at the Red Army Armour Centre at Voronezh. The importance of these limited but invaluable exchanges on the development of each army's ideas on the combat employment of tanks is difficult

BELOW: Red Army fitters check the tracks of a T-27 *Tankietka* (tankette). It was based on the VCL design and included several improvements, the most obvious of which were the hinged hatches to give overhead protection. In addition to this, the T-27A had an extra set of wheel bogies to improve mobility. The tankettes were useful training vehicles, enabling the Red Army to become familiar with tracked vehicles and the concept of mechanized warfare.

T-27A MODEL 1932 TANKETTE

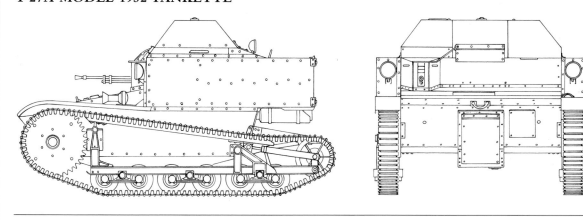

SPEED: 42km/h (26mph)

DIMENSIONS: Length 2.59m (8ft 6in); Width 1.83m (6ft);
Height 1.45m (4ft 9in); Weight 2700kg (2.65 tons)

ARMOUR: 10mm (0.39in)

WEAPONRY: One 7.62mm (0.3in) MG

EFFECTIVE RANGE: 120km (75 miles)

CREW: 2

to assess. Both looked extensively to the British Army's successful experience in World War I as well as its developments during the post-war period.

As would be expected during any period of change in military affairs, German and Soviet military texts and articles at this point were translated and studied closely by both sides. But so were those of a wide number of other combative nations. Many of the conclusions about tactics which were reached during this era by the Reichswehr and the Red Army had strong parallels, but it stands to reason that they are so manifestly logical that it would be fruitless to try and argue which nation's designers and engineers inspired the other.

What can be said with some certainty about this period is that between 1920 and 1930, the Red Army was a vibrant and imaginative organization that was busily engaged in developing its own unique ideas about the combat employment of tanks. These ideas were not a pale imitation of Germany's, or of other nations. In fact, in some areas, the Soviets were to prove startlingly original.

LEFT: The T-27A saw action on the outer edges of the Soviet Empire when it was used by NKVD security troops in operations against the Basmachi bandits of the Karak desert on the borders with Afghanistan. By the time production ceased in 1933, some 2540 had been built. The tankettes were still in service in 1941, though by this time they were no longer used as machine gun carriers, but rather as tractors for pulling 37mm (1.46in) and 45mm (1.77in) antitank guns.

CHAPTER TWO

DEEP BATTLE

It is often assumed that Germany was the first country to develop and perfect deep penetration armoured tactics. In fact, in the USSR in the 1930s, armoured theorists and vehicle engineers were pioneering tactics and tanks that would eventually win the war with Nazi Germany.

The First Five Year Plan (1929–34) and its successors created a massive industrial base that was vital to creating the massed tank forces being envisaged in the late 1920s by senior Red Army officers. In 1929 the Red Army possessed just 340 tanks; this had risen to 7633 by 1935, giving the Soviets the largest tank fleet in the world. Massive losses inflicted by the Germans between 1941 and 1942 cut the Soviet tank park from a colossal 28,800 (these figures include replacement and training vehicles) to just 1503. By 1945, the resilience of the Soviet people and thorough industrial planning had restored the Red Army's tank park to 16,200 operational, replacement and training vehicles.

The sheer weight of materiel undoubtedly made an enormous contribution to Soviet victory in World War II, but this factor must be treated with some caution. Until the late 20th century, the prevailing view of the Red Army was typified by the remarks of Colonel Albert

LEFT: IS-2 heavy tanks churn along a forest firebreak during the final months of World War II. The IS-2, with its thick armour and 122mm (4.8in) gun, was the most powerful tank of World War II. Its only drawback was the two-piece ammunition that made loading the weapon slow.

RIGHT: KV-1 tanks making their way through Leningrad. The Red Army's attempts at up-armouring the KV-1 yielded only a poor power-to-weight ratio with the result that the tank's performance was severely reduced. This decrease in effectiveness was a high price to pay for a tank that was protected by the same type of armament as the more agile T-34. However, the chassis of the KV-1 was to provide the design basis for the successful Iosef Stalin (IS) series of heavy tanks, as well as some self-propelled guns like the ISU-152.

Seaton, who wrote that the Soviet armed forces at that time (the interwar period) had no soldiers of genius and experience, and the Red Army was an indifferent imitation of the German Army. Soviet victories during World War II were explained as being the result of brute force and ignorance. Red Army operations lacked sophistication in their planing and execution, using sledge-hammer blows rather than the finesse and precision of the German rapier blows.

These arguments were not without substance. During the war, the Red Army mounted offensives that had all the hallmarks of a crude battering-ram, composed of vast amounts of men and equipment, and which incurred massive casualties. At the same time, such an interpretation rests upon a number of false premises about the conditions under which the Red Army fought, and the peculiar nature of Soviet views on the conduct of armoured warfare.

Basically, at the outbreak of war, the Red Army was ill trained and inappropriately equipped. The massive casualties it

suffered in the first two years forced the Soviet High Command (STAVKA) to commit troops as quickly as possible to the fighting, a decision which denied them the time to train to the high tactical standards of the German Army. Although mass was a key factor in Soviet operations, STAVKA did not possess an inexhaustible supply of manpower. As early as 1943, it had anticipated increasing manpower shortages in the future. In 1945 Soviet rifle divisions had only one-quarter of their strength on paper, in a force that stood at 2700 men.

That the Soviets were able to compensate for this deficiency can be attributed to the skillful planning and handling of their forces to create massive concentrations of tanks, infantry and guns at specific points along the front to conduct deep, armoured thrusts that overwhelmed German positions. More significantly, the Red Army's success stemmed from the years 1925–41, when it created an original and sophisticated doctrine and organization for its tank and mechanized forces. These ideas, with a different emphasis on the methods of fighting, make it is misleading to judge Soviet conduct of operations by Western standards. When viewed within the context of Soviet society and military thought, a totally different perspective emerges on the Red Army, and its design and employment of tank forces. It was not an indifferent imitation; on the contrary, it was boldly original.

THE INTERWAR RED ARMY

In the 1920s the Red Army was concerned with three major questions regarding future war: first, the nature of war between modern industrialized states; second, the problems of overcoming powerful enemy defences with frontal assaults in order to achieve decisive success; and third, the potential impact of advanced technology on the conduct of battle. The Red Army set about answering these questions through rigorous analysis of the two most recent wars: World War I (1914–18) and the Russian Civil War (1919–21).

Careful study of these recent conflicts provided the basis for predicting the nature of the next major conflict involving the Soviet Union, and the methods of fighting that would be needed to achieve victory. Understanding these two issues enabled the Soviets to make balanced speculations about the potential impact of future advances in technology on the battlefield. This knowledge was invaluable in creating the organization and doctrine of the Red Army, and also for focusing Soviet scientific research on developing the weapons required to fight and win a future war.

The Red Army's ability to solve its problems in such a sophisticated manner was the product of an open and vibrant atmosphere of intellectual debate. Marshal M.V. Frunze organized a staff consisting of Russian Civil War commanders, former Tsarist military specialists (*voenspatsy*) and radical Communist officers. The result of this unique mix of ideological, practical knowledge and theoretical thought was the creation of the

LEFT: ISU-152 Model 1944 SP guns on the move. The ISU-152, armed with a 152mm (5.9in) ML-20S with 20 rounds of HE and APHE ammunition, had a crew of five. The big gun fired a 43.4kg (96lb) shell to a maximum range of about 10,000m (10,935yd) and was more than capable of destroying the largest German tanks, as well as providing close support to infantry assaults against German fortifications and fixed positions.

concept of the 'Deep Battle' at the end of the 1920s, followed by the radical 'Deep Operations' idea in the mid–1930s. These two related concepts combined to establish the broad guidelines for the organization of Soviet tank forces and the types of tanks which would be required, as well as their roles in combat.

Ultimately, the ideas created by two decades of openness and innovation were crushed after 1937 by Stalin's ruthless purge of the officer corps, which killed most of the originators of the Deep Battle and Deep Operation concepts, while fear silenced the survivors. Only in the desperation of defeat during the war did Stalin relent and allow the pre-war concepts to be re-introduced.

THE THEORY OF MODERN WAR

Of central importance to the evolution of Soviet military art was an appreciation of the conditions of modern war. Citing evidence from World War I, Red Army theorists concluded that the million-man armies created by modern industrialized states were too resilient and physically large to be defeated in a single campaign. Strategic victory in future conflicts

would come through an accumulation of victories. With millions of troops engaged, the vast scale of the battlefield meant that numerous individual battles would occur. There was a real danger that these battles would become localized events, leading to a random pattern of success or failure in each one, which might ultimately lead to great loss, but definitely no substantial gains.

To avoid this chaotic battlefield and to make sure that resources were used effectively for maximum gain, Soviet officers – amongst whom A.A. Svechin, M.N. Tukachevsky and V.K. Triandafillov were the most influential – argued that it was necessary to carefully coordinate multiple individual tactical battles based on sound logistics, towards achieving a single aim, which was known as the operation.

The method by which a higher-level commander prioritized and coordinated the tactical battles to achieve the operation's aim was known as operational art. Rather like the conductor of an orchestra, the operational commander's task was to blend numerous instruments, each playing their own solos, within the framework of one musical score. Alone, a single operation would still be inadequate for overcoming the enemy's vast resources; rather, strategic victory would stem from the sum of several operations, planned and conducted one after the other and interconnected in time.

DEEP BATTLE AND ARMOUR

Having established the idea that strategic victory in future war would result from an accumulation of operational successes, each flowing from the ability to link individual battles to a common aim, the Red Army turned to the issue of achieving tactical success in battle. The Soviets paid particular attention to the nature of combat during World War I.

Given that the Red Army concluded that tactical defence was based upon the concept of a succession of fortified lines in depth, it logically followed that the attacker would need to structure his forces in a similar fashion. Successive echelons would be necessary in order to retain sufficient force to overcome the entire defence. A detailed analysis of numerous battles in the war, most notable of these being the British attack at Amiens on 8 August 1918, involving over

BELOW: *Tyazholy Tank IS* Heavy Tank 'Iosef Stalin' IS-2 tanks of the 1st Ukrainian Front camouflaged in a concentration area in woods near Berlin in April 1945. The IS-2 was armed with a 122mm (4.8in) M1943 gun with 28 rounds as well as a 12.7mm (0.5in) AA gun and three 7.62mm (0.303in) machine guns. The IS-2 was the most powerfully armed tank in World War II and its improved fire-control meant that it could fight German Tigers and Panthers on more than equal terms.

400 tanks, emphasized the need for close tactical cooperation between infantry, artillery and other service arms. The Russian 1916 offensive under General Brusilov demonstrated that an attack on a broad front would tie down enemy forces, thereby creating the conditions for a breakthrough with overwhelming force at pre-selected points on the front line.

In 1929 two works outlined a coherent doctrine incorporating Soviet observations on combat, termed Deep Battle; these were the 1929 Field Regulations (PU-29) and, more significantly, Lieutenant-General V. K. Triandafillov's book, *The Nature of Operations of Modern Armies*. The aim of Deep Battle was to penetrate all of the enemy's tactical defences, to a depth of approximately 10–15km (6.2–9.3 miles). Partially echoing the Brusilov offensive, Triandafillov argued that only a simultaneous attack across the front and entire depth of the enemy's tactical position could break the line and subsequently restore mobility to operations.

On the main axes of attack, Deep Battle was to be conducted simultaneously by long-range artillery and air strikes against the enemy rear, and frontal attacks by deeply echeloned all-arms formations, in order to achieve a swift breakthrough. These concentrations of force were to be concealed from the enemy by *maskirovka*, a combination of deception, dis-information, security and camouflage, thereby creating conditions of maximum surprise, and further weakening the enemy's ability to respond.

TACTICS FOR DEEP BATTLE

The significance of Triandafillov's work went beyond the idea of Deep Battle because it outlined the conduct of an operation, not just the tactical means, which was the focus of PU-29. His book also established the potential impact of massed tank formations in future combat, a subject largely ignored in the Field Regulations. Triandafillov's book was written on the eve of the First Five Year Plan which provided the Red Army with the tank forces he had outlined.

In 1930 an experimental armoured brigade was created under the command of K.B. Kalinovsky. Initially, it consisted of a tank regiment, an infantry regiment, an artillery division, and a reconnaissance

battalion. In total the brigade had 60 MS-1 tanks and 32 T-27 tankettes. By 1932 four regiments of increased size had been created at Smolensk, Leningrad, Kharkov and Moscow, while several territorial tank battalions also existed. These new forces were partly a result of the great tank programme of 1931, which had re-structured industrial production to create the massed tank forces which were advocated by Triandafillov and Marshal M.N. Tukachevsky.

A commission to determine the organization of tank and mechanized forces was established in 1932. On advice received from this commission, the decision was taken to form the 11th and 45th Mechanized Corps in autumn 1932. Each corps contained a mechanized brigade of T-26 tanks (three tank battalions, a rifle battalion, an artillery division, an engineer battalion, and antiaircraft machine-gun company); a second tank regiment with an identical order of battle but equipped with BT tanks; a rifle brigade, and units under corps command

ABOVE: Stalin watches an air display over the Tuchino Aerodrome in Moscow in the summer of 1939. Watching with him were members of the Politburo and their wives, including Klimenti Voroshilov. Stalin took an active part in the development of the tanks that equipped the Red Army, and some designers would appeal directly to him if they felt their design was being compromised.

RIGHT: Trailing clouds of exhaust smoke, an ISU-152 Model 1944 SP gun grinds up a hill on a summer day in 1944. In post-war tank designs, Soviet engineers included the ability to produce instant dense white smoke-screens by injecting unburned diesel fuel into the exhaust. This was later copied in the west with tanks like the British Challenger II.

BELOW: Infantry of the 1st Ukrainian Front dash forward supported by an IS-2 heavy tank in the summer of 1944 in the Ukraine. The long 122mm (4.8in) M1943 gun with its distinctive overhang was an extremely powerful weapon. However, it fired two-part ammunition, where normally tanks had one part 'fixed' ammunition, and so only 28 rounds could be carried. The IS-2 was used in action for the first time in February 1944 at Korsun Shevcherkov.

(reconnaissance, engineers, flamethrowing battalions, antiaircraft artillery division, traffic-control company and a technical supply base). Worth emphasizing is that in broad outline, this was close to German Panzer division organization, but with one exception: the first Panzer division was not created until 1935.

In fact, K.B. Kalinovsky's experimental brigade played a vital role in testing Triandafillov's idea about the tactical employment of tanks in Deep Battle and the types of tanks required to fulfil each mission. There were three groups of armour: NPP (infantry support), DPP (long-range infantry support) and DD

(long-range action/exploitation). The definitions of these groups was not related to their range of action, but to the particular tactical task to be performed in effecting a breakthrough of the entire depth of the enemy's defences.

NPP tanks were designed to clear a path for the infantry through the enemy's initial defences in order to effect a break-in. Their roles included crushing barbed wire left uncut by the artillery preparation, and destroying enemy strongpoints and tanks. They were also to assist in beating off enemy counterattacks. Trials established that 15–16 NPP tanks were required to successfully attack 1km (0.6 miles) of the front line. The tanks were to advance at intervals of 15–30m (16.4–32.8yd), following directly behind the creeping artillery barrage.

Infantry were to follow in waves not more than 100m (91yd) behind the tanks in order to mop up surviving enemy positions. If the tanks encountered obstacles, or defences that they were ill-suited to tackle, then the infantry were to move forward and attack under covering fire from the tanks. Once the enemy was destroyed, or engineers had created passages over or through the obstacles, the NPP tanks were to resume their position in the vanguard of the attack, once the artillery had resumed fire. These tactics were first used to varying degrees of effect during a series of border clashes with the Chinese in 1929.

Tanks in the DPP echelon were tasked with supporting the second echelon of infantry in continuing the breakthrough of the enemy's positions in depth. They operated with infantry and artillery in the same tactical pattern as the NPP tanks. DPP tank groups were also tasked to seek out and destroy enemy artillery positions in depth ahead of the infantry, and destroy enemy sub-units in reserve to

BELOW: With the battered Brandenburg Gate in the background, a column of IS-2 tanks rumbles through Berlin following the surrender of the German capital in May 1945. The photograph shows clearly the wide tracks that gave the tank good cross-country performance on snow and mud, resulting from a low track-weight ratio and good traction.

prevent them supporting units in more forward positions. The DD tanks would assist those forces carrying out the final stages of the breakthrough

The T-26 light, T-28 medium and heavy T-35 tanks developed in the late 1920s were designed to carry out NPP and DPP roles. By the outbreak of war, these vehicles had been replaced by the stronger KV-1 and KV-2 heavy assault tanks. As the war progressed, the more powerful KV-85, IS-1 and IS-2 tanks – as well as SU-122/152 and ISU-122/152 self-propelled guns capable of withstanding improved antitank weapons – were introduced. The T-34 was used during all phases of the assault, depending on the strength of enemy defences.

DEEP OPERATIONS
The ideas of Deep Battle were crystallized in the 1936 Field Regulations (PU-36). Although banned during Stalin's purges, the 1936 regulations were re-introduced during World War II as the 1944 Field Regulations (PU-44), forming the basis for successful Soviet military operations in the latter stages of the war. However, Deep Battle was only one part of a more sophisticated Soviet approach

to armoured operations whose outline was sketched out in the early 1930s by Lieutenant-General V.K. Triandafillov. Although Triandafillov died in an air crash in July 1931, notes he had made earlier provided the basis for a series of posthumous lectures given in 1933 which was entitled 'Fundamentals of the Deep Operation', in which Triandafillov, in conjunction with a number of other theorists, pointed out that the Deep Battle was only the opening phase of an operation, and as such was designed to breach the enemy's front by the application of overwhelming force in order to annihilate the enemy's forces.

The next, and key, phase was to exploit the attack into the enemy's rear to inflict a decisive blow over a wide area in order to gain time and space. This concept, termed the Deep Operation, was based on Soviet realization that modern mass armies were systems whose ability to function and carry out their missions was dependent upon effective interaction between the front and rear. If the fighting mass of the enemy at the front could be separated from headquarters, supplies and reserves in its rear, it would cease to function and lay itself open to defeat. Unlike

BELOW: In what is probably a propaganda picture, a BT-5 fast tank advances with supporting Soviet infantry – the 'shell bursts' look a little too neat to be genuine. The photograph was taken on 22 July 1942 in the Crimea. Changes in tactical doctrine following Stalin's purges of the 1930s had relegated the BT tanks from deep-penetration attacks to this infantry support role, for which they were not ideal. The BT was the most important tank in the Soviet order of battle from 1939 to 1941, with the T-26 making up 75 per cent of the Red Army's tank strength.

Deep Battle, which emphasized encirclement and physical destruction of enemy forces in order to break through the front line, the Deep Operation was concerned with disrupting, or paralysing, an enemy's organization, command and control to great depth, an effect termed 'operational shock'. It was concluded that an enemy force which was suffering from the after-effects of operational shock would be far easier to defeat in detail because it would not be capable of coordinating a large-scale resistance.

The Deep Operations concept was startlingly original. It should be emphasized that it was radically different to the German Army's ideas for conducting large-scale offensives, which would utilize new technology to carry out their traditional method of encirclement and then total annihilation of the enemy. Beyond a tactical level, the Germans would never emphasize disruption of the enemy as the key to success.

In conducting the Deep Operation, the Red Army outlined the procedure for the use of four echelons that were to interact simultaneously to generate maximum tactical and operational shock: the holding force; the strike force; the development echelon; and the desanti echelon. The holding forces were to fix the enemy across the whole front, and in the meantime the strike forces – with their NPP, DPP and DD tank groups – were to smash a series of large holes throughout the entire depth of the enemy's tactical defences.

This was the Deep Battle, and its aim was to create the conditions for the development and *desanti* echelons to implement the Deep Operation. The former was to be conducted by large tank, mechanized and cavalry formations driving at great speed into the opponent's deep rear. The *desanti* echelon involved the landing of paratroops ahead of the armoured formations in order to increase the effect of the deep strike. Radically for the time, the Soviets experimented with landing light tanks and vehicles from aircraft in order to increase the firepower, mobility and consequently the shock-effect of their airborne forces.

A variety of techniques were envisaged for employing the armoured forces.

ABOVE: T-34/76B tanks emerge from a tree line in Russia. The first appearance of these fast, well-armed and armoured tanks caused panic among German troops, who discovered that their 3.7cm (1.45in) PaK 35/36 antitank guns would not penetrate the tank's armour. The 8.8cm (3.4in) FlaK was pressed into an antitank role, and its high velocity ammunition and the steady nerves of the crews were often essential to stop the T-34s breaking through.

ABOVE: Tank riders of the Southern Front have dismounted from their T-34 steeds and are engaged in the unenviable process of advancing against German positions in the Donbass Region. The year is 1942. Out in the open, the tank riders are vulnerable, but all are armed with the robust and very effective PPSh 41 submachine gun. This weapon used simple production techniques of stamping and brazing, weighed a total of 3.56kg (7.8lb), and was fitted with a 71-round drum or 35-round box magazine. It fired at 900 rounds a minute.

The frontal blow was designed to slice up the whole front and rear of the enemy into a series of isolated groupings. The turning movement involved placing a large strike group of armoured forces in the enemy's rear to threaten his line of retreat, or strike his front-line forces from behind. It was also designed to psychologically disrupt the enemy by forcing him to deal with the equally unenviable choices of fighting to his front and rear, or risking a retreat with a powerful Soviet armoured force along his exposed flanks. A double envelopment of enemy forces by armoured groups was a possibility, depending on the circumstances.

Whichever of these techniques was adopted, it was the interaction between fighting across the front and the forces manoeuvring at great depth that was responsible for generating the operational shock, collapse and success which would come about during an offensive.

SOVIET ARMOUR IN DEFENCE

In defensive operations the Soviets envisaged the use of armour in several ways. Forward tactical defences comprised strongly fortified and deeply echeloned lines supported by massed artillery and antitank fire. Tanks were employed on likely avenues of enemy attack to support

the infantry in an antitank role and to spearhead local counterattacks. At the operational level, large Soviet tank- and mechanized forces were deployed as a second echelon in the deep rear.

The task of these forces was twofold. The first was purely defensive; if the enemy managed to breach the main line of defence, then the second echelon armoured forces were to move up and counterattack in order to restore the front line. The second was offensive. The Red Army's primary aim in a defensive operation was to grind the strength of the enemy's main assault forces down in its deep tactical defences. This would create the opportunity for the use of the second echelon tank and mechanized forces to deliver a counteroffensive. This blow was intended not simply to restore the front line, but also to develop a major attack beyond Soviet territory into the enemy's rear in order to inflict a decisive defeat on him.

In this manner, the Red Army was able to establish a close relationship between defensive and offensive operations, in which it first created the conditions for a seamless shift to the latter. During World War II, it was the fighting during the Battle of Kursk which demonstrated the Red Army's use

of a strong defence to wear down a German attack before an offensive.

TESTING DEEP BATTLE AND OPERATIONS

The principles of the Deep Battle and the initial ideas about Deep Operation were extensively tested by the Soviets in manoeuvres during the 1930s. The two largest were those held in the Kiev Byelorussian Military Districts in 1935 and 1936 respectively. The Kiev manoeuvres, which were supervised by Army Commander First Rank I.E. Yakir, involved VIII and XVII Rifle Corps, XXXXV Mechanized Corps, II Cavalry Corps and 9th Cavalry Division.

The exercise involved the penetration of a strong enemy defence and its exploitation by the cavalry, coordinated with airborne landings deep in the enemy's rear by elements of a parachute and two air-landed rifle regiments. In the summer of 1936 the Byelorussian Military District tested deep armoured manoeuvres in conjunction with airborne landings under the supervision of the district commander, I.P. Uborevich. The foreign military observers who were present at these trials were, on the whole, impressed by the sheer scale and sophistication of the Soviet forces they saw at work out on the testing grounds.

However, despite the sophistication of Soviet theory and the skillful organization demonstrated during manoeuvres, the Red Army was not a fully effective combat force. Deficiencies in tactical training and handling of troops were starkly exposed in the Russo–Finnish War. The mobilization of manpower reserves in the face of the threat from Germany between 1939 and 1941 prevented and inhibited effective reform because of lack of training resources and instructors as the army numbers rose to a strength of over five million.

When war with Germany broke out on 22 June 1941, the Red Army suffered a series of massive defeats because it was caught unprepared, with troops and officers who were poorly trained and equipped. In the opening months of the war, damning after-action reports from officers of the armoured inspectorate revealed the dire state of the tank forces: over 30 per cent of tanks needed extensive repairs. Command staffs were not adequately trained, lacked radios and, in some cases, even went without maps.

Logistic and maintenance support was poorly appreciated and badly organized, leading to 40–50 per cent of tanks being lost through lack of fuel or mechanical problems. Crews had not mastered the

ABOVE: The tank riders have moved forward in front of their tanks in order to close with the enemy German positions. This was a common Soviet tactic that required the infantry to neutralize antitank positions before their own tanks made the breakthrough. However, the grim reality was that oncoming German machine-gun fire would often cut down the Soviet infantry before they had even reached their objectives. Accordingly, when tank support was not available, Soviet infantry were deliberately intoxicated with vodka so that they could be sent forward cheering, with arms linked, against the German positions.

new KV and T-34 tanks and had no training in field repairs. Some examples of the tactical handling of tanks was inept in the extreme. In one engagement when the lead tank of a column of Soviet tanks was destroyed, rather than deploying into a firing line, each remaining tank filed past the disabled vehicle. As the next leading tank was disabled, the unit, still in column, side-stepped round again. In minutes, the whole unit was destroyed.

Neither had the Soviets managed to resolve all the issues concerning the use of armoured forces in Deep Operations. Critically the question of whether to commit the tank exploitation forces during the last phase of the breakthrough or after its completion was not answered. Neither was the distance between tank forces operating in the enemy's rear. Pre-war work on resolving these issues had been cut short by Stalin's purges of the officers corps, which ended research into Deep Operations. These problems, as well as the tactical and command skills required to implement Soviet theory, would have to be learned during the war, and learned often at great cost.

TANK FORCES' ORGANIZATION 1938–45

The evolution of then Deep Operations concept led to a change in the organization of Soviet armoured and mechanized forces in order to meet the requirements for large-scale offensive actions. Principally this involved the concentration of tanks in large tank corps rather than the mechanized corps. After August 1938, 4 tank corps were formed, each with 2 light tank regiments and 1 rifle regiment, 12,364 men and 660 tanks. Other units included 6 independent tank brigades and 6 tank regiments as well as 23 tankette battalions.

The new organization of the Soviet tank forces and the Deep Battle and Operation techniques for employing them received a severe reverse between 1937 and 1940. In 1937 Stalin began a ruthless purge of the Red Army's officer corps. In just under two years, 50 per cent of all officers of the rank of brigade commander and above were shot, imprisoned or removed from duty. M.N. Tukachevsky and most other Deep Battle and Deep Operation theorists were executed and their ideas banned, a great loss to the Soviets in the early war years.

In conjunction with the purges, a commission chaired by Deputy Commissar for Defence, G.I Kulik, undertook a flawed analysis of tank operations in the Far East and Spanish Civil War. This concluded that deep raids with tanks were increasingly impractical because of new, more powerful antitank

BELOW: Whitewashed T-34/76D tanks of 1st Ukrainian Front pulled over on the side of the Zhitomir Shosse highway on the outskirts of Kiev in December 1943. A distinctive feature of these and all Soviet tanks were the wide tracks that spread the weight over a larger area and allowed the tanks to cross snow and soft ground. The tanks have been brought forward to repel an attack by the well-equipped and experienced XLVIII Panzer Corps that eventually forced them back.

guns. It was argued that the tank corps were too cumbersome to be controlled in battle. Despite the majority of the commission voting in favour of retaining the tank corps, in November 1939 the Main Military Council agreed with the minority position and ordered the corps disbanded. Tanks were to be used in groups no larger than brigade strength, and for infantry support.

The experience of the disastrous Russo–Finnish War (1939–40) and the impressive performance of German armoured forces during the campaigns in Poland (1939) and France (1940) exposed the stupidity of this mistake. In late 1940, orders were given to reform the mechanized corps. At the start of the war, there were 29 mechanized corps in different stages of formation. These were supposed to have three divisions, totalling more than 36,000 men and 1031 tanks, including 256 BT-7, 17 T-37/T-38s, and 546 KVs and T-34s. However, the formation of such a large number of corps proved impossible, given shortages in

personnel, tanks, weapons, and vehicles. By mid–1941, the great losses that had been suffered meant that the mechanized corps were disbanded.

Tank regiments were nominally reduced from 93 to 67 tanks. Problems in the efficient handling of regiments in battle caused by the dual system of brigade and regimental commanders were resolved by the dissolution of the latter in combat formations. The preference for equipping tank brigades with a mixture of heavy-, medium- and light tanks in each battalion severely impaired their effectiveness because of the different capabilities of each tank type. This led to the establishment of a uniform organization for all tank brigades in July 1942, which was slightly modified at the end of 1943 to provide more appropriate support units for the new and formidable standard-issue T-34/85 tank.

The experience gained in the winter offensive of 1941–1942 validated the basic principles of Deep Battle, but lack of large tank formations under Army

ABOVE: Soldiers sit on the rear deck of T-34/85s as they advance over rough terrain towards a Soviet collective farm. Though the men who were assigned to this role often suffered heavy casualties, they were invaluable for the tank crews, since they could fight through infantry strongpoints and antitank gun positions. Moreover, for Soviet infantry, riding into battle on the warm rear decks of tanks was a much more appealing option than slogging on foot through the dust, mud and snow of the Russian landscape.

RIGHT: The crews of two antitank guns, a 76.2mm (3in) Model 1942 and a 45mm (1.77in) Model 1942, wheel their guns across a shallow river; in the background T-34/76 tanks carry infantry forward. This is almost certainly a posed photograph: the bunched crews and the combination of guns and tanks makes little tactical sense. The officer on the left seems to be ambling up the riverbank.

BELOW: A parade by T-26 tanks shows clearly the results of the mass-production programme of 1931 and 1941 which produced 12,000 T-26s of all marks. In the same period, French tank production was 4000 and German a mere 3400. In 1941 the Red Army had many obsolescent tanks like the T-26 and BT series, and STAVKA lacked the operational skills to use massed armour correctly.

Front headquarters control restricted exploitation beyond tactical depth to inflict operational shock. To implement the Deep Operation, in March 1942 the commander of Red Army Tank and Mechanized Forces, General Fedorenko, began the formation of the first four tank corps. They consisted of 2, and later 3 tank brigades, and 1 motorized rifle brigade, giving a strength of 5603 men and 100 tanks (20 heavy KV tanks, 40 medium T-34 and 40 light T-60 or T-70). These were unbalanced forces, having no artillery, engineer or reconnaissance units. The mistake in allocating only a small group of officers to coordinate the brigades was demonstrated during fighting around Voronezh in spring 1942, where lack of tactical flexibility greatly hampered operations. The need for

greater autonomy of action from higher command was also noted.

Formation of mechanized corps began in September of 1942. Based on the experience gained with the tank corps, the new formations included the specialized and auxiliary units right from the start. Their were three types of organization for the six mechanized corps formed at the start of 1943. I and II Mechanised Corps had 175 tanks each and III and V had 224 tanks each, while the IV and VI had 204 tanks each. In due course, the organization of the first two corps became the basis for the organization for all new mechanized corps.

At the same time as the creation of the tank and mechanized corps, large operational units termed tank armies started to be formed. The first two tank armies (Third and Fifth) were formed in May–June 1942. By the end of July, the First and Fourth tank armies were formed under the Stalingrad Front, before huge losses led to them being disbanded a month later.

In the beginning, the standard organization for tank armies depended on the orders for their formation and thus varied widely. The experience of the using the Third Tank Army at Kozelsk and the Fifth Tank Army in the Stalingrad counteroffensive provided insights about their fighting capabilities and organizational structure. The varying mobility and fighting power of the tank army's complement of rifle divisions, tank corps and cavalry corps created serious problems in terms of cooperation, command and supply, making the 1942 establishment tank armies unwieldy, hard to manoeuvre and difficult to control.

A special meeting of the Main Defence Committee (GKO) was held in January of 1943 to develop guidelines for the organization of the tank armies. Preliminary suggestions from several prominent military commanders were heard. It was decided to rid the tank armies of any non-motorized rifle formations and organizationally emphasize their tank nucleus. Thus a tank army as a rule would have consisted of two tank and one mechanized corps, as well as an AA division, a multiple missile launcher 'Katyusha', howitzer artillery, AT artillery and motorcycle regiments, plus auxiliary and support units. In reality, however, the organization of an army was defined according to the orders for its formation. In 32 out of the 64 offensive operations which involved tank armies, they had only 2, not 3, corps. Only the Third Guards Tank Army had three corps throughout World War II.

The tank army's firepower, shock strength, mobility and self-sufficiency in combat were steadily increased between 1943 and 1944 by regular changes to the structure and weapons of the tank and mechanized corps. During January 1943 mechanized corps received a mixed self-propelled artillery regiment (8 SU-122s and 17 SU-76s) and a reserve of 40 tanks. In August 1943 the antitank artillery regiment was replaced by a self-propelled artillery regiment of 21 SU-76s, and a

BELOW: A parade of SU-76 SP guns gives a dramatic impression of the phenomenal rate of production of Soviet tank factories. Without a complex traversing turret, the SU-76 was quick and easy to produce; by the end of World War II the GAZ factories had manufactured over 12,500. By 1945 many had been converted to ammunition carriers or recovery vehicles. Subsequently some were transferred to China and North Korea and saw action in the Korean War.

RIGHT: British officers inspect a T-26S Model 1939. It was part of the joint Anglo–Soviet force that occupied Persia in 1941 in order to ensure the free flow of oil and also to prevent a possible Axis incursion via Syria and Iraq. The T-26S as shown here was an improved version which had been fitted with a drop-forged front for the turret, as well as a re-designed hull superstructure protected by sloping armour.

BELOW: An improved version of the T-26 with Christie suspension was built as the T-46, seen here with a frame radio antenna. However, the T-46 was too complex and expensive and production ceased after only 70 tanks had been built, these vehicles seeing action with a Soviet armoured brigade against the Finns in 1940.

regiment of 15 SU-85s with a T-34 command tank. In 1944 the mechanized brigade's tank regiment lost its remaining light tanks, giving it a total of 35 T-34s. The tank corps' combat power was improved in a similar manner in August 1943 with the addition of two self-propelled artillery regiments (SU-76 and SU-152). A year later a light regiment of artillery was added.

In 1944 self-propelled and light artillery brigades were included in the tank armies. To further increase success in operations, they received additional reinforcements of artillery, antitank brigades, and antitank regiments. At the end of the war, a three-corps tank army usually had more than 50,000 men, 850–920 tanks and SP guns, about 800 field guns and mortars, and more than 5000 trucks and

other vehicles. However, in reality, they rarely deployed their full complement of personnel and equipment.

While the creation of the tank armies provided the tools for implementing Deep Operations, throughout the war the Red Army enhanced its ability to carry out the Deep Battle concept by the creation of independent tank and self-propelled artillery regiments that could be used to reinforce rifle formations during the breakthrough of the enemy front line. This process began as early as 1942, when independent tank regiments were created in order to support rifle formations during combat.

In October 1942 this process was developed further with the creation of independent breakthrough heavy tank regiment for use on the main axis of an attack. These regiments consisted of four companies, each of five KV-1 tanks. These formations were initially formed by heavy tanks which had been withdrawn from the mixed independent tank battalions, and recently disbanded heavy tank brigades. In February 1944 the heavy breakthrough regiments were converted to a new organization and renamed 'heavy tank regiments' with 21 IS-2 tanks and support units. These regiments were immediately given the honorary status of 'Guard' upon formation. Independent tank regiments were also re-organized by removing light tanks and strengthening administration and supply units. Independent Guards heavy tank brigades with 65 heavy IS-2 tanks were created in December 1944.

CONCLUSION

The Red Army of the interwar years was a paradox. On the one hand, its gifted intellectual commanders developed one of the most sophisticated doctrines for using armoured forces in the world. To implement its ideas, it created large tank formations equipped with some of the most advanced tanks in the world. Yet even before Stalin's crippling purges and the Kulik commission, it had created forces deficient in many equipment areas, and troops and officers inadequately trained to carry out the new and complex tactical and operational ideas. Only in the brutal cauldron of war would the Red Army finally master the techniques for Deep Battle and Deep Operations.

BELOW: A Soviet tank crew pose in front of their T-34/76. One of the reasons for the dramatic losses suffered by the tank arm in the early part of the war was the lack of proper training for crews. Until the German advance was successfully stemmed in 1943, units were rushed to the front and thrown into battle unprepared for combat with the experienced German crews. As the war progressed, however, Soviet tankmen became more adept and tactically aware.

CHAPTER THREE

LIGHT TANKS

Light tanks were used as reconnaissance vehicles, scouting ahead of the main forces. In theory, they used agility, speed and a low silhouette to compensate for thin armour and modest firepower, but their crews on the Eastern Front were extremely vulnerable and suffered heavy losses.

The industrialization of the Soviet economy in the late 1920s and throughout the 1930s was a daunting and complex challenge. The speed at which the Soviets achieved their aim of converting Russia into a first-rate industrial power was an impressive achievement, but was not without errors and limitations. One of the most significant restrictions on the development of industry was a lack of experienced technical personnel, especially design engineers. This had a strong impact on the Red Army's armaments programme at the start of the First Five Year Plan. Designs and prototypes for heavy- and medium tanks were rapidly developed, but the numbers delivered to the Red Army were low, because the designs were too complex for the infant Soviet industry. In contrast, the experience gained in light-tank design such as the T-18, and the simplicity of their construction, meant that they could be built in the vast numbers required by the Red Army's mechanization programme. At the outbreak of war in 1941, light tanks were the most numerous type in the Soviet inventory.

LEFT: Draped in the vestiges of camouflage, a T-60 light tank burns in a Soviet street. As its turret is facing to the rear, it suggests the tank was fleeing from its eventual destroyer. The T-60 had a high-velocity 20mm (0.78in) ShVAK aircraft cannon as its main armament and a co-axial 7.62mm (0.3in) DT machine gun.

ABOVE: A T-26TU Model 1931 fitted with a Model 28 37mm (1.46in) gun in the left turret and a DT 7.62mm (0.3in) machine gun in the right. It carried 180 rounds of main armament ammunition on board, had a crew of three, and was usually assigned to platoon and company commanders.

Like most Red Army weapons, the design, production and combat roles of light tank types underwent a variety of changes between 1929 and 1945. The initial emphasis on light-tank construction placed them at the forefront of the characteristic pattern of tank design that emerged in the Soviet Union of the 1930s. At the start, Soviet tank design relied on the purchase of foreign tanks, which were either directly copied, or

served as the inspiration for native models. By the start of the 1940s, this situation changed as a mature Soviet tank industry evolved original designs from first-generation concepts.

The experience of war between 1941 and 1945 led to a decline in light-tank production. In the opening two years of the war, production remained high for three reasons. First, the need to quickly replace the catastrophic losses suffered between 1941 and 1942 (7000 tanks in the first year alone) forced the Soviets to continue manufacturing existing tank types – despite their poor performance in battle – rather than disrupt production with the introduction of improved models. Second, light tanks were simple and cheap to construct. Third, and perhaps most significant, because they did not require scarce armour plate and powerful engines, they could be manufactured in large numbers in smaller and less specialized factories. This was of vital importance between 1941 and 1942, when the evacuation of large Soviet industrial plants to the east in order to avoid capture by the advancing Germans seriously disrupted production of medium T-34 and heavy KV tanks. Once the relocation and expansion of the armaments industry was completed in 1942, light-tank manufacture was diminished in preference of these heavier, more battleworthy types. Production was terminated in late 1943.

The war also saw an increase in the armour and firepower of tanks and anti-tank weapons, which reduced the battlefield effectiveness of light tanks, drastically altering their role. Originally, interwar Soviet military thought had envisaged the use of light tanks for reconnaissance, and in direct support of infantry during the assault. This latter role

was gradually reduced during the Great Patriotic War (World War II) because of the increase in defending firepower, which made it impossible, or suicidal, to extensively employ light tanks in an infantry support role. In early 1944, light tanks were removed from tank- and mechanized brigades and regiments. Their infantry support role was completely taken over by the superior T-34 medium tank and SU-76 self-propelled gun, which were available in abundance. The remaining examples of the T-60, T-70 and T-80 light tanks were used for reconnaissance (although armoured cars and British and American Lend-Lease tanks were often preferred), as escorts to supply convoys, artillery tractors, command tanks, and in the role of protecting headquarters.

PRE-WAR LIGHT TANKS: T-26

The 13 February 1931 order of the Revolutionary War Council (RVS) to begin mass production of the T-27 tankette signalled the birth of the massive armoured and mechanized formations which were envisaged in the General Staff's Programme for the Armoured-Automobile supply to the Red Army. But arguably it was the decision, taken on the same day, to manufacture the T-26 light infantry support tank that heralded the creation of an effective Red Army armoured force. The T-27 was only

T-26S MODEL 1939 LIGHT TANK

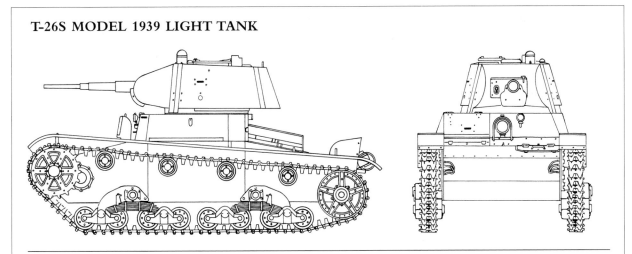

SPEED: 28km/h (17mph)

DIMENSIONS: Length 4.80m (15ft 9in); Width 2.39m (7ft 10in); Height 2.33m (7ft 8in); Weight 10,465kg (10.30 tons)

ARMOUR: 25mm (0.9in)

WEAPONRY: One 45mm (1.77in), two 7.62mm (0.3in) MG

EFFECTIVE RANGE: 200km (125 miles)

CREW: 3

BELOW: T-26B-2 Model 1933 tanks on a May Day parade in Red Square. Initially armed with a new long-barrelled 37mm (1.46in) gun, the T-26 was up-gunned with a 45mm (1.77in) weapon. Though it was intended to fit all tanks with radios, only a fraction received them; these, with their distinctive horseshoe-shaped frame antenna, were reserved for platoon and company commanders.

intended for the reconnaissance role, as it was the T-26 that was to carry out the first phase of the Red Army's concept of Deep Battle by providing direct support to infantry when breaking through enemy defences. The T-26 was central to conducting future offensive operations. When production ended in 1941, over 12,000 variants had been manufactured.

The T-26 was based upon the British Vickers-Armstrong 6 ton (6.09 tonne) E Light Tank, purchased by the Directorate of the Mechanization of the Red Army (UMM), led by I.A. Khalepsky, on 28 May 1929. The Vickers E models arrived

in the Soviet Union in 1930, but before production began, Soviet designers were allowed to develop their own prototypes based on the British design. Two such prototypes, the TMM-1 and TMM-2, were developed and underwent comparative tests with the Vickers E at the Kubinka testing ground near Moscow. The superior British design was selected for production, under a licence agreement which was previously agreed with Vickers-Armstrong, and designated T-26. The first large-scale public display of the new tank took place in Red Square on 7 November 1931.

T-37 MODEL 1934 SMALL AMPHIBIOUS TANK

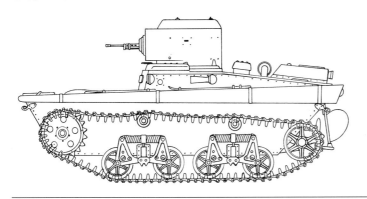 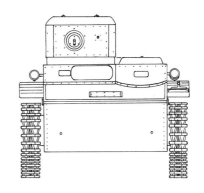

SPEED: 35km/h (21mph)

DIMENSIONS: Length 3.75m (12ft 4in); Width 2.07m (6ft 7in);
Height 1.82m (5ft 11in); Weight 3200kg (3.15 tons)

ARMOUR: 10mm (0.39in)

WEAPONRY: One 7.62mm (0.3in) MG

EFFECTIVE RANGE: 185km (115 miles)

CREW: 2

T-26 designs between 1931 and 1933 were distinguished by the diversity of weapons installed on them, and most strikingly the use of twin turrets. The standard T-26 support tank was initially armed with two DT 7.62mm (0.3in) machine guns. A commander's variant was also manufactured with a 37mm (1.46in) gun replacing the machine gun in the right turret. An Armstrong-Siddeley petrol engine (renamed GAZ T-26), also manufactured under licence, gave the T-26 a road speed of 32km/h (20mph) and an impressive road range of 140km (87 miles). The use of twin turrets created some limitations in the tank's combat effectiveness. The two gunner's seats did not automatically rotate with the turret's mechanism; instead, they had to be swung round manually. Locks were fitted to the turrets, restricting their traverse to 265 degrees in order to prevent them from fouling each other.

The use of multiple turrets remained a distinctive feature of Soviet tank design until the late 1930s, but as early as 1933 it was discarded for the T-26 and subsequent light tanks in favour of a single turret. Initially the single turret variant was created by the crude technique of removing the right-hand turret. This proved unsatisfactory because the German Rheinmetall 37mm (1.46in) gun, which was selected for installation in the remaining turret, was difficult to load in the confined space. The turret ring also

had a tendency to fracture under the more powerful gun's recoil. The solution to the problem of mounting a larger gun was solved by designing a stronger, purpose-built turret. Designed by the Bolshevik Leningrad factory and KhPZ Kharkov works, the larger turret could mount the new 45mm (1.77in) Model 1932 gun. After further refinements, both the turret and gun became the standard production fit for the T-26 Model 1933, BT-5 and T-35 tank classes.

The T-26 Model 1933 became the most numerous production model of the class, with over 5000 manufactured up to 1937. However, thin armour and an underpowered engine meant that the tank was not universally liked by crews. The riveted armour was dropped after the border clashes with the Japanese in Manchuria between 1934 and 1935 revealed that machine-gun fire split the rivet, sending the inner part careening about the crew compartment, with lethal results. After this, all Soviet tank armour was welded. Repeated modifications to the engine design between 1931 and 1941 made only modest improvements from 90bhp (67kW) to 97bhp (72kW). It was intended to fit horseshoe radio antenna to all tanks, but resources proved inadequate. The large, exposed antenna also proved vulnerable to artillery splinters and was later abandoned. The last models of the T-26 Model 1933 produced in 1936 received two more DT

ABOVE: In the snow, Finnish officers examine a couple of captured T-37 Model 1934, which would have been classified by the Soviets as Small Amphibious Tanks. The track has come off the vehicle in the foreground, leaving its bare wheels exposed, and has been draped over its rear deck. The machine guns have been removed from the tanks, undoubtedly so that they could be used by the Finns in the age-old practice of aiming captured weapons at their former owners.

machine guns: one in the turret rear, the other on top for antiaircraft duties. However, by the late 1930s, the limited use of the T-26 in several conflicts raised the question about its ability to survive against new direct-fire weapons.

T-26 LIGHT TANKS IN ACTION

The first combat tests of Soviet tanks came in the Spanish Civil War (1936–39), clashes in the Far East with Japan (1938–39), and the Russo–Finnish War (1939–40). The great contrasts in weather, terrain and nature of the opponents in these conflicts provided diverse lessons about the tactical employment of armour, and revealed both the strengths and weaknesses of the T-26.

In Spain the T-26 was to suffer from lack of coordination with Republican infantry forces that often left the tanks exposed to enemy counterattacks or artillery. With no influence over the tactical employment of Republican forces, there was relatively little Soviet commanders could do to improve cooperation with supporting forces. The T-26 itself did perform effectively on a number of occasions. During the attack on Sesena on 29 October 1936, T-26s of the 1st Battalion succeeded in penetrating Nationalist defences, and went on to shoot up their positions in the village, overrun an artillery battery, and destroy two CV 3/35 tankettes, for minimal loss. Throughout the war the 45mm (1.77in) gun on the T-26 gave it the edge against Spanish Nationalist tanks and those of their German and Italian allies. It proved so superior that the Nationalist Army offered a bounty of 500 pesetas for any tank captured. The T-26 demonstrated a similar superiority against Japanese armour at Lake Khasan (1938) and Khalkin Gol (1939). Unlike Spain, terrain and the all-Soviet nature of the forces allowed the T-26 to be used *en masse* and in coordination with supporting arms. The result was that Japanese forward defences were overwhelmed by infantry

supported by rapid fire from the massed 45mm (1.77in) guns of the T-26.

Yet serious weaknesses were also revealed in Spain, the Far East and Finland. The weakness of the 15mm (0.59in) frontal- and 6mm (0.23in) side armour to new antitank weapons and direct artillery fire led to heavy losses in all three conflicts. Fighting on the Jarma River in Spain cost Soviet formations 40 per cent of their strength to 37mm (1.45in) antitank gunfire. Lack of artillery and infantry support led to heavy casualties in Finland, and even when this

BELOW: Battalion and company commanders lead their battalion in a pre-war May Day Parade in 1937. The vehicle in the front is the T-37(V) commander's version, recognizable by the frame antenna around the hull. The T-37 was closely derived from the Vickers Carden-Loyd amphibious tank that had been purchased by the USSR during 1931.

support was provided, as at Khalkin Gol, substantial losses occurred. The conclusion to be drawn was that by the late 1930s, the T-26 was already highly vulnerable in performing its direct-assault role, and that the emergence of more powerful antitank weapons in the near future would make it obsolete.

LATE T-26 MODEL

In light of the T-26 combat experience, Soviet designers undertook a series of modifications to upgrade and extend the service life of the T-26. Fuel capacity was increased and some models received searchlights for nightfighting. In 1937 the re-designated T-26S received stronger frontal armour (25mm/0.9in) and a turret with thicker and sloping armour. Defensive improvements continued in 1939 with sloping hull armour. In light of the Finnish War, plates were added to a number of tanks to increase their armour to 50mm (1.9in). However, despite these modifications, when the Germans attacked the Soviet Union in June 1941, the T-26 proved obsolete against modern antitank weapons, although its 45mm (1.77in) gun could destroy all German armoured vehicles it faced except the Panzerkampfwagen IV. Many T-26s were also lost because of technical problems

with gearboxes and clutch failures. Of course, lack of crew training, inept command, fuel- and ammunition shortages, and woeful repair facilities exacerbated losses but, as the Soviets had already acknowledged by halting production in 1940, the T-26 was due for replacement. The first tank action of the war confirmed this view. Between 22 and 23 June, a counterattack against the 18th Panzer Division south-east of Brest Litovsk by two brigades of General Bogdanov's 30th Tank Division, composed chiefly of T-26 tanks, made no appreciable progress, whilst suffering heavily at the hands of German antitank gunfire and air attacks.

T-26 ENGINEERING VEHICLES

The utility of the T-26 design was exploited by Soviet designers to create a number of variants to undertake specialized combat roles. Based on the T-26 Model 1931, the OT-26 had a flamethrower with a range of 25m (82ft) mounted in the right turret. The need to increase space for larger fuel tanks led to the left-hand turret being omitted from later versions. Even so, limitations on fuel and difficulties in operating the flamethrower in the small turret led to the development of the OT-130, based on the larger Model 1932 turret.

After 1937, the new OT-133 flamethrower, based on the more reliable and better-armoured T-26S, was introduced. Both the OT-130 and OT-133 saw action in the Russo–Finnish war, but their performance was poor because the limited range of their armament forced them to come within range of Finnish defences which concentrated their fire against these detested weapons. Lack of a machine gun also made them defenceless when they had expended their main armament. This experience led to the development of better-armoured KV and T-34 flamethrowing tanks with improved weapons, although the OT tanks were still being used in 1941.

A bridge-carrying variant, the ST-26, was developed and used between 1934 and 1938. Its 7m (23ft) bridge was used for crossing narrow gaps or obstacles. Other roles the T-26 was adapted for included towing tractors and forward-observation vehicles for the artillery, and as smoke- and chemical weapon tanks.

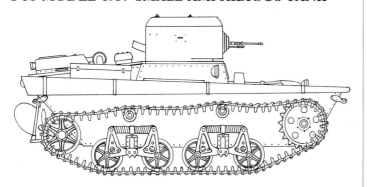

T-38 MODEL 1937 SMALL AMPHIBIOUS TANK

SPEED: 40km/h (25mph)

DIMENSIONS: Length 3.76m (12ft 4in); Width 1.95m (6ft 5in); Height 1.62m (5ft 4in); Weight 3332kg (3.28 tons)

ARMOUR: 10mm (0.39in)

WEAPONRY: One 7.62mm (0.3in) MG

EFFECTIVE RANGE: 150km (93 miles)

CREW: 2

T-40 MODEL 1940 AMPHIBIOUS TANK

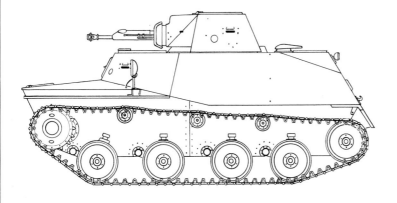

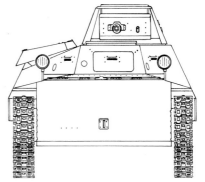

SPEED: 45km/h (28mph)

DIMENSIONS: Length 4.43m (13ft 6in); Width 2.51m (8ft 3in);
    Height 2.12m (6ft 11in); Weight 5590kg (5.50 tons)

ARMOUR: 13mm (0.51in)

WEAPONRY: One 12.7mm (0.5in) MG and one 7.62mm (0.3in)
    MG; or one 20mm (0.78in) cannon and one 7.62mm (0.3in)
    MG EFFECTIVE RANGE: 350km (215 miles)

CREW: 2

T-46 AND T-50

The low mobility of the T-26 across country compared to the BT Fast Tank, and its increasing vulnerability towards the end of the 1930s, caused the Soviets to design two prototypes to replace it: the T-46 and the T-50. The T-46 was begun in 1935 by an OKMO team in 1935. The aim was to enhance the T-26's mobility by adapting it to fit the BT American-designed Christie suspension. A small number of T-46 tanks were manufactured, but the complexity of design, the cost and the basic fact that it was an unnecessary, and inferior, rival to the BT Fast Tank meant that mass production was never actually sanctioned by the Soviet higher powers.

The T-50 development programme of 1939–41 was a seemingly more pragmatic affair, being designed to supersede the increasingly obsolescent T-26 and BT tanks in their infantry support and exploitation roles. Prototypes from the Voroshilovsky and Kirovsky factories were tested in 1940, the latter being accepted for production. Externally the T-50's sloping hull armour and welded turret gave it a strong resemblance to the T-34 medium tank, but internally it was closer to the layout of the T-26. The 37mm (1.46in) frontal armour was actually inferior to that of the T-34, but it was over twice the thickness of the BT-7

armour, and three times the armour of the standard T-26 tanks. The 40–57 degree slope of the hull further enhanced the tank's protection.

A weight of 13.7 tonnes (13.5 tons) combined with a torsion bar suspension and V-4 diesel engine gave the T-50 a remarkably low ground pressure and top road speed of 60km/h (37mph). It was armed with the standard 45mm (1.77in) gun and one co-axial 7.62mm (0.303in) DT machine gun. In the end, the T-50 was manufactured in negligible numbers for three reasons: first, the disruption caused to the tank industry by the outbreak of war; second, insurmountable difficulties in manufacturing the V-4 engine; third, the British Lend-Lease Valentine tanks and the T-34 had proved themselves to be more than capable of carrying out its envisaged roles.

LIGHT AMPHIBIOUS SCOUT TANKS

Another area in which British designs had a strong influence on early Soviet tank types was the development of amphibious light armoured vehicles. The series of tank types bought from Vickers-Armstrong/Carden Loyd in 1929 had included the innovative VCL Amphibian tank. A light 3.04 tonne (3 ton) vehicle with a machine gun, it could cross small waterways. The Amphibian inspired a generation of Soviet amphibious tank

ABOVE: Soviet soldiers in snow camouflage move off from a column of *Lyokhy* Tank T-70 light tanks. The T-70 entered service in January 1942; it had a crew of two and was armed with a 45mm (1.77in) gun and a 7.62mm (0.3in) DT machine gun. It was made at the Gorki Automobile Works and when production ceased in 1943, the factory had built 8226 vehicles. Despite its narrow tracks, a weight of 9960kg (9.8 tons) meant that drivers could move it across firm snow.

designs, until the demands of war terminated production.

In 1931 a design team at Zavod Nr 47 near Moscow simultaneously developed two prototype amphibious tanks which were based on the VCL design. The T-33 (originally designated the MT-33) had a crew of two and weighed 3.04 tonnes (3 tons). The T-41 was similar in design and armament, carrying a single, turret-mounted DT 7.62mm (0.3in) machine gun, with the main difference being in the body, which was slightly larger for greater buoyancy when crossing a waterway. Unsatisfactory performances during trials of the two vehicles, and especially problems with the T-41's waterproofing and the unsuitability of the VCL suspension, led to the development of a further alternative prototype.

The T-37 was a refinement of the earlier models rather than a radically new design. A modified Horstmann spring coil suspension was adopted with improved tracks and drive system for the single propeller. The hull was strengthened and sheet-metal track guards encasing balsa-wood floats were added for extra buoyancy. These modifications were dispensed with as the T-37 came to the end of its production run in 1936. Waterproofing problems persisted because of the hull's river construction, but this was on the whole overcome in 1935 by welding together and riveting the tank's armour plates.

The durability of the T-37 design was shown during rigorous trials in 1933 when over 11 days, 7 T-37s travelled 1126km (700 miles), over 965km (600 miles) in water. Like most Soviet tank designs, dedicated command variants were constructed, which were termed T-37TU. A production run of 1200 vehicles was completed between 1933 and 1936. They served in a reconnaissance role with tank, mechanized and cavalry units in all Red Army operations up to 1942.

THE T-38

Plans to modernize the T-37 in the mid–1930s led to such extensive changes by the Zavod Nr 37 team that it was decided to designate it T-38. Improved hull design gave a lower profile and a decrease in weight. Coupled with a new suspension, wider tracks and improved steering, the T-38 was easier to handle, more manoeuvreable, and altogether a better swimmer than the T-37. Armament, however, remained the same as the T-37, although a 20mm (0.78in) gun fitted in a low turret with the driver was rejected because it restricted his ability to control the vehicle.

In addition to its reconnaissance role, the T-38 underwent several experimental combat roles. During the 1936 Kiev Military District manoeuvres, a number of T-38 and T-27 vehicles were air-landed deep behind enemy lines in a radical test of the potential of airborne forces. In 1940, several T-38s were adapted for radio control and fitted with explosives

for use against enemy bunkers. An estimated 1300 vehicles were manufactured between 1937 and 1939.

THE T-40

Common to many pre-war Soviet tank designs, the T-37 and T-38 proved to be too vulnerable to heavy machine-gun fire and shell splinters. This problem had been foreseen as early as 1938, when a special research department at Zavod Nr 37, led by chief engineer N.A. Astrov, was instructed to design two variants of a new light scout tank, of which one was to be amphibious. Several prototypes of the amphibious vehicle (initially designated T-30A) were in trials between July and August 1939. Once orders to rectify defects were complied with, the vehicle was accepted for production and service as the T-40 on 19 December 1939.

The vehicle had a torsion suspension and, in the water, was driven by a single propeller and steered by two rudders at the rear. A more powerful engine, hermetically sealed hatches and a better-shaped front with a special water deflector enabled the T-40 to cross wider rivers with strong currents, like the Dniepr and Dnestr (although as a precaution the crew were supplied with lifebelts). Despite ambitious plans, production was low, and in 1940 the addition of extra armour and the need to

---

T-46

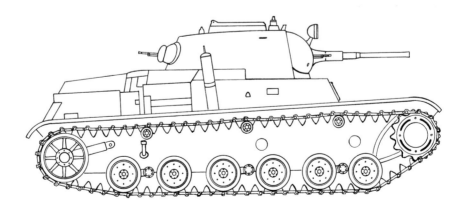

SPEED: 60km/h (36mph)

DIMENSIONS: Length 5.5m (18ft); Width 2.33m (7ft 8in); Height 2.29m (7ft 6in); Weight 9072kg (10.2 tons)

ARMOUR: 15mm (0.59in)

WEAPONRY: One 45mm (1.77in) L/46 and two 7.62mm (0.3in) MGs

EFFECTIVE RANGE: 499km (310 miles)

CREW: 3

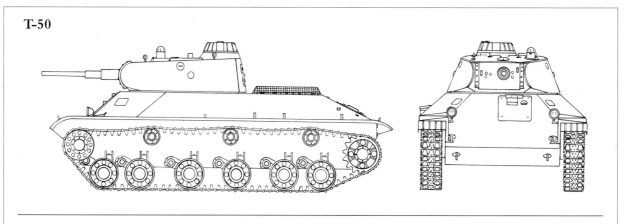

T-50

SPEED: 50km/h (31mph)

DIMENSIONS: Length 5.18m (17ft); Width 2.48m (8ft 1in);
    Height 2m (6ft 8in); Weight 13,715kg (13.5tons)

ARMOUR: 37mm (1.46in)

WEAPONRY: One 45mm (1.77in); two 7.62mm (0.3in) MG

EFFECTIVE RANGE: 352km (220 miles)

CREW: 4

increase tank production led to the non-amphibious T-30B prototype being given priority, also as the T-40.

At 6.09 tonnes (6 tons), both T-40 variants weighed twice the weight of the T-37 and T-38, but the cause of this increase − welded thicker 14mm (0.5in) bulletproof armour − did not make it any less vulnerable in battle to light weapons than they were. The inability of its 12.7mm (0.5in) DShK main gun, while firing armour-piercing rounds, to penetrate armour 16mm (0.62in) above 300m (984ft) also restricted its combat worthiness. Possibly if the T-40 had been used in its reconnaissance role, its armour and gun might just have proved sufficient, but the tendency of Soviet commanders to use them like regular tanks led to heavy losses in 1940 and 1941.

LIGHT TANKS OF WORLD WAR II

Scepticism about the ability to manufacture the projected T-50 light tank and poor performance of the T-40 led N.A. Astrov's Zavod Nr 37 team to develop a new light tank which would be capable of rapid production in order to satisfy the Soviet Union's desperate need for tanks after catastrophic losses in summer 1941. They retained the suspension, chassis and engine of the T-40, but a new hull with an improved silhouette and an increased armour protection of 25mm (0.98in) frontal was designed. A distinctive eight-sided conical turret that was cheaper to

manufacture than the T-40's was also developed. The ineffective 12.7mm (0.5in) gun was retained with a co-axial DT 7.62mm (0.3in) machine gun.

THE T-60

The basic design was completed by the Zavod Nr 37 team in an amazing 15 days. Having created the T-60 concept on his own initiative, Astrov, seconded by Lieutenant-Colonel V.P. Okunev, wrote to Josef Stalin contrasting the advantages of mass-producing the T-60 with the more complex T-50. The following inspection by a high-ranking minister resulted in two decisions. First, to replace the 12.7mm (0.5in) machine gun with a 20mm (0.78in) ShVAK, an improvement over earlier light tanks, but still inadequate against the standard German Panzer III and IV models that the T-60 would have to engage whilst a shortage of medium T-34 tanks persisted into 1942. Second, the Main Defence Committee (GKO) headed by Stalin ordered production of 10,000 T-60s to commence immediately. Some sources claim that Stalin's interest in the T-60 was so great that he actually attended the vehicle's final trials in person.

Displacement of Soviet industry to the east in 1941 disrupted production and further refinement of the T-60. In Autumn Zavod Nr 37's move east saw work on the T-60 transferred to Zavod Nr 38 at Kirov and GAZ at Gorki. Soon

T-60 MODEL 1942 LIGHT TANK

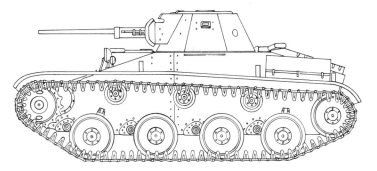
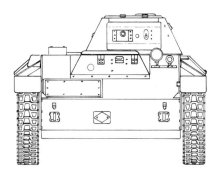

SPEED: 45km/h (38mph)

DIMENSIONS: Length 4.29m (14ft 1in); Width 2.46m (8ft 1in);
   Height 1.89m (6ft 2in); Weight 5150kg (5.07 tons)

ARMOUR: 20mm (0.78in)

WEAPONRY: One 20mm (0.78in) cannon; one 7.62mm
   (0.3in) MG

EFFECTIVE RANGE: 615km (380 miles)

CREW: 2

afterwards, additional industrial evacuation left GAZ as the sole developer. Modifications made by that company in 1942 included an increase in frontal armour to 35mm (1.37in). The increased weight from the new armour exacerbated the T-60's sluggish performance characteristics, most notably its inability to keep up with the T-34 on cross-country operations. A series of modifications failed to remedy this shortfall.

Installation of the GAZ-203 engine gave the T-60 theoretical speeds of 44km/h (27.3mph) by road and 22km/h (13.6mph) across country, but the latter was difficult to achieve and sustain. Replacing the spoked roadwheels on the 1941 model with disc wheels, as well as the enforced adoption of an all-metal construction because of rubber shortages had no real impact. Mobility over marshy- and snow-covered terrain was

BELOW: Soviet recruits hear a lecture on the transmission of the T-60A light tank; this tank seems to have had its armament removed for the lesson. Firing its 20mm (0.78in) ShVAK cannon, the T-60 could penetrate the same armour as the 37mm (1.46in) gun which was proposed for the T-60.

RIGHT: A wary-looking German soldier has his picture taken while seated on a captured T-70. The tank, which was mass-produced at the Gorki Automobile Works, was given the same chassis as the T-60, but with the drive taken to the front, instead of to the rear. It had a newly designed turret and its armament comprised a 45mm (1.77in) gun as well as a co-axial 7.62mm (0.303in) DT machine gun. The hull armour was given better angles for protection than previous tanks and the driver was equipped with an armoured visor.

enhanced by the development of removable track extensions, but again, they could not solve the difficulties of cooperating with T-34s. Similar attempts to up-gun the T-60 with the 37mm (1.46in) ZiS-19 and 45mm (1.77in) ZiS-19BM guns proved abortive because of the tank's small turret. By the time a re-designed turret capable of mounting the 45mm (1.77in) ZiS-19BM gun had passed its trials, the project was cancelled because the new T-70 light tank had been accepted for service. When production switched to the T-70 during February 1943, a total of 6022 T-60 light tanks had been manufactured.

T-70 AND T-80

N.A. Astrov's team developed the T-70 with the intention of creating a light tank with more robust armour, stronger armament and greater mobility than the T-60.

T-70 MODEL 1942 LIGHT TANK

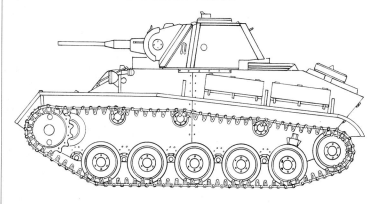

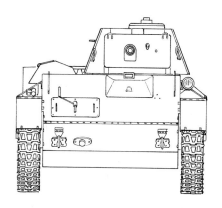

SPEED: 50km/h (31mph)

DIMENSIONS: Length 4.66m (15ft 2in); Width 2.52m (7ft 8in); Height 2.10m (6ft 9in); Weight 9950kg (9.79 tons)

ARMOUR: 60mm (2.36in)

WEAPONRY: One 45mm (1.77in); one 7.62mm (0.3in) MG

EFFECTIVE RANGE: 450km (280 miles)

CREW: 2

After modifications to the power system, re-designing the turret in flat armour plate rather than copying the T-40's construction, and placing it on the left of the hull with the engines on the right for easier construction, the T-70 was accepted for production in March 1942. Despite the Astrov team's best endeavours, the T-70 was at best a modest improvement on its predecessor, and in some areas, even worse.

At first glance, the T-70's 45mm (1.77in) ZiS-19BM gun – which was mounted in a turret on the left of the hull – and 45mm (1.77in) frontal armour did increase its protection and firepower. However, at that time, German modifications to the guns and armour of their medium Panzer III and IV tanks largely negated these armament developments which had been made in the T-70M.

Further problems in combat stemmed from a having a two-man crew. This forced the commander to double up as gunner, greatly inhibiting his ability to direct the driver and his fire accuracy when in contact with the enemy. The restrictions caused by a two-man crew were common to all Soviet light tanks, other than the T-26.

The T-70 design's greatest shortfall was in its mobility. The T-70 chassis was a copy of the T-60, modified to front-rather than rear-wheel drive. Reliance on other existing technology to cut costs and speed construction led to the unusual design of using two GAZ-202 lorry engines side by side, each powering a single track. This was not a complete success in manufacturing terms; more critically, the T-70's speed was only slightly greater than the T-60's, and its

BELOW: A T-70A Model 1942 in the classic reconnaissance role. Using a building as cover, the crew has moved up into the outskirts of a village. The tank appears to have suffered some operational damage, since the left headlamp has been knocked out of alignment. A spare roadwheel is bolted to the rear deck.

cross-country range of 180km (111.8 miles) was 70km (43.5 miles) less, and half that of the T-34 Model 1943. Clearly the T-70 was even less suited to taking part in the fast, deep-armoured operations envisaged by Soviet military planners. The overall unsuitability of the T-70 saw production end in 1943 after 8226 vehicles had been built.

The T-80 appeared in late 1943 and was again the result of work by the Astrov team. Their main aim was to install a larger turret with an electrical traverse to accommodate a commander and gunner, thereby improving the vehicle's performance in combat. The hull of the T-80 was identical to that of the T-70, the only other significant changes being a stronger suspension and wider tracks. Sound a design as it was, the T-80 did not alter the problems of survivability in

battle that confronted the T-60 and T-70. Many of the functions of light scout- and infantry-support tanks were also being undertaken either by the heavier British Valentine tanks provided through Lend-Lease, or by the T-34. The introduction of the SU-76 self-propelled gun, with many components of the T-60 and T-70 but with heavier firepower, was a better use of resources than light-tank production.

T-60 AND T-70 IN ACTION

As mentioned earlier, the performance of the T-60 and T-70 light tanks in combat was far from satisfactory because of a combination of inferior armour and lack of firepower. A noted critic of these two tank types was Major-General M.E. Katukov. In a meeting with Stalin in autumn 1942, Katukov told him that his crews did not like the T-60:

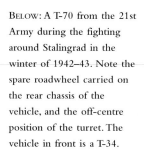

BELOW: A T-70 from the 21st Army during the fighting around Stalingrad in the winter of 1942–43. Note the spare roadwheel carried on the rear chassis of the vehicle, and the off-centre position of the turret. The vehicle in front is a T-34.

It has only a 20mm [0.78in] gun. In serious combat with armoured forces it just does not have it ... To attack in mud or snow is a deadly affair. In the battles around Moscow, we continually had to drag them in tow.

He was more cautious, however, about the new T-70, but nonetheless noted, somewhat sceptically, 'It has not shown us anything special.'

Katukov was right about the crews' intense dislike of the T-60: they nick-named them BM-2, meaning *Bratskaya Mogila na Dovoikh*; quite literally, 'a brother's grave for two', referring to the tank's vulnerability to German antitank fire. On the other hand, they were better than nothing during the dark days of 1941 and 1942, and as commander of I Tank Corps during fierce fighting earlier in 1942, Katukov was forced to acknowledge the debt he owed them:

And now, in this fateful hour, when the Germans had almost defeated us, those 'ridiculous' tanks saved our positions. It was lucky that the rye in the area was over a metre high, as the T-60s were almost hidden by it. Using this rye field, both of our T-60 tanks were able to infiltrate to the rear of the German infantry and then open fire. After several minutes of intensive fire, the German attack was halted.

The T-70's most dramatic engagements came in July 1943 at the Battle of Kursk, the climax of the German summer offensive. On 12 July, the Soviet Fifth Guards Tank Army and German II SS Panzer and III Panzer Corps clashed on a 32km (20 mile) front before the village of Prokhorovka. In all, during the heavy fighting, 429 German tanks and 870 Soviet tanks were engaged, and this number included 261 T-70 light tanks.

ABOVE: A Soviet SU-76M light SP gun covers a crossroads in Berlin in May 1945. With its open top and rear, the SU-76M was not popular with its four-man crews; however, with the exception of the T-34, it was the most widely produced armoured vehicle in the USSR during World War II. Armed with a 76.2mm (0.3in) ZiS-3 field gun, it had a maximum speed of 45km/h (28mph).

Although Soviet tank losses were significantly greater than those of their opponents (perhaps even as much as three times as high), the German advance was contained and the battle subsequently swung in favour of the Soviets. At the height of the battle on 12 July, the Red Army's 31st Tank Brigade succeeded in penetrating the rear elements of the 1st SS *Leibstandarte Adolf Hitler* Panzergrenadier Division. The 1st SS Divisional history recorded the sheer ferocity of the tank action:

the remaining three Panzers ... could fire at the Russians from a distance of 10 to 30 metres [30–90ft] and make every shell a direct hit because the Russians could not see through the dust and smoke that there were German tanks rolling along with them in the same direction. There were already 19 Russian tanks standing burning on the battlefield when the *Abteilung* [2nd Panzer Regiment] opened fire for the first time ... destroying 62 T-70s and T-34s in a three hour long battle that could almost be termed hand-to-hand combat.

Soviet losses were inflated by the Germans, but it seems clear that a large number of T-70s were lost. For the rest of the war, the T-60 and T-70 were gradually removed from combat roles and used for convoy duties, reconnaissance, training and defending headquarters.

BELOW: A pair of T-70s are used as gun tractors by the crews of two M1942 ZIS-3 76.2mm (3in) antitank guns to move their weapons up to the front across the frozen ground. This photograph was taken near Leningrad in February 1943.

SU-76 Self-propelled Gun

In 1942 the Soviets initiated a number of projects to produce mechanized artillery guns to support infantry and armoured formations. The design of the light gun was given to the Zavod Nr 38 team at Kirov. They began by basing their design on the existing T-60 chassis. The prototype OSU-76 had mounted a 76.2mm (3in) ZiS-3 gun at the rear of the hull in a crude casemate armour box. Problems with the T-60 chassis mounting the gun's weight led to the adoption of the longer, more robust T-70 chassis.

This vehicle, designated SU-12, was a joint project between the Zavod Nr 38 and the Zavod Nr 92 team from Gorki. The GKO accepted the prototype for production in December 1942 as the SU-76. A major re-design of the forward hull was undertaken by Astrov's team in spring 1943, and engine performance enhanced by replacing a side-by-side configuration for the GAZ-202 engines with an in-line set-up. This improved design was manufactured as the SU-76M, and all earlier models withdrawn.

The SU-76M appeared too late in the war to make an effective tank destroyer, but was valued in an infantry support role. The open top and rear and thin armour made the SU-76M vulnerable to light weapons and small-arms fire, especially in built-up areas. It was unpopular with crews, earning it the nicknames *Suka* (bitch) and *Golozhopil Ferdinant* (Naked Ass Ferdinant, after its profile's similarity to the German Ferdinand). Even so, the number produced in World War II was only surpassed by the T-34.

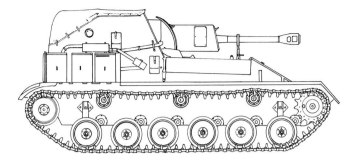

SU-76M MODEL 1944 LIGHT SP GUN

SPEED: 44km/h (27mph)

DIMENSIONS: Length 5m (16ft 5in); Width 2.74m (9ft); Height 2.20m (7ft 3in); Weight 11,200kg (11.02 tons)

ARMOUR: 35mm (1.3in)

WEAPONRY: One 76.2mm (3in) gun M1942

EFFECTIVE RANGE: 265km (165 miles)

CREW: 4

LEFT: Although despised by its crews, the SU-76M was an effective weapon which used the T-70's chassis. The vehicle was built in large numbers by the Soviets, and after the war continued to serve with a number of client states. In this photograph a Republic of Korea soldier inspects a captured SU-76M near Hayang in 1950, during the Korean War.

CHAPTER FOUR

MEDIUM AND FAST TANKS

The Red Army's experiments with the BT series of fast tanks paved the way for the development of the T-34, arguably the finest tank of the last century. The German invasion in 1941 led to the rediscovery of the doctrines of deep battle that had first been tested with BT tanks in the 1930s.

The Soviet classification of *Sredni* (Medium) tanks embraced the types T-12, T-22, T-24, T-28, T-29, T-32 and also the superb T-34, covered elsewhere, which was developed between 1930 and 1941. The BT, or *Bystrokhodnii*, Tank series were Fast Tanks that used the suspension developed by the irascible American inventor, J. Walter Christie. When in the late summer and autumn of 1941 a total of 17,000 tanks – which were largely BTs and T-26s – fell victim to Panzer divisions, the Germans were convinced that they had broken the back of the Soviet tank arm. This was understandable, since 75 per cent of the Soviet tank strength at the time was BTs and T-26s.

Left: Finnish troops in training leap from a moving BT-5 (V) captured early in 1940 – albeit without its frame antenna. To prevent destruction by 'friendly fire' they have painted a bold swastika emblem (a Finnish identifying symbol, not a mark of allegiance to the Nazi Party) on the tank's turret.

ABOVE: Developed around 1925, the T-12 had a 45mm (1.77in) gun with 100 rounds stowed on board. It was initially fitted with the distinctive 'tail' of the Renault FT-17 light tank. The T-12 was given a more powerful engine and also had a bigger crew than the FT-17. The commander had his own cupola with a machine gun. Although the 1930 budget had funds to develop 30 T-12s, the project was cancelled in favour of the T-24.

However, the BT series and T-26s were not the end-products of the 1930s tank-development programme. The USSR had learned valuable lessons about engines, armour, ballistic angles, track widths and firepower, and these were now being incorporated into new and formidable designs. The appearance of the T-34 and KV tank models which had been built in new or relocated factories beyond the Ural mountains came as an ugly shock to the German tank crews after the first two years of the war in the east, when they enjoyed a tactical edge over their Soviet adversaries.

In the late 1930s, Soviet armoured doctrine had changed, partly in the light of experience in the Spanish Civil War. In Spain General Pavlov had attempted deep penetration tactics with his BTs and T-26s, notably with 50 tanks at Esquivas on 29 October 1936. In March 1937 he launched an improvised counterattack with a larger force against the Italians near Guadalajara in fighting near Madrid. However, his tank tactics failed because inappropriate arrangements had been

made to support them – there was a lack of equally mobile infantry and artillery capable of keeping up – and because the tanks' fuel supply broke down.

The changes to Soviet tank doctrine had also happened because many of the more innovative officers in the Soviet Army had been been executed and others imprisoned. However, after 1941, those who were languishing in Gulags would return to lead the Red Army to victory in 1945.

EARLY MEDIUM TANKS: THE T-22

Developed by a German engineer named Grotte, the T-22 was also known as the TG-1, or Tank Grotte 1. It was the brain-child of the OKMO bureau in Leningrad, headed by N. Barykov, that was also developing the T-28. In 1932 the Grotte TG-1 was built as a prototype in three variants. One was armed with a 37mm (1.46in) gun and four machine guns, one with a 76.2mm (3in) gun and four machine guns, and the third with a 76.2mm (3in) and a 37mm (1.46in) gun and one machine gun. Grotte also proposed a heavier vehicle, the TG-3, that received the designation T-29.

The T-22 was a remarkably modern-looking vehicle for its time. It was large for the period – 7.5m (24ft 6in) long, 3m (9ft 8in) wide and 2.8m (9ft 1in) high – and had a crew of 11. Its M-5 engine developed 186kW (250bhp), giving a maximum road speed of 35km/h (21 mph). Armour protection was between 8mm (0.31in) and 20mm (0.78in), and it weighed 2500kg (27.5 tons). The TG-1/T-22 was not accepted for production due to its complexity and the problems this would pose for the tank industry.

T-24

Built in the 1930s, the T-24 was derived from the T-12 that had been developed from the MS series, which in turn was derived from the French Renault FT-17.

The MS was the first purely Russian design. The MS-1 resembled the Renault and was soon given a more powerful engine as the MS-2 and finally uprated to the MS-3. The MS-3, produced in 1923, had a crew of two and was armed with a M1916 37mm (1.46in) gun and two machine guns. It weighed 5500kg (5.41 tons) and was 3.5m (11ft 6in) long, 1.76m (5ft 9in) wide, and 2.12m (5ft 11in) high. It was powered by a six-cylinder 31kW (65bhp) petrol engine, and had a road

speed of 12km/h (10mph) and a road range of 60km (38 miles).

The T-12, built around 1925, had a simple hull structure between two tracks with small-bogie suspension. It had a cylindrical turret with a rounded commander's cupola and a crew of four. It weighed 17,236kg (19 tons) and was 7.5m (24ft 6in) long, 3m (9ft 8in) wide and 2.8m (9ft 1in) high. Armed with a Model 32 45mm (1.77in) gun with 100 rounds, it also had four DT machine guns. It was an unreliable design and was soon replaced by the T-24.

The T-24 was a good design but was let down by poor mechanicals. The hull was widened to overlap the tracks and the superstructure had a V-shaped front with the driver at the apex. The turret was roomy and had a cupola. However, after 25 were built, the drive train and suspension caused problems, and the project was cancelled.

The tank had a crew of three and was armed with a Model 32 45mm (1.77in) gun and three machine guns. Maximum armour was 25.4mm (1in) and the tank weighed 18,500kg (18.20 tons). It was 6.5m (21ft 3in) long, 3m (9ft 8in) wide and 2.8m (9ft 1in) high. Powered by an eight-cylinder 222kW (300bhp) petrol engine, its road speed was 24km/h (15mph) and it had a road range of 200km (125 miles).

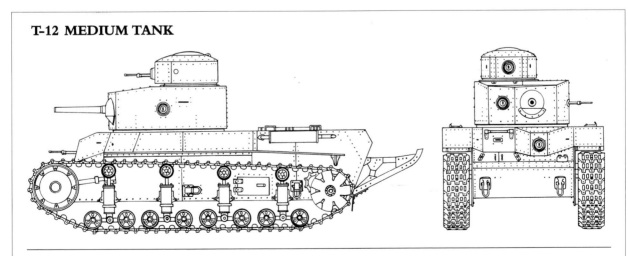

T-12 MEDIUM TANK

SPEED: n/a

DIMENSIONS: Length 7.5m (24ft 5in); Width 3m (9ft 8in); Height 2.8m (9ft 1in); Weight 19,800kg (21.8tons)

ARMOUR: 22mm (0.86in)

WEAPONRY: One 45mm (1.77in); four 7.62mm (0.3in) MG

EFFECTIVE RANGE: n/a

CREW: 4

ABOVE: The T-28A, with the short 76.2mm (3in) (L/16.5) gun in the main central turret and two auxiliary turrets, looked formidable. Despite its shape and bulk, it was fast for the period and up-armoured for its use in Finland in 1940.

T-28

Though a medium tank, with its three turrets the T-28 looked superficially like a heavy tank and could be mistaken for the multi-turreted T-35. The T-28 had been developed in 1932 at the Leningrad Kirov Plant or Bolshevik Factory as a break-through tank, and it drew on the British A6 medium and German NbFz Grosstraktor design. The Soviet forces had seen this German vehicle when they were employed in field exercises at the Kazan training area in 1929. After trials with the prototype, heavier armour and more powerful armament were requested, and the original Model 27/32 45mm (1.77in) gun was replaced by a 76.2mm (3in) gun. The first model was

T-28 MODEL 1934 MEDIUM TANK

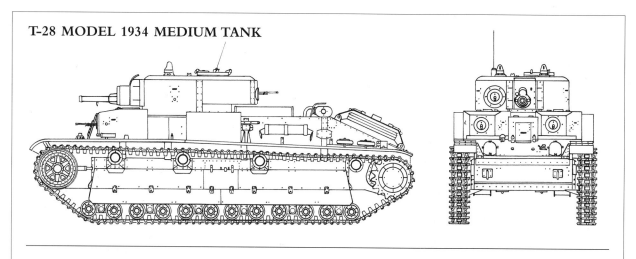

SPEED: 37km/h (22mph)

DIMENSIONS: Length 7.44m (24ft 5in); Width 2.86m (9ft 3in); Height 2.86m (9ft 3in); Weight 32,000kg (31.50 tons)

ARMOUR: 80mm (3.14in)

WEAPONRY: One 45mm (1.77in) or one 76.2mm (3in); three 7.62mm (0.3in) MG

EFFECTIVE RANGE: 220km (135 miles)

CREW: 6

accepted for adoption by the Red Army on 11 August 1933.

The T-28 had a crew of six who manned the central turret armed with a very effective dual-purpose 76.2mm (3in) gun with three DT machine guns, a co-axial DT, and two in two forward turrets. During 1938, further modifications saw the existing 16.5-calibre gun being replaced by a 26-calibre L-10, and this tank was designated the T-28 Ob.1938. The T-28 carried 70 rounds of main armament ammunition and 7938 for the DT machine guns.

The tank weighed 32,000kg (31.50 tons), and it was 7.44m (24ft 5in) long, 2.86m (9ft 3in) wide, and 2.86m (9ft 3in) high. It was powered by a M-17L V-12 372kW (500bhp) petrol engine that developed 1400rpm. The maximum road speed of 37km/h (22mph) was quite fast for vehicles of this type, while cross-country it was 20km/h (12.4mph) and the road range was 220km (135 miles). Maximum armour protection was 80mm (3.14in) and minimum 20mm (0.79in). The T-28 had multi-wheel suspension with a front idlers and rear drive; much

of this suspension was covered by skirting with mud chutes.

When the decision was taken to authorize production of the T-28, production was taken over by the Red Putilov Factory in Leningrad, because by now the Bolshevik Factory was fully committed to manufacturing the T-26 light tank. The first production batch of 10 vehicles took part in the May Day parade in Moscow in 1933.

The T-28 went through four modifications during its production run from 1933 to 1940. The T-28A that appeared in 1933 had modified suspension that consisted of 12 bogie rollers with four return rollers. It had increased frontal armour. German intelligence designated it the T-28V. The T-28B was a further modernization that the Germans designated T-28M. Work for this was undertaken between 1938 and 1939. A ball-mounted machine gun was fitted in the turret rear and the main gun uprated.

By the time the Winter War against Finland had begun, there were two T-28 Brigades: these were the 10th and 20th Heavy Tank Brigades. Both suffered

BELOW: On a May Day Parade T-28s rumble across Red Square. The multi-turret design was also popular in Britain, France and Germany in the 1930s, but only the Soviet Union saw its tanks go into action. The idea of a land-based battleship was appealing but the vehicles were easy targets for agile German tanks with their better command and control.

heavy losses from the small number of Finnish antitank gun crews, who nicknamed the clumsy vehicles 'The Mail Train'. In an attempt to improve the level of protection, the T-28C was developed. The frontal armour on the hull and turret was increased from 50mm (1.96in) to 80mm (3.14in) and the rear and sides to 40mm (1.57in) by additional 'screened armour'. The weight increased to 32,513kg (32 tons). The up-armoured tank performed extremely well in the breakthrough attacks against the Mannerheim Line in 1940.

The BT tank that was the mainstay of the prewar tank forces was known to its crews as 'Betka' – (Beetle) – the affectionate girl's diminutive 'Betushka', or 'Tri-Tankista' (Three Tank Men). It had originally been intended for an independent mechanized cavalry role, complemented by the T-28 that would provide infantry support. By the late 1930s, this distinction had disappeared and all tanks, including the BTs, were relegated to infantry support. The designations given to this vast range of light tanks differ in Western literature. In the 1930s when they were being developed, the USSR was highly secretive, and even the plants that built BTs were often more interested in technical improvement than recording by date and designation exactly when these changes were made. By the time production

ceased, a total of some 7000 BT tanks had been manufactured.

The significance of J.W. Christie's suspension, used in the BTs, cannot be over-emphasized. It transformed Soviet tank design and laid the foundations for a large and successful line of AFVs. Before World War I, Christie's Front Drive Motor Company had built tractors, a racing car and fire engines, and in 1919 it designed and built a light tank.

With the promise of cash reward in mind, Christie had produced a new tank in 1928. It proved very unreliable in testing at Fort Benning and it had inadequate engine cooling. Nevertheless, seven designated Medium Tank T3s or Combat Car T1s were ordered in June 1931 and they were produced by Christie's US Wheel Track Layer Corporation. The T3 was armed with a 37mm (1.46in) M1916 Trench Cannon and powered by a Liberty V-12 engine. The improved T3E2 had a completely new two-man turret, five machine guns, thicker armour, a 324.6kW (435bhp) Curtis engine and higher speed: 56.3km/h (35mph) on tracks and 96.6km/h (60mph) on wheels.

In 1929 a US cavalry officer, C.C. Benson, had enthused in two US military journals about the vehicle that he called 'The New Christie, Model 1940' because, he said, it was 'easily ten years ahead of its time'. These articles had

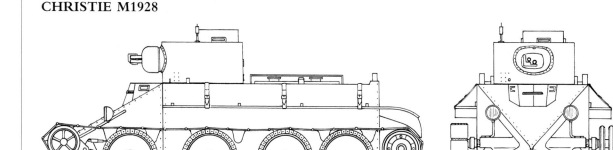

CHRISTIE M1928

SPEED: 113km/h (70mph) – wheels; 68km/h (42mph) – tracks

DIMENSIONS: Length 5.18m (17ft); Width 2.13m (7ft); Height 6ft (1.82m); Weight 8740kg (8.6 tons)

ARMOUR: 13mm (0.51in)

WEAPONRY: Two MGs

EFFECTIVE RANGE: n/a

CREW: 3

attracted the interest of a Soviet officer, Innokenti Andreyevich Khalepsky, who was at that time head of the Red Army Military Technical Board.

The USSR had set up purchasing organizations in the United Kingdom and the USA to buy new technology. In the UK the company was Arcos Ltd, and it made considerable efforts to acquire tanks and technical intelligence from Vickers-Armstrong. The British-based team bought commercially available tanks, but the War Department put a bar on the export of vehicles that were in service with the British Army. Moscow soon realized that their operation in the USA had found something far more valuable. In the USA, that organization was the Amtorg Trading Company.

The facility to operate with or without tracks fascinated the Soviet engineers; however, it was the suspension

that enabled tanks to move at high-speed cross-country that was the lasting benefit of the Christie system. The track-and-wheel system was attractive, since it would allow a fast approach march on wheel along roads and then, after an operation that took about 30 minutes, the crew would switch to tracks. In the 1930s all tank designs were plagued by unreliable tracks whose performance was blighted by a short running life.

Five T3E2s were built by fire-engine maker La France, since Christie was too busy with his next project. He was also too inclined to make changes in designs when they were already in production, such as improving the angle of the armour or turret design.

On 29 April 1930, Christie signed a contract with an Amtorg vice-president, A.V. Petrov, for two improved models of his tank. The ceremony was witnessed by

ABOVE: The preliminary test of a Christie M1930, bought from the US designer, travels along the Leningrad road near the village of Buzlanovo. The driver glances at the photographer, having just taken the tank across a shallow river in August 1931. This particular vehicle does not have a turret and armament, the main factor which enabled Christie to export it out of the USA to the USSR under the guise of being a 'tractor', rather than a tank.

ABOVE: The trial production batches of the BT-2 Model 1932 had several minor changes introduced to them, such as the new concave wheels, as well as a simplified mantlet for the gun. There were two models of the BT-2, one which was armed with a 37mm (1.46in) Model 1930 gun, and the other which was armed with DT 7.62mm (0.3in) machine guns. However, the machine-gun variant was not popular with crews for its lack of firepower, and all BT-2 production was eventually to turn entirely to the gun-armed variant.

Khalepsky and Joseph Michael, Amtorg's resident attorney. Michael had drafted a tough contract. It would be effective for 10 years, and in it Christie agreed not to 'transfer or otherwise dispose of his patent rights or interest in said tanks to any third party'. In addition, he agreed 'not to assign [the] agreements to any third parties without the previous written consent' of Amtorg. In addition, Christie was expected to provide technical aid, such as drawings, parts and instructions. In order to monitor the tanks' construction effectively, Khalepsky assigned an engineer to work with the US Wheel Track Layer Corporation.

Two turretless T3s were bought by the Soviet Union and shipped out in the guise of agricultural tractors. Lieutenant-Colonel J.K. Crain of the US War Department and S.L. Parker from the State Department's Division for Eastern European Affairs had attempted to halt the export to a country that the USA did not recognize officially. By the time they began to question Christie, it was too late: the 'tractors' had been shipped out of New York on 24 December. Soviet engi-

neers were impressed by its speed and the suspension that gave it an enhanced cross-country mobility, and these vehicles were to form the basis of the BT-2, which would enter full production in September 1931.

At the same that Christie had signed an exclusive contract with the USSR, he had also entered into negotiations with Poland, had contacted France and would eventually sign a separate contract with the UK. The British used his suspension in a series of fast but poorly-armoured (and poorly-armed) so-called 'cruiser' tanks, like the Crusader and Covenantor. However, by the end of the war, the suspension had matured into tanks like the Comet and Cromwell, the forebears of the superb Centurion.

The Soviet Army, Andreyevich Khalepsky and the Amtorg Trading Company had by now become increasingly suspicious of Christie who, as his company faced bankruptcy, was making increasingly unrealistic demands for payment in gold. Christie died during World War II, still embroiled in lawsuits with the US Government.

BT-1

Developed in 1932, this may have been a straight copy of the T-3, even down to the 166kW (350bhp) V-12 Liberty petrol engine with maximum road speed on tracks of 65km/h (40mph) and on wheels of 105km/h (65mph). Some assert that the BT-1 was in fact the designation for the original Christie vehicles. Whatever the truth, the tank had a crew of three, weighed 10,200kg (10 tons), was 5.49m (18ft) long, 2.23m (7ft 4in) wide and 1.92m (6ft 4in) high. Maximum armour protection was 13mm (0.51in) and minimum 6mm (0.24in). The armament consisted of two machine guns. Only a small number were built at the Kharkov Locomotive Works (KhPZ Nr 183) to evaluate the basic design.

BT-2

Using the same hull as the BT-1, Soviet engineers mounted a 37mm (1.46in) M1930 gun with a co-axial 7.62mm (0.3in) DT machine gun. The 37mm gun had 96 rounds and the machine guns 4000. It entered service in 1932, and some were still in armoured divisions in 1941. The first three prototypes were completed without armament, and they took part in the November Revolution Parade in Moscow in 1931.

The more powerful armament raised the vehicle's weight to 11,000kg (10.82 tons) but in all other respects it was identical to the BT-1. The BT-2 was capable of 110km/h (68.4mph) on roads, 50km/h (31mph) cross-country and had a road range of 300km (186 miles). Drive was on the rear sprockets and via a chain link to the rearmost road wheels when not running on tracks. It had clutch and brake steering and mechanical brakes.

A machine-gun armed version of the BT-2 with three DT guns was not popular with crews. The BT-3 was a further improvement on the BT-1 with solid disc roadwheels in place of spoked, and a

BELOW: Recruits watch as a BT-2 clears a bank; the Christie suspension was well capable of absorbing the shock of the landing. The 'flying tank' picture was widely circulated in the war as a dramatic propaganda image; ironically, the tank was by then obsolete.

BT-2

SPEED: 112km/h (70mph) – wheels; 65km/h (40mph) – tracks
DIMENSIONS: Length 5.49m (18ft); Width 2.33m (7ft 4in);
Height 2.21m (7ft 3in); Weight 9253.3kg (10.2 tons)
ARMOUR: 13mm (0.51in)

WEAPONRY: One 37mm (1.46in); one 7.62mm (0.3in) MG
EFFECTIVE RANGE: 90km (55 miles)
CREW: 3

45mm (1.77in) gun in place of the 37mm (1.46in). Only a few were built and, along with T-26s and T-28s, most were later modified as bridgelayers. A small number were modified with a flamethrower replacing the main armament. The BT-4 was a prototype with a twin DT machine-gun turret.

BT-5

This tank went into production at the end of 1932 in a new factory in Kharkov and brought together all the lessons learned so far in the programme. It would be the backbone of the Soviet Army armoured force in the late 1930s. About 50 BT-5s were sent to Spain to operate within the assembled Russo–Spanish Republican tank units.

The tank had a crew of three, a larger turret with a 45mm (1.77in) M1932 tank gun, and a co-axial machine gun. It carried 72–115 rounds for the 45mm gun and 2394 for the machine gun. It also had a new and more powerful engine and better vision equipment. The M-5 aero engine, a V-12 petrol, was capable of developing 260kW (350bhp), and on tracks the BT-5 was capable of 65km/h (40mph), and on wheels a remarkable 112km/h (70mph) on roads.

The maximum armour protection was now 13mm (0.51in) and minimum 6mm (0.24in) and it included a riveted glacis plate. The tank weighed 11,500kg (11.31 tons). It was the same length and width as

the BT-1, but the height had increased to 2.21m (7ft 3in). The BT-6 or BT-5(V) was the commander's version. It had a radio in the turret bustle and a frame antenna which, when fully rigged, extended around the turret sides and rear.

Small numbers of BT-5 tanks were used for trials and experiments. The BT-5PKh was fitted with a snorkel and rubber sealing for crossing rivers under water. The 4th Motorized Regiment, part of the 4th Don Cossack Division, tested BT-5PKh tanks in the 1936 summer manoeuvres in Byelorussia near Slutsk. A flamethrower version had the flame projector mounted in the hull, allowing the gun to be retained. However, the fighting compartment became so cramped that it was almost impossible to service the gun. BT-5s saw action in Finland, but the close woodland and the crews' tactics exposed them to Finnish infantry tank-hunters.

BT-5s were used for trials as armoured engineer vehicles carrying fascines for filling in antitank ditches and bridges. The tracks were fitted with primitive grousers, which were called 'supplementary track', to assist movement across snow or soft ground.

BT-7

Experience in the Far East in combat in 1934 and 1935 with the Japanese Army of Manchuria had shown the vulnerability of riveted tank construction, and so the decision was taken to produce a tank with welded armour. It was in this remote theatre that at Khalkin Gol in 1939 the unknown general Georgi Zhukov demonstrated his brilliance as a tank commander. His skillful handling of five armoured brigades expelled the Japanese Sixth, or Kanto, Army from positions they had captured on the Mongolian Manchurian border by the Khalkin River.

The Japanese commander who had disobeyed orders and invaded Soviet territory had air superiority, and had assembled 3 infantry divisions, 180 tanks, 500 guns and 450 aircraft. The Russians had 100,000 infantry with 498 tanks, strong artillery and 580 outclassed aircraft. Zhukov used his infantry to hold the Japanese front and then launched his armour in a pincer attack. The Soviet losses were about 10,000, but the shaken Japanese withdrew after suffering losses of about 18,000.

The new tank that grew out of this battlefield experience became the BT-7, the next improvement to the BT family. It had a conical turret, thicker armour, more fuel and ammunition capacity, a ball-mounted machine gun in the turret rear, and stronger transmission. The Model 35 45mm (1.77in) gun on the BT-7 had 146 rounds, a marked improvement on the BT-5 that had carried a maximum of 115 rounds.

The later production types BT-7-2 were fitted with twin horn periscopes. The BT-7 was powered by the new M17-TV-12 petrol engine that developed 372kW (500bhp) at 1760rpm. It was a copy of a German BMW engine that had originally been designed for aircraft use, and gave a road speed of 72km/h (45mph), a cross-country speed of 50km/h (31mph), and a road range of 430km (265 miles). The weight had risen to 13,900kg (13.68 tons), and the hull was now 5.66m (18ft 7in), the width 2.29m (7ft 6in) and height 2.42m (7ft 11in). Maximum hull armour was increased to 22mm (0.86in), but minimum remained 6mm (0.24in). In 1939 it was the major Soviet fighting tank.

Variants included the BT-7A, a close support vehicle mounting the 76.2mm (3in) regimental howitzer in a larger turret with 50 rounds and two DT machine guns. It was intended to support cavalry tank formations, and carried 50 rounds of main ammunition and was slightly heavier than the BT-7. The OP-7 was a flamethrower version that had the fuel cell for the projector in an armoured pannier on the right hull side. The BT-7 (V) or BT-7TU was the commander's model with the turret of the BT-5(V) with radio and frame antenna, though later models had a whip antenna that made them less of an obvious target in tank-on-tank actions.

BT-5 FAST TANK

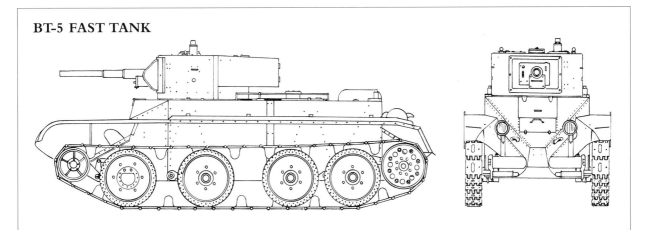

SPEED: 112km/h (70mph) – wheels; 65km/h (40mph) – tracks
DIMENSIONS: Length 5.49m (18ft); Width 2.33m (7ft 4in);
 Height 2.21m (7ft 3in); Weight 11,500kg (11.31 tons)
ARMOUR: 13mm (0.51in)

WEAPONRY: One 45mm (1.77in); one 7.62mm (0.3in) MG
EFFECTIVE RANGE: 90km (55 miles)
CREW: 3

tons), was 6.11m (20ft) long and 2.46m (8ft) high and was powered by a V-12 liquid-cooled diesel engine based on a Hispano-Suiza 12Y aircraft engine that gave a top road speed of 86km/h (53.4mph) and cross-country of 50km/h (31mph). Diesel conferred a number of advantages: it increased the radius of action by approximately one-third over the petrol engine for the same amount of fuel; it reduced the fire risk; and it simplified maintenance and production, as well as simplifying logistics.

The BT-7M had a full-length sloping glacis instead of the pointed 'prow' of the earlier BT designs, though the armour protection was the same as the BT-7. It reverted to wheel-and-tracks, a system that Mikhail Koshkin of the Kharkov bureau saw as an added weight for no operational benefit and which he fought to exclude from the T-34. The BT-8 had a 45mm (1.77in) Model 38 gun with 146 rounds, and two DT machine guns with 2394 rounds. It was with the BT-7s and BT-8s that Zhukov went on to achieve his victory at Khalkin Gol.

BT-IS

Developed in 1939, this single experimental tank was the last of the BT series and was in effect the BT-7M hull improved by sloping the side armour in the same way as the glacis plate. Though the tank had a BT-7 turret with 45mm (1.77in) gun, this was probably for trials purposes only. It had a crew of three and maximum armour protection of 30mm (1.18in). Its shape was a precursor of the T-34. The tank weighed 15,600kg (15.35 tons) and was 5.76m (18ft 11in) long, and 2.28m (7ft 6in) high and wide. The M17-T-V-12 diesel produced 372kW (500bhp) and gave a top road speed of 65km/h (40mph) and a road range of 400km (250 miles).

PT-1

The BT provided many of the components for the prototype PT-1 (*Plavayushchiy Tank-1*, or Amphibious Tank-1). Developed by a team which was headed by N. Astrov and N. Tsiets in 1932, it had a larger hull. This wider hull was designed to give sufficient buoyancy in order to ensure that it would float. It was propelled through the water by means of a propeller fitted beneath the

ABOVE: The BT-5 shown as a roadrunner without its tracks and with the driver's and commanders hatches open. The wheels were linked by a chain drive to the engine, and running on wheels offered two advantages: it not only was faster on roads but it also reduced track wear. Being capable of driving without wheels was, however, a luxury that would have been unnecessary had the vehicle enjoyed a better track design.

The BT-7 saw action in Finland and also during the Soviet invasion of eastern Poland in 1939. Its nemesis would come in 1941 with Operation Barbarossa, the German invasion of the USSR. Captured tanks were employed by German forces, painted field grey and boldly marked with black crosses on all vertical surfaces as well as hatches. As with the practice of using captured T-34s, the necessity to mark them clearly to avoid 'friendly fire' would often nullify any attempts made to camouflage the tanks.

BT-7M/BT-8

Though only about 700 of these tanks were built between 1939 and 1940, they represent a transition vehicle that had many of the characteristics of the early T-34. The BT-7M weighed 14,650kg (14.4

BT-7 FAST TANK

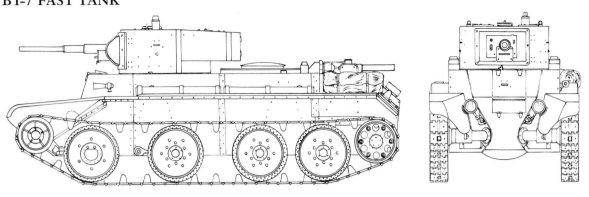

SPEED: 72km/h (45mph)

DIMENSIONS: Length 5.66m (18ft 7in); Width 2.29m (7ft 6in);
   Height 2.42m (7ft 11in); Weight 13,900kg (13.68 tons)

ARMOUR: 22mm (0.86in)

WEAPONRY: One 45mm (1.77in); two 7.62mm (0.3in) MG

EFFECTIVE RANGE: 430km (265 miles)

CREW: 3

hull and it had a rudder for underwater steering. During two years of trials, a new version, designated the PT-1A, was proposed. It was designed with various modifications, including a shorter pitched track. Even though it was not accepted by STAVKA for mass production, due to its design complexity, a small production run was authorized by the Directorate of Mechanization and Motorization and RVS, in order that tactical trials could be made with amphibious vehicles.

LEFT: An inspection of a Soviet BT-5 platoon; in the foreground is a BT-5U with its distinctive radio antenna. The BT-5 was effectively a BT-2 fitted with a 45mm (1.77in) gun. The original production batch had a very small rear bustle on the turret, while the production model had a more ample turret bustle. The tank went into production at the end of 1932 in a new factory in Kharkov and was the Soviet Army armoured force's backbone in the late 1930s. It had a crew of three, a new and more powerful engine, and better vision equipment. On tracks it could reach 65km/h (40mph) and on wheels a remarkable 112km/h (70mph) on roads.

CHAPTER FIVE

THE T-34

The T-34 may have come as a surprise to the Germans, but it was the result of several years of research and development as well as battles by the engineers with Soviet bureaucracy. The design was, however, rugged and versatile, and allowed the tank to be up-gunned and improved without breaks in production.

The head of the Directorate of Armoured Forces (ABTU), General Dmitri Pavlov, drew mixed conclusions from the performance of Soviet tanks in the Spanish Civil War, but his assertion that massed armour was ineffective would be disastrous for the Red Army's mechanized forces in 1941. Pavlov was heavily involved with the re-evaluation of future Soviet tanks following the war in Spain. To his credit was his proposal that the Red Army needed a new tank. This vehicle would become the T-34.

The Soviet BT and T-26 tanks' vulnerability in Spain had shown how much antitank weapons had improved. The Soviets therefore set to work producing a so-called 'shellproof' tank, with greater survivability against small-arms fire, shell splinters, small-calibre artillery and contemporary antitank weapons; and, more specifically, proof against a hit from a 37mm (1.46in) gun at any range and a 76.2mm (3in) antitank gun at ranges over 1000m (1100yd). Soviet tanks had shown an alarming propensity to catch fire when hit, largely due to their petrol engines, and this also stimulated a Soviet interest in diesel-powered engines with a low flash point.

LEFT: A captured T-34 M1941 guards a road through a village as a Renault ADK light truck drives past in December 1941. The Germans used a huge variety of captured vehicles – particularly the excellent T-34, which was better than any German tank currently in service – but this posed major logistical problems.

Pavlov wanted a replacement for the BT, essentially an improved version of the BT-IS. He tasked the design team at the Kharkov Locomotive, or Komintern, Factory in November 1937 with the production of a fast AFV using the convertible wheel/track system and BT Christie suspension. The new 20.2 tonne (20 ton) tank, which was given the designation the A-20, was to have a 45mm (1.77in) gun and 20mm (0.8in) armour.

It was not a particularly revolutionary design specification in itself, but Pavlov evidently wanted to combine heavier protection with the existing firepower and mobility of the BT series. The Kharkov factory, however, eventually delivered to the Director of Armoured Forces a superb fighting vehicle.

THE KHARKOV DESIGN TEAM
In 1936, the head of the Kharkov bureau, Mikhail Koshkin, who had been posted in to work on BT improvements, assembled a talented and experienced team. His deputy and old friend Alexsandr Morozov – who had already designed the new V-2 diesel engine first used on the BT-8 and the Voroshilovets artillery tractor – was responsible for the power train. The suspension team was led by Nikolai Kucherenko and P. Vasihev, who had been part of the T-29-4 tank project which tested the Christie-type suspension on medium tanks that were considerably

heavier than the BT. M. Tarshinov, who was responsible for the armour, had worked on the BT-IS and the BT-SV test tanks at Kharkov under Koshkin's predecessor, A. Firsov, and the BT-SV project had made ground-breaking use of 25mm (1in) sloping armour.

The team presented a wooden model of the A-20 to the Defence Council of the Soviet of People's Commissars (Soviet Narodnykh Komissarov, or SNAKE) in May 1938. However, they had doubts about the A-20 design specification, in particular the wheel/track feature. Koshkin argued that it added needless weight, and combat experience had shown it to be pointless.

The armour needed to be at least 30mm (1.2in) thick to withstand existing and future threats, and Koshkin considered that the 45mm (1.77in) gun was also inadequate and that a considerably larger 76.2mm (3in) weapon was needed to defeat similarly-protected enemy tanks. He made these points strongly at a presentation at which Josef Stalin was present. Stalin was evidently impressed, and the Main Military Council subsequently gave permission for the Kharkov factory to build a prototype, both of the A-20 and also of a heavier up-armoured and up-gunned version, which was given the designation A-30.

The wheel/track issue still remained unresolved. The unnecessary combination of tracks and road wheels was unduly heavy, and the complex technology involved increasingly convinced the Kharkov design team that the system would hamper mass production and if it were produced, would cause difficulties with maintenance. Simplicity had always proven to be a virtue with equipment for the Red Army soldier.

Therefore, on their own initiative, Koshkin and Morozov designed a heavier, purely-tracked medium tank, based around the A-30, which incorporated the suggestions that Koshkin had made to the Main Military Council. They submitted drawings of a 19.2 tonne (19 ton) tank, the A-32 (also called the T-32), to a conference on medium tank design in August 1938, with positive results. The Main Defence Committee and Stalin approved the project and demanded the production and evaluation of a prototype of the A-32 as soon as possible.

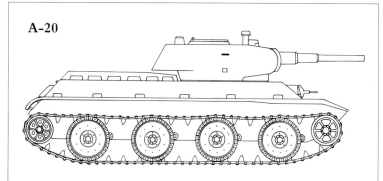

A-20

SPEED: 65km/h (40mph)
DIMENSIONS: Length 5.7m (18ft 7in); Width 2.7m (8ft 8in); Height 2.4m (7ft 8in); Weight 18,000kg (19.8 tons)
ARMOUR: 20mm (0.8in)
WEAPONRY: One 45mm (1.77in); two 7.62mm (0.3in) DT MG
EFFECTIVE RANGE: n/a
CREW: 4

The process that led to the approval of the A-32 illustrated the fickle but occasionally-inspired influence of Josef Stalin. The Main Military Council had criticized the A-32 because it did not have the wheel/track feature, but Stalin saw the logic of Koshkin's argument that the weight saved by losing the wheel/track feature could be used to add extra protection, and so he backed the design of the A-32. This meant that the Kharkov design team now had three projects: the A-20, A-30 and A-32.

THE PROTOTYPES

The prototype of the A-20 was further advanced and stuck closely to ABTU specification. The 18.2 tonne (18 ton) design retained the wheel/track configuration of the BT series. Like its BT forebears, it ran on four pairs of road wheels powered by the new, compact and powerful 373kW (500bhp) V-2 diesel tank engine. The chassis was based on that of the BT-7M. It was armed with the 45mm (1.77in) high-velocity gun, like most of the BT series, as well a co-axial and hull-mounted machine gun.

The shape of the tank, however, was more interesting, as it provided the first glimpse of the hull and turret shape that would later be adopted in the T-34. The A-20 had a new 25mm (1in) rolled armour plate turret. The A-20's wide, V-shaped glacis plate was set at 60 degrees. The hull overhung the tracks, and the hull sides above track level were angled and 25mm (1in) thick. This conformed to the same specifications of another attempt to produce a shell-proof tank: the T-46-5 (or Izdeliye 111). This 32.3 tonne (32 ton) tank had reached the prototype stage and but was cancelled. However, its armour protection schemes had some influence on the A-20.

The attempt to up-gun the A-20 in the shape of the A-30 soon proved to be a dead end. The design team made an attempt to place the short-barrelled 76.2mm (3in) (L/30.5) gun used on the BTU in the A-20 turret. This failed comprehensively because the turret was far too small for the larger weapon, making it extremely difficult to operate. More fundamentally, the turret ring could not absorb the recoil of the 76.2mm (3in)

ABOVE: An A-20 drives up a hill during trials, and it shows the classic shape of the future T-34, with well-angled armour and low silhouette. The engineers had a clear vision of the tank they wanted to design, and first presented it to the Defence Council of the Soviet of People's Commissars (SNAKE) in May 1938. But they first had to contend with political and military interference, and ironically it was only after a presentation in front of Stalin, and his subsequent direct intervention, that the successful design was given approval for development.

gun. Eventually , the basic impracticability of the project ensured that the A-30 was quietly dropped.

The A-32 was a far more promising design and a major development on the BT. The wheel/track system was dropped, although the tank retained the Christie suspension system. As it did not have to move on wheels, the weight saving was considerable, and the amount of armour on the new hull shape could be increased to 30–60mm (1.2–2.4in) without violating the weight limit. The designers also gave the A-32 a new steering system that used the conventional method of levers, rather than the steering wheel used in the BT and the A-20. They had discovered on the BT series that while a steering wheel was certainly not the best method of steering a tracked vehicle, it had proved impossible to steer a wheeled vehicle with levers. The road wheels were increased to five. Finally, true to Koshkin's original proposal for a tank with a larger gun as well as thicker armour, it was given a 76.2mm (3in) gun.

Prototypes for both the A-20 and A-32 were ready by July 1939 and were sent to the Scientific Test Institute of Tank Technology (NIB) at Kubinka, where they both proved mechanically reliable and superior to all other models. The A-20's performance without tracks was poor but, like the A-32, with tracks it was very satisfactory. On 1 September 1939 both the A-20 and A-32, along with the KV heavy tank and the expensive and complex T-50 and T-40 amphibious tanks, appeared in a display of new Red Army vehicles which was held for the Main Military Council.

The inclusion of the two tanks in the display indicated official satisfaction with the design, although there was no consensus amongst the Main Military Council. Koshkin was adamant that the A-32 was the superior model, and reckoned it ought to be considered a universal tank to replace the variety of Soviet types and fulfil the roles of the BT, T-26 light and T-28 medium tank. Its disadvantage was that it was comparatively

BELOW: A camouflaged and slogan-painted T-34/76B tank of Yakunin's subunit drives through the town of Izyum during an offensive near Kharkov in January 1942. The large turret hatch is open and shows clearly the problem that it posed for the commander, who had either to sit high in the turret to see forward, or to drive closed up.

expensive, and some of the council expressed serious concern that the A-32 would cost three times as much as the T-26. Pavlov supported the A-20, which was the ultimate product of his initial ABTU design specification.

THE UP-ARMOURED A-32

The issue was finally settled at a meeting of the Defence Committee of the SNAKE on 19 December 1939. The debate turned to the latest reports from the fighting in Finland, which had been invaded by the USSR in November 1939. The experience appeared somewhat similar to that in Spain and Khalkin Gol, stressing the vulnerability of Soviet tanks to the small number of Finnish antitank guns. In addition, their armament – which was usually the standard 45mm (1.77in) or short, low-velocity 76.2mm (3in) gun – proved inadequate against emplaced Finnish bunkers.

Koshkin told the committee that, after considering these developments, his team had prepared estimates which demonstrated that the A-32 could be up-armoured even further without an unacceptable loss of performance and mobility. Koshkin produced drawings and models to back up his case, and convinced Stalin – who was chairing the committee – to approve the up-armoured version of the A-32 medium tank. In service, this medium tank would replace the BT and T-28.

With the outset of war in Europe in 1939, the committee ordered into production a project that Koshkin emphasized was incomplete: a prototype had not yet been built. Representatives of the Committee for Medium Industry were told that the High Command wanted 200 built in the following year. All that remained now was to give the tank a suitably resounding name.

ABOVE: This photograph of a T-34 production line does not show how grim the conditions in the factories in the Urals were in reality. It was cold, noisy and dirty, with women, older men, and youngsters alike working 16-hour shifts by day and by night. Although they were administered with meagre rations, their efforts proved very effective, and they succeeded in manufacturing huge numbers of T-34s: 3000 in 1941 alone.

ABOVE: A tank formation, commanded by Major Baranov in a concentration area near the Crimea in October 1941. The smooth, well-angled glacis plate of the T-34/76B can be seen, with only a machine gun and the driver's hatch breaking the integrity of its armour protection.

THE FIRST T-34S

The heavy tank design bureau in Leningrad had reversed many years of Soviet practice by naming their new tank the Klimenti Voroshilov, or KV, after the egregious Defence Commissar. With some courage, Koshkin told Voroshilov that the new tank should not be named after another hero of the Soviet Union; rather they should return to using the traditional designations. Koshkin suggested the designation T-34 to commemorate the 1934 state decree which ordered a massive expansion of the Soviet armoured forces. It was also the year that Koshkin had had his first ideas about the new tank. Accordingly, Koshkin's proposal was accepted.

Once the team received official sanction to build a purely tracked medium tank, they had returned to their original design for the A-32. The T-34 required thicker armour, but it also needed to be equipped with more firepower as well as a reliable transmission. Morozov and the transmission group devoted considerable time and effort to finding a solution to these problems.

The two prototypes were ready by January 1940, and Koshkin took them on a gruelling trial march to prove the hardiness of the design. He drove them from Kharkov to Moscow, and here the tank was presented to the Red Army. Following this presentation, they were sent on to Finland for combat tests against the Mannerheim Line, but unfortunately they arrived too late to see any action. However, Koshkin and his team were able to demonstrate the power of the T-34's armament against captured Finnish bunkers. There were further firing trials in Minsk, and then it was on to Kiev, and finally back to Kharkov. This round trip had covered a distance of 2880km (1800 miles) in the bitter weather of February and March.

During June the drawings were completed and mass production began. The first production T-34 Model 1940 rolled out of Kharkov in September 1940. During the gruelling winter test-drive, Koshkin had contracted pneumonia, and he died on 26 September 1940. Morozov, now head of conceptual design, took over the T-34 project.

THE CHASSIS AND SUSPENSION

The chassis, based on the Christie system, had five pairs of large road wheels with a gap between the second and third. Each wheel's suspension was independently mounted, and transversely swung on a vertical coil spring inside the hull. The drive sprocket was mounted at the rear to reduce vulnerability. It was the same roller type used on the BTs. The drive sprockets drove wide, 483mm (19in) skeleton-type cast-manganese steel tracks with centre guide horns positioned on alternate track links.

The system had an interesting and ingenious method of retaining its track pins. The roundhead pins were inserted from the inside; there was no retaining device used on the track itself. Instead, a curved wiper plate was welded to each side of the hull at the rear, level with the top run of the track. Therefore, any loose track pin passing the wiper plate in motion was immediately knocked back into place. The method also allowed the rapid removal and replacement of track blocks, considerably easing and speeding up maintenance and repairs in the field. The wide tracks provided a small specific ground pressure not exceeding 0.7–0.75kg per cm (10–10.6lb per in), while that of British, German and American medium and heavy tanks was 0.95–1kg per cm (13.1–13.9lb per in). Track guards covered the top of the suspension system and extended 25cm (9.8in) beyond the hull at the front and 10cm (3.9in) at the rear. The suspension permitted the T-34 to retain high speeds even when moving over rough terrain, while the wide tracks on the tank, weighing only 28.3 tonnes (28 tons), meant that it could traverse muddy terrain, as well as snow-covered ground.

THE HULL AND ARMOUR

The hull, which was designed by Nikolai Kucherenko, overhung the tracks and had sloped sides. It was of homogeneous rolled-steel plate and electro-welded

BELOW: The breach of the 76.2mm (3in) L-11 gun of a T-34 seen through the open turret hatch with ready use ammunition stowed to the right. The tank had 77 rounds stowed on board and 4725 rounds of 7.62mm (0.3in) ammunition for the two DT machine guns. When the hatch was open, the crew was vulnerable to shell airbursts or close-in attack by infantry.

ABOVE: Fresh off the production line, T-34/76B tanks roll through a Russian town. In the field the tanks carried spare fuel in drums which were attached to the hull sides and rear, and they also carried canvas to erect as a tent for the crew. When fighting closed in on industrial cities, tanks came off the production line and rolled straight into battle, and many of them left the factories without being fitted with such 'extras' as periscopes or radios.

throughout using only three thickness of armour plate: 45mm (1.77in) front and sides; 40mm (1.57in) at the rear; and 20mm (0.78in) on the top. The standard of welding was poor, but not so bad as to allow weld failures. The glacis plate, set back at 60 degrees, was 45mm (1.77in) thick and was free of apertures, apart from the driver's hatch and the ball-mounted hull machine gun. The driver's hatch also contained his periscope. The sloping armour gave excellent ballistic protection and provided the equivalent protection of 75mm (2.95in) of vertical plate, making the T-34 a virtually invulnerable tank in 1941.

The rear deck behind the turret was slightly raised to accommodate the row of engine compartment louvres and access plate with exhaust pipes on either side. The upper rear plate and the engine cover plate were fastened with screws and these could be removed if repairs on the transmission or engine were ever to become necessary

THE DRIVER AND HIS CONTROLS

The driving compartment was separated from the engine by the tank's single bulkhead. The driver sat on the left front of the hull with a large, one-piece hatch that hinged forward to allow access. It mounted the observation periscopes. The driver steered the tank through the use of a clutch-and-brake system, and this was controlled by two steering levers and gear-change lever and a manual clutch pedal and foot brakes. The controls were linked to the transmission at the rear by metal rods which ran along the tank's floor. They required more strength to operate than Western tanks, where the transmission and gearbox were positioned close together.

There was no power-assisted control gear. T-34 drivers often had a mallet to use on the controls if they seized up. The four-speed gearbox was replaced by a five-speed type on the last 100 T-34 Model 1943s, making it easier to change gear and increasing the tank's speed.

There was a fuel-injection pedal on the floor with the clutch and brake pedals. In a position at the bottom of the hull was another pedal (often referred to as the Desantov) which immobilized the tank. There were also two compressed-air bottles for cold-weather starts.

LEFT: A T-34/76D crew refuel their tank in the winter of 1942. The new tank had twin hatches in the turret and grab rails for tank *desants* – tank riding infantry. The hexagonal T-34/76D turret had no rear overhang that in earlier marks had proved vulnerable to attack by German infantry, who would wedge Teller antitank mines underneath it.

T-34 MODEL 1942 MEDIUM TANK

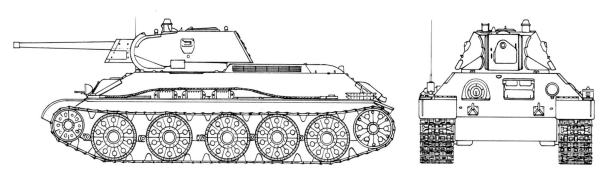

SPEED: 50km/h (31mph)

DIMENSIONS: Length 6.19m (20ft 3in); Width 2.92m (9ft 7in);
Height 2.39m (7ft 10in); Weight 26,720kg (26.30 tons)

ARMOUR: 80mm (3.14in)

WEAPONRY: One 76.2mm (3in); two 7.62mm (0.3in) MG

EFFECTIVE RANGE: 300km (190 miles)

CREW: 5

THE GUNNER/RADIO OPERATOR

The hull gunner/radio operator sat in the front right of the hull, with an escape hatch in the floor in front of him. In combat he operated the ball-mounted Degtyarev DT 7.62mm (0.3in) machine gun with a 24-degree horizontal fire arc and elevation of between -6 degrees and +12 degrees. The machine gun which was fitted into the Model 1942 tanks had an armoured sleeve.

Although early in the war many T-34s lacked radios – and during some of the Red Army's acute manpower crises, this position was occasionally left unfilled as the war progressed – the proportion of radio-equipped tanks grew steadily. In 1941 the company commander's tank

RIGHT: A T-34/76C Model 1943 named 'Leningradyets' of the 30th Guards Tank Brigade advances into Krasnoye Selo in January 1944. It had spudded tracks, single horn periscope, cast turret, twin driver's periscopes and an armoured shield on the hull machine gun, welded nose and claw tow-hooks on the glacis.

was usually equipped with a 71-TK-3 radio, and efforts were made to extend the available sets to platoon leaders. In the first two years of the conflict the Soviets also used the 71-TK-1. The situation improved with the widespread introduction of the 9-R radio in late 1942. Although technically the 9-R's range was 24km (15 miles), on the move it was effectively 8km (5 miles).

The Germans, who attached considerable importance to the universal provision of radios to their tank crews, noted the poor tactical cooperation of Soviet tanks. In the absence of radios, the Soviets relied on flag signals. There was even a special hatch in the main turret hatch for signals even when it was closed down. This proved impractical in action, as the platoon commander had enough to deal with controlling his own tank and aiming its gun. Often he would simply tell the other crews to follow his lead. The situation improved as radio production increased, and by the summer of 1943 around 75–80 per cent of all tanks

were radio equipped. Inside the tank the crew communicated through the TUP interphone system. The crew's *Tankobyi Shlem* (padded cloth helmets) had built-in earphones and a throat microphone.

THE TURRET

The turret on all models was low. Although a low silhouette is useful in combat, it restricted the depression of the main and auxiliary armament, particularly on the reverse slope or at close range. The low turret also made the interior cramped, as did the small size of the turret ring. As there was no turret basket, the driving compartment led directly into the turret's fighting compartment at any position of traverse. On later models, grab rails were welded to the turret and hull for tank-borne infantry.

THE COMMANDER AND LOADER

The most serious flaw of the whole T-34 was poor ergonomic design of the turret. German tank turrets had a three-man crew: gunner, loader and the commander

ABOVE: A T-34/76D tank advances across ground frozen solid in a hard frost in 1943. The big road wheels of the American-designed Christie suspension were less likely to jam up with mud and dirt when compared to the German tanks that had small road wheels and return rollers above them for the track. The German suspension system also left the side of the hull vulnerable to hits by antitank weapons.

ABOVE: A column of T-34/85 with their turrets traversed to the rear in the winter of 1944. Early production models either lacked mushroom vents altogether or had one only and were designated T-34/85/1. The bigger turret allowed an extra crewman to be carried. The tank *desants* have collected on the louvres in order to enjoy the warm air which is wafting from the engines. An underching beam has been lashed to the hull.

who was responsible for observing the terrain, directing the crew and coordinating the tank with the rest of the unit. The situation was different in the cramped confines of the two-man turret of the T-34. The commander had the same tasks, but in addition he also had to aim and fire the main gun, which was a task enough in itself, and a very serious distraction from his main command functions in action.

Loading was also a full-time role, and despite its demands, there was a brief and naturally unsuccessful experiment at giving the responsibility of loading the gun rather than firing it to the commander. As there was no turret basket, the turret crew sat on stools which were suspended from the turret ring. The commander sat to the left of the gun, and the loader, who was also tasked with firing the co-axial machine gun, sat on the right of the gun.

The T-34's optical devices were poorer than the German equivalents. The main x 2.5 telescopic sight on earlier models, the TOD-6, was replaced by the TMFD. In 1942 T-34s from the Stalingrad tractor plant were often driven straight off the production line and into battle. They lacked gun sights and could only be aimed at almost point-blank range by the loader peering down the barrel.

For general viewing the commander and loader both used the PT-6 periscope. Later tanks were fitted with the PT-4-7 and PT-5. Wartime shortages often meant the loader's periscope was deleted. These provided a very narrow field of vision, and this was not much improved by the provision of armoured viewing ports at shoulder level for the loader and commander. There were pistol ports below these and also one in the rear, although these were sometimes omitted on later models of the tank.

Many German tank commanders liked to fight with their heads out of the turret for a 360-degree view. If the T-34 commander attempted this, his view was severely curtailed by the large, forward-opening one-piece hatch. He was obliged to sit on the turret roof, risking not only enemy fire, but also injury from the extremely heavy hatch. Such was its size that opening it also exposed the loader. The T-34 Model 1943 introduced separate hatches for the commander and loader, but only on the final models was a 360-degree commander's cupola fitted.

The turret itself was originally made of rolled plate with the gun in a cast-contoured cradle. On the Model 1941 the cast gun-cradle was replaced by an angular bolted type. During the production run of the Model 1942, a second version entered service with a 52mm (2in) cast turret, although it was virtually the same as the original rolled turret.

THE NEW HEXAGONAL TURRET

The Deputy Peoples Commissar for Defence and head of the Central Artillery Directorate (GAU), G.I. Kulik, disliked the T-34 and insisted on various changes. This disrupted early production and led to the Council of People's Commissars ordering an improvement programme for the T-34. Designated the T-34M, it would have the torsion bar suspension system used on the KV and T-50 tanks, and the hull and turret re-designed with an increase in armour.

The project broke down when it became clear that it would seriously disrupt production. Morozov had designed a new turret for the T-34M in response to some of the flaws of the earlier turrets that had shown up in combat. German tank-killing infantry squads could climb onto the back of the tank and wedge a Teller AT mine under the turret overhang. The overhang also created a shell

BELOW: The crew of a T-34/76D with soldiers of the Twenty-First Army huddle on the turret of the tank during the fighting near Stalingrad in Operation Uranus. The Twenty-First Army, part of the South-western Front under General Nikolai Vatutin, initially had a hard fight with the Third Romanian Army on the northern Don, but punched through them and swung south behind the Sixth Army. The T-34 with its wide tracks could move across snow at speed, allowing armoured crews to use the *Blitzkrieg* tactics of fast, deep penetration that the Germany Army had used in 1941–42 against them.

BELOW: Tank riders dismount
from a rather overcrowded
T-34 near the town of
Communarsk in the
Voroshilov district in 1942.
The photograph is probably
posed since the number of
soldiers on the tank is
unrealistic and the tank
appears to be halted. The
men would have obscured
the crew's periscopes and
vision blocs and restricted
the operation of the turret.
Normal practice was for
men to ride on the rear
deck or later on the sides,
holding grab rails that had
been welded onto the turret;
they would dismount as it
went into the attack and
flush out the infantry in
trenches and bunkers.

trap that deflected incoming rounds into the vulnerable turret ring. Morozov's new, cast, hexagonal turret that appeared on the Model 1943 eliminated the overhang, was also considerably easier to manufacture and larger than the original turrets, giving the turret crew a little more space. However, the problem of the small turret and overworked turret crew was only adequately solved with the introduction of a large three-man turret on the T-34/85 that entered production in the winter of 1943.

ARMAMENT

The early T-34 Model 1940 was armed with the short 76.2mm (3in) L-11 Model 1938 rifled gun with a length of 30.5 calibres. During 1941 a very small number of T-34s were fitted with the 57mm (2.24in) ZiS-4 long-barrelled high-velocity weapon, which was intended for engaging lightly armed vehicles at longer ranges. The high velocity of this weapon

compensated for the loss of calibre, and the L-11 remained the standard gun on the Model 1940 production run, although it was not exactly up to the standard that the Soviets were seeking for a gun, and the T-34 designers were not totally satisfied with the weapon.

Fortunately there was a better gun available, although Soviet bureaucracy and the interference of Kulik, the head of the GAU, did much to hamper its introduction. Grabin and his team at Zavod Nr 92 already had a new 76.2mm (3in) gun in production. The F-32 was being fitted to the new KV heavy tank and was achieving much better antiarmour performance than the T-34 Model 1940s L-11, due to its longer barrel.

By the end of 1940 a member of Grabin's team, P. Muraviev, had adapted Grabin's F-32 gun for the T-34 and produced a weapon (the longer F-34 with 42 calibres) considerably superior to the

L-11. In a move showing considerable initiative and courage, Grabin and the director of Zavod Nr 92, A. Elyan, began producing the F-34 alongside the L-11 and shipped them to the Kharkov plant which was building the T-34. The initial F-34 guns were completed in January 1941 and the first T-34s, usually classified as the T-34 Model 1941, armed with the F-34, rolled out in February 1941.

They were mainly used as platoon- and company commander tanks, and proved very popular in combat after the German invasion, due to their increased hitting power. Stalin became aware of the new version through front-line correspondence. So as units involved in the fighting demanded more tanks equipped with the F-34, rather than the less effective L-11, the Main Defence Committee finally authorized the F-34 in the summer of 1941. The 76.2mm (3in) F-34 Model 1940 (42-calibre length) gun equipped all subsequent models of T-34 until increases in German armour pro-

tection led to the adoption of an 85mm (3.34in) gun in late 1943, though tanks armed with the F-34 remained in service until the end of the war.

The F-34 had a conventional semi-automatic drop breech and the commander fired the main gun either by hand or by using a foot pedal. The gun elevated from -3 degree to +30 degrees while the L-11 could depress to -5 degrees. The commander was responsible for the manual or electric turret traverse on the latter at a rate of 26 degrees a second. The standard Soviet armour-piercing round at the start of the war was the BR-350A, weighing 6.3kg (13.9lb) with an initial muzzle velocity of 655m/s (720yd/s). In the F-34 gun it could penetrate the PzKpfw III and deal with the latest German tank, the PzKpfw IV Ausf. F, which had 50mm (1.96in) frontal armour, at almost all ranges.

The F-34 gave the T-34 such a considerable advantage in range and hitting

ABOVE: T-34/76D tanks of the Third Guards Tank Army of the 1st Ukrainian Front parked in a concentration area at the edge of the Puscha-Voditza Woods on the outskirts of Kiev. This picture was taken on 5 November 1943. The Third Guards Tank Army had driven north from Bukrin on the River Dniepr and punched through the German defences to the north of Kiev, before swinging south and east to trap the Hessian 88th Infantry Division in a pocket in the city.

ABOVE: The surviving population of a Ukrainian village – largely made up of the young, female or very old – line a road to greet a column of T-34/76D tanks as it drives through in the summer of 1943. The huge losses in manpower suffered by the Soviet Union in World War II meant that in the 1950s and early 1960s, many heavy manual jobs like construction work, heavy industry and farming that formerly would have been done by the men, were undertaken by women.

power that the Germans scrambled to overcome it; the Mark IV Ausf. H with 80mm (3.2in) frontal armour was introduced in the spring of 1943. The Soviets maintained their lead with the 3kg (6.6lb) APDS round, the BR-350P. It could penetrate 92mm (3.7in) of armour at 500m (550yd), the average range of a tank engagement.

However, the introduction of the new German tank models designed specifically to defeat the T-34 in 1943 shifted the balance drastically. The F-34 gun proved largely incapable of penetrating the frontal armour of the Tiger and Panther at normal combat ranges. At Kursk in July 1943, the T-34s were forced to close to point-blank or manoeuvre to engage the side or rear. The situation was only resolved with the adoption of the 85mm (3.34in) gun in late 1943.

The T-34 carried 77 rounds for the main gun. This was increased to 100 on

the T-34 Model 1943. The standard combat load was 19 rounds of BR-350A AP, 53 F-354 or OF-350 HE rounds and 5 SH-350 rounds of canister. Three ready-use rounds were on the hull side near the loaders feet, and six more were on the wall beside the commander. The rest of the ammunition was on the hull floor, covered by neoprene matting. The loader pulled back the matting to access the ammunition bins, but the stowage was slightly awkward and often required the hull machine-gunner's help. The floor would become a mess of open bins and discarded matting that degraded the crew's performance in combat.

SECONDARY ARMAMENT

The first 115 Model 1940 produced had a rear-mounted DT gun in the turret. The gas-operated DP Model 1928 had an effective range of about 800m (880yd) and fired at 600 rounds per minute (rpm). This was kept down to 125rpm to avoid jamming and overheating. The DT had a retractable metal stock and wooden pistol grip, and used a separate optical sight rather than the tangent leaf sight of the infantry weapon. Its drum magazine held 60 rounds in two tiers. The 35 drums for the two machine-guns were stored half in racks at the back of the turret, and the other half forward in the hull near the hull gunner.

THE ENGINE

The engine mounted at the rear of the hull was flanked by cooling radiators with a cooling fan in the centre. It was the V-type four-stroke 12-cylinder, water-cooled diesel that had been developed for the BT-7M. The 3.8 litre (0.84 gallon) version fitted to the T-34 could produce an impressive 367kW (493bhp) at 1800rpm and gave an excellent power-to-weight ratio of 14kW (18.8bhp) per tonne (13.3kW/17.9bhp per ton). This gave the T-34 a road speed of 54km/h (34mph) and a cross-country speed of 10–11.25km/h (16–25mph), depending on terrain, at an average 1.84 litres per km (0.65 gallons per mile). This improved considerably on the road. The V-2 also gave an increased range of operation of 464km (290 miles) compared to tanks powered by conventional petrol internal combustion engines. The main fuel tank was in the hull, with four auxiliary cylinder tanks on the side of the hull and two smaller ones on the rear plate.

The transmission was at the rear, therefore the driving/fighting compart-

BELOW: Standing on a knocked-out German PzKpfw IV Ausf. H fitted with *Schürzen* spaced armour, a Soviet Army cameraman films SU-85 assault guns as, laden with infantry of the 1st Ukrainian Front, they drive through a Russian village in the Lvov area in 1944. Approaching from the opposite direction is a US-supplied 4 x 4 Weapons Carrier. With US-supplied vehicles and its own excellent tanks, the Soviet Army was a mobile, powerful force capable of its own *Blitzkrieg* tactics.

ABOVE: In his T-34/76D the commander of a T-34 company wearing a sheepskin coat uses a signal pistol to order the start of an attack with tank-borne infantry in the winter of 1943–44. As the commander, his tank is distinguished from the others by its radio antenna on the front hull. The lack of radios in Soviet tanks continued to restrict their tactical flexibility throughout the Great Patriotic War (World War II).

ment was not cluttered by a drive train. The transmission proved troublesome early in the war; some crews carried spare transmissions secured to the engine compartment deck by steel cables.

SOVIET INDUSTRIAL EVACUATION

The Soviet military revival of 1942–43 in which the T-34 played such a vital part was intrinsically linked to the recovery of the battered Soviet industrial economy. That there was any Soviet industry left to revive was due to the remarkable evacuation of machines, equipment, and manpower that took place before the German advance. The Soviet leadership showed considerable prescience by setting up a Committee of Evacuation two days after the launching of Operation Barbarossa. As the situation worsened and the key industrial centres of Riga and Minsk were lost, the State Committee for Defence ordered Voznesensky, the Chairman of the Gosplan, to draw up a

plan for a second line of industrial defence in the East and to organize a coherent productive combination between the industry already existing in the East and those transported. The plan envisaged the evacuation of industry to the Urals, Volga, Eastern Siberia and Central Asia. Priority was given to the armaments factories.

When describing this vast undertaking, however, coherence is not a word that springs immediately to mind. Engineers and workers dismantled their factories, hauled the machinery to a railhead and loaded it on to a waiting flatcar. Workers arrived without their equipment, equipment without its workers. Nonetheless, some 1.5 million wagonloads of evacuated industrial equipment were moved eastwards with the estimated 16 million Soviet citizens necessary to man it. Between July and December 1941, 1523 enterprises – the bulk of the western Soviet Unions iron, steel and engineering plants – were moved out of reach of the German invaders.

Every effort was made to marry evacuated plants with existing factories, but many industries had to set up in undeveloped areas and many of these were in the most inhospitable areas of the Soviet Union. Soviet propaganda had little need to embellish the accounts of endurance and heroism involved in the establishment of these factories in temperatures of –40°C (–40°F), and there is no reason to doubt the newsreels' veracity.

PRODUCTION OF THE T-34 MOVES EAST

In August 1941 the Kharkov Locomotive Plant began to be evacuated to Nizhni Tagil. It was renamed the Uralvagon Plant No 183 and, married to the existing Chelyabinsk tractor works and the equipment from the Kirov Plant from Leningrad, the giant complex became Tankograd. The workforce was made up of women, old men and teenagers who laboured 12 to 16 hours a day on rations that were one-fifth of that of the British population. On average, this was merely 0.45kg (1lb) of bread and scraps of meat or fat, and this meagre ration would be supplemented by whatever food they could grow themselves.

Although the efforts of the Soviet population were awe-inspiring, much of their production achievements were down to the talents of Morozov and the T-34 design team who moved to Nizhni Tagil with the rest of the Kharkov plant. The main aim of the team was to cut costs and make production by an unskilled labour force easier. V. Buslov and V. Nitsenko developed a cast turret that, while similar in appearance to the welded turret, was altogether much more simple to manufacture.

This was adopted on both the Model 1940 and Model 1941 T-34 that had either a cast- or welded turret, depending on where they were manufactured. Of the plants set up to take the slack as the Kharkov plant was moved eastwards, Krasnoye Sormovo at Gorki, near Moscow, was responsible for production of the tanks with the new cast turret, while the STZ Plant in Stalingrad continued to make the welded turrets.

The Model 1942, introduced in late 1941, was very similar to the previous model, apart from the fact that many of its components were simplified. For example, the F-34 gun on the Model 1941 had 861 parts, while on the Model 1942 the number was down to 614. They

BELOW: A T-34/85, with the grab rails on the hull and turret for tank-riding infantry clearly visible. The T-34/85 had armour ranging between 60mm (2.36in) and 18mm (0.71in). The co-axial machine gun can be seen to the right of the 85mm (3.34in) ZiS S-53 gun. The T-34/85 was approved for adoption by the Red Army on 15 December 1943.

BELOW: Tank *desants* have jumped clear of their T-34/85 vehicles and started to run forward to attack. The infantry were largely equipped with the PPSh 41 submachine gun, a short-range weapon that, to be effective, obliged the user to close with his enemy. This meant that an attack by a tank and *desant* force would be very aggressive and usually end with hand-to-hand fighting.

also managed to drive down the cost of producing the tank, so that it went down from 269,500 roubles in 1941 to 193,000 roubles in 1942.

Perhaps more important than any of these savings in materials, the man hours needed to produce a T-34 dropped from 8000 in 1941 to 3700. Admittedly craftsmanship also declined, but that did not matter, as the apparent crudity seems to have affected neither the protection afforded by the armour, nor the actual performance of the tank.

In the autumn of 1942, production at Stalingrad was closed down due to the heavy fighting in the city. Production was further extended in Tankograd, and the

Ural Heavy Machine Tool Factory in Sverdlovsk was converted to production of T-34s. By now the Soviets were beginning to out-produce the Germans and wear them down through a terrible war of attrition.

HIGH SOVIET PRODUCTION LEVELS

The Soviet economy out-produced the German economy from a far smaller resource base and with a less-skilled workforce. Much of this was down to the simplicity of production goals and the single-minded concentration on the production of proven types. The Soviet Union only produced two tanks in great quantity. Only towards the end of the

war did they introduce a new tank, the IS (Iosef Stalin), but even that was simply a re-designed KV. The T-34 design was mechanically simple, facilitating quantity production with limited resources in specialized machine tools and skilled labour. It had a great number of parts that were interchangeable with the other successful design, the KV, including the engine, gun, transmission, and vision devices.

PRODUCTION OF THE T-34

The war on the Eastern Front was a tank war. While large infantry formations were involved in the fighting, and while there was street-fighting at battles like

Stalingrad, in which case tanks were of limited use, the war in Russia witnessed the biggest tank battles in history. In the year 1941 alone, Russia produced a staggering total of around 3000 T-34s.

At first the problem was finding crews to man the tanks, as so many Russians had been killed or taken prisoner in the vast encirclements of Soviet defensive positions by the Germans in their initial advance following Operation Barbarossa. The movement of factories and the workers to staff them safely out of the German's reach east of the Urals also meant that many potential recruits were employed in building the T-34 rather than crewing it.

ABOVE: Infantry ride on the back of a T-34/85 that has been equipped with a Mugalev mine-roller, or trawl. Two multi-disc wheels were fitted to a T-shaped configuration to the beam. The first mine-roller detachments were formed in May 1942, and eventually there were at least five regiments with PT-34 mine trawls. A trawl could withstand 8 to 10 detonations by 5–10kg (11–22lb) mines before it needed to be repaired.

Unlike the German tanks it would come up against, the T-34 was not a sophisticated fighting machine. While the original T-34s exhibited high levels of craftsmanship, the exigencies of war meant that later models were crudely

RIGHT: T-34/85/1 tanks of the Third Guards Tank Army of the 1st Ukrainian Front wait in woodland close to Berlin in April 1945. The T-34/85 had a cast steel turret and was armed with an 85mm (3.34in) ZiS-53 gun that had originally been an AA gun with 55 rounds. Though the chassis was virtually unchanged from the T-34/76 the increased armour, 60mm (2.3in) in contrast to 45mm (1.5in), and armament had reduced speed to 50km/h (31mph).

manufactured. As production increased, many of the hull fittings were simplified, and some features, such as a second roof periscope for the loader, were simply omitted. The T-34 was rugged and simple, and as such seemed to symbolize the whole spirit of the Russian war effort, concentrating on the three characteristics that made the tank so deadly: gun, armour and mobility.

UPGRADING THE T-34

Battle performance was (and indeed, still is) the ultimate determinant of the effectiveness of any weapons system. The battles in front of Moscow in 1941 had shown the Russians that changes needed

to be made to the T-34. As a result, the T-34 went through numerous cosmetic changes as the war unfolded, and the different tank factories adapted their production lines to meet changing battlefield needs.

The overhang of the turret was reduced and the fuel supply was increased; the gearbox was also improved. A new style of driver's hatch was introduced, the rectangular transmission access hatch on the rear plate giving way to a circular hatch, and the engine grille was simplified. A new, wider 500mm (19.6in) track with a waffle pattern improved traction (vehicles with these modifications were known as the T-34 Model

ABOVE: A column of T-34/85 tanks on the move in the spring of 1945. Spare track links have been attached to the glacis plate. This had two functions: first, the tracks added a modest increase in armour protection; and second, they were also readily available if links in use on the tracks were broken or damaged by mines or gunfire.

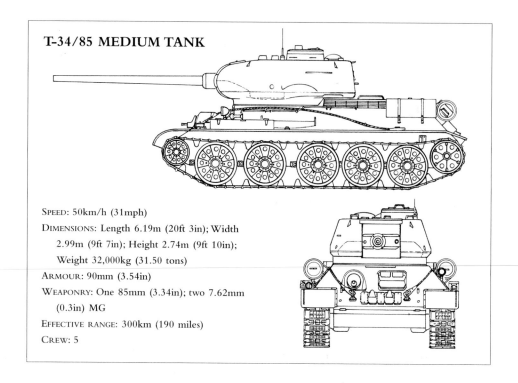

T-34/85 MEDIUM TANK

SPEED: 50km/h (31mph)

DIMENSIONS: Length 6.19m (20ft 3in); Width
2.99m (9ft 7in); Height 2.74m (9ft 10in);
Weight 32,000kg (31.50 tons)

ARMOUR: 90mm (3.54in)

WEAPONRY: One 85mm (3.34in); two 7.62mm
(0.3in) MG

EFFECTIVE RANGE: 300km (190 miles)

CREW: 5

1942). More importantly for the crew, extra armour was welded on to some models (spare track attached to the body of the tank was one way of quickly doing this), while later models came off the production lines with turret protection of 90mm (3.5in) of armour as standard.

Having said this, a shortage of rubber at many of the T-34 production plants led to an all-steel wheel being temporarily introduced in 1942. This all-steel wheel was unpopular with tank crews as contact with the metal track at high speeds set up harmonic vibrations that were noisy and unpleasant for those inside, and could cause damage to the T-34 itself by loosening parts. As rubber became available again, rubber-rimmed wheels were used in the fifth and sixth position. With increased rubber supplies in 1943, the all-steel wheel was phased out. While in 1942, T-34 production jumped to over 5000 tanks, more radical changes needed to be made to the basic design to take into account the newer German models arriving on the Eastern Front. By 1943, the T-34 had become a much more effective fighting vehicle. The re-designed turret held a crew of three, vision was improved with the addition of a new cupola, and radios were added as standard. These changes culminated in a totally new T-34 model, which was designated the T-34/85.

THE T-34/85

The modifications outlined above produced the other main variant of the T-34 tank, the T-34/85, that would continue as a fighting machine well beyond World War II. The T-34/76 had a two-man turret that was cramped and inefficient. Therefore, the existing T-34 chassis was adapted to take a cast, three-man turret and a more powerful gun. The three-man turret freed up the commander who had previously operated the main gun. The new gun in the T-34/85 was the long 85mm (3.34in), adapted from an anti-aircraft gun. The up-gunned T-34/85 was capable of firing a 9.8kg (21.5lb) round at a muzzle velocity of 780m/s (2600ft/s). This compared favourably to the German 8.8cm (3.46in) on the Tiger that fired a 10.1kg (22.25lb) shot at 797m/s (2657ft/s). The 7.5cm (2.95in) on the Panther fired a much smaller shot of 6.8kg (15lb), but it did compensate for this with a higher muzzle velocity of 920m/s (3068ft/s).

The extra armour, turret space and firepower meant an increase in weight for the T-34/85. Having said this, the design team that produced the T-34 with the long 85mm (3.34in) gun managed to combine the new features without reducing overall efficiency. While the weight of the T-34/85 rose from 27.3 to 32.3 tonnes (27 to 32 tons), and its range fell from 448km (280 miles) to 304km (190 miles), the T-34/85 was the most powerful tank in the Allied arsenal when it went into production in late 1943, and of all the tanks on the field, it was only slightly less formidable than the Panther.

The T-34/85 also used existing industrial production lines, and so the new design could be produced rapidly and in great numbers for the Red Army. In 1943, of the 6000 T-34s built, only a small proportion were the T-34/85. But in 1944, 65 per cent of the new tanks rolling out of the tank factories in the Urals were the new T-34s with the 85mm (3.34in) gun. These new T-34s were decisive in providing a

counter to the heavier German machines produced by this time. By 1944, production of the T-34/85 dwarfed that of the T-34/76. Wartime production of the T-34s of both types approached 40,000, making it the most widely produced tank of the war.

SUMMARY OF ALL T-34 VARIANTS

As the T-34 was produced from different factories, models and types varied. In August 1939, the Soviet Main Military Council accepted the T-34 as the Red Army's medium battle tank. The new design was completed during December 1939 and became known as the T-34 (Model 1940). On 19 December 1939, the drawings and models of the new T-34

BELOW: Black exhaust smoke streams from a T-34/85/1 tank of the 1st Ukrainian Front as it crosses a deserted railway bridge over the Elbe in May 1945. In the background are the gutted ruins of the city of Dresden. In controversial raids between 13 and 15 February 1945, RAF and USAAF bombers had attacked Dresden. The city was full of refugees from the east, and in the intense firestorm that followed the bombs, between 30,000 and 60,000 people were killed.

ABOVE: The T-44 developed by the Morozov design team retained the same turret as the T-34/85, as well as roadwheels, track and engine; however, the hull and engine layout was completely re-designed. New torsion bar suspension was added and armour protection for the turret front went up to 120mm (4.72in). A small number of T-44s saw action in the final months of World War II.

were submitted to the High Command, which accepted them for production, even though the prototype had not yet been completed.

DIESEL ENGINES

The first production-line models were fitted with V-2 diesel engines, but shortages meant that some of these early models were equipped with the older M-17 petrol engine. Problems with transmissions were such that the T-34/76 (Model 40) often went into battle with spare transmission units secured to the engine compartment deck by steel cables.

The Model 40 had a rolled plate turret and a short 76.2mm (3in) L/30.3 (L-11) Model 1938 tank gun mounted in a distinctive cast cradle welded to a flush outside mantle. The Model 40 established a standardization pattern among the T-34 variants of having a great number of interchangeable parts, such as engine, armament, transmission and periscopes. Mechanical simplicity was a prime concern. The hull was of a welded construction throughout, with only three different thickness of rolled plate armour.

The Christie suspension had five large, double road wheels on each side, with a

LEFT: A T-34/85 which is equipped with a snorkel submerged underwater during a river-crossing operation. In contrast to the standard postwar NATO practice in amphibious tank design, Soviet practice was to fit a snorkel which allowed in just enough air for the crew and the engine during short underwater crossings of obstacles such as rivers and creeks. However the air vent was not wide enough for the crew to escape through if the tank broke down under water – which could have fatal consequences for them.

noticeably larger gap between the second and third wheels. The drive sprocket, located for safety to the rear, was of the roller type used on the BT series and powered a cast manganese-steel track with centre guide horns on alternative track links. This first model of the T-34 had a distinctive turret overhang and a clumsy turret hatch occupying the entire rear part of the turret. The Model 40 had one periscope fitted on the front left-hand side. In late 1941, a small number were fitted with the long-barrelled, high-velocity 57mm (2.24in) ZiS-4 gun, to

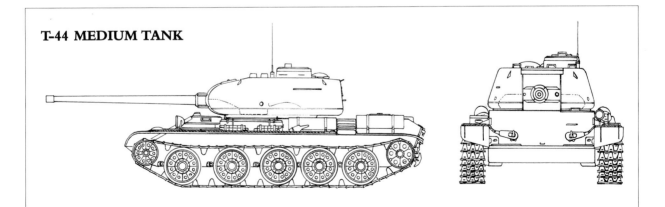

T-44 MEDIUM TANK

SPEED: 50km/h (32mph)
DIMENSIONS: Length 6.50m (21ft 4in); Width 3.28m (10ft 9in);
    Height 2.49m (8ft 2in); Weight 34,545kg (34 tons)
ARMOUR: 120mm (4.72in)

WEAPONRY: One 85mm (3.34in) or one 100mm (3.9in) gun;
    two 7.62mm (0.3in) MG
EFFECTIVE RANGE: 250km (155 miles)
CREW: 4

SU-85 TANK DESTROYER

SPEED: 48km/h (30mph)

DIMENSIONS: Length 6.58m (21ft 7in); Width 2.99m (9ft 10in); Height 2.54m (8ft 4in); Weight 29,600kg (29.13 tons)

ARMOUR: 54mm (2.1in)

WEAPONRY: One 85mm (3.34in) gun

EFFECTIVE RANGE: 320km (200 miles)

CREW: 4

engage light armoured vehicles at greater ranges than the 76.2mm (0.303in) L-11.

T-34 (MODEL 1941)

The second model of the T-34 appeared in 1941 and was essentially a commander's Model 40 with a rolled plate turret mounting a more powerful Model 1940 76.2mm (3in) L/41.5 gun. The same clumsy turret hatch was retained, but some of these variants had twin periscopes. While there was no change in the layout of the hull, these commander's tanks had a stowage box on the right-hand track guard. The most noticeable feature of the 1941 model was the replacement of the peculiar cast gun cradle by an angular, bolted type. During 1942, a model appeared with a cast turret and it also had new, wider tracks. Some were fitted with a flamethrower (ATO-41) and had an armoured fuel container on the rear plate of the hull.

T-34 (MODEL 1942)

In 1942 the cast turret (as opposed to rolled plate) became standard in the Model 1942. The new turret weighed 4.4 tonnes (4.32 tons) and had a ring diameter of 1.38m (4.6ft). The Model 1942 had various improvements, taking into account reports from the battlefield. The commander and gunner now had separate hatches, and a new hull machine-gun mounting made the

7.62mm (0.3in) DT machine gun more effective in close-quarter battle.

In early 1942 a team designed a new T-34, the T-34M, with a chassis similar to the KV tank (with smaller road wheels), and a completely new hull and turret layout. However, this tank was not accepted for production, and only the hexagonal shape to the T-34/M turret was retained for the next variant of the T-34, the T-34/76 Model 1943.

As discussed earlier, the T-34 Model 1943 was manufactured in response to battlefield reports which showed that one drawback of the current T-34 design was the turret overhang at the rear that was vulnerable to attack by Teller mine-armed infantry tank-hunters. The new, cast hexagonal turret with no overhang became the Model 1943 and included other changes, such as improved fuel capacity and welded armour plate components.

T-34/76E

Subsequent T-34/76 models are best known by their British classification. The Models E and F were both produced in 1943. While the basic hull and turret structure of the T-34/76E remained the same, it had a more effective air-cleaning and lubrication system. The hull design was also improved by using automatic welding processes with improved materials that gave stronger, higher-quality joins. The Model 'E' clearly demonstrated the advances made in Soviet industry. This new confidence in tank construction meant that each new T-34 model was more rugged and better equipped.

T-34/76F

The Model 'F' had a distinctive appearance as, while it had no commander's cupola, the model had contoured undercuts around all the sides and the front. The main difference to the F was, however, in its internal workings. The T-34/76F had new, highly efficient automotive components. The old four-speed gearbox was replaced by a five-speed box that made gear-changing easier and increased the speed of the T-34. The air filter was refined further and a level of care and thought went into the mechanics of the T-34/76F that set it apart from earlier models. However, only a limited number of this type were produced as production began to move in a much more radical direction.

By 1943 it was apparent that the 76.2mm (3in) gun on the T-34 was inadequate. The model incorporated many new design features, and had added armour protection, but it was still under-gunned. The appearance of the German long-barrelled high-velocity 7.5cm (2.95in) (L/48) and 8.8cm (3.46in) tank guns finally proved that the T-34 had to be up-gunned, and this was to lead to the genesis of the T-34/85.

T-34/85-I

With its 85mm (3.34in) gun, the T-34/85-I that appeared in 1943 was basically an up-gunned T-34. The T-34/85 had a new turret originally designed for the KV-85 tank with a ring diameter of 1.56m (5.2ft). This created the space for an extra crewmember and simplified the tasks of the tank commander, who previously had helped with the gun. The T-34/85-I was first issued to élite Guards Tank units, and the new gun soon proved its worth. Based upon the pre-war M-1939 85mm (3.34in) anti-aircraft gun, it had an effective range of 1000m (1100yd) and, it was claimed, was able to penetrate the frontal armour of the German Tigers and Panthers.

T-44

Introduced in 1944, the T-44 with its crew of four was a total re-design of the

BELOW: A knocked out SU-85 SP antitank gun. Built at the Uralmashzavod and Kirov plants, the SU-85 fired HE, APHE and HVAP with a muzzle velocity of 795m/sec (2620ft/sec) and was designed to counter German Tiger and Panther tanks. However, once the T-34/85 armed with the same gun was in service, production ceased, though the SU-85 remained in the front line until the end of the war.

SU-100 TANK DESTROYER

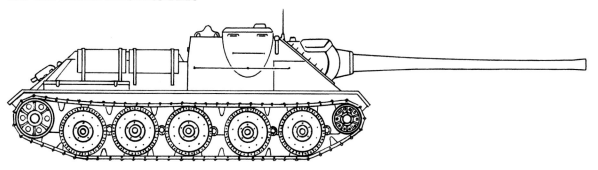

SPEED: 56km/h (35mph)

DIMENSIONS: Length 5.92m (19ft 5in); Width 3m (9ft 10in);
Height 2.54m (8ft 4in); Weight 32,515kg (32 tons)

ARMOUR: 110mm (4.3in)

WEAPONRY: One 100mm (3.9in) gun

EFFECTIVE RANGE: 300km (186 miles)

CREW: 4

T-34/85. It was longer and lower, had a larger turret, thicker armour up to 120mm (4.75in) and torsion bar suspension. There was no hull machine gun and the V-12 381kW (512bhp) diesel engine was mounted transversely. It was initially armed with an 85mm (3.34in) gun, and this was later replaced with a 100mm (3.9in), but the turret was too small for this big gun and the weight of the tank was 34,545kg (34 tons). The hull was 6.5m (21ft 4in) long, and it was 3.28m (10ft 9in) wide and 2.49m (8ft 2in) high. The V-12 381kW (512bhp) diesel engine gave a road speed of 50km/h (32mph) and range of 250km (155 miles). The T-

RIGHT: A column of captured Soviet vehicles are started up by the Germans ready for use against their former owners. In the front is a SU-85 with a length of track attached to its glacis plate. Note that its jettionsable fuel tanks have been discarded, only the brackets remaining. Behind the SU-85 is a T-34. Most Russian roads were mud baths in spring or autumn. In winter the mud froze, immobilizing unwary vehicles. In summer it turned into a choking dust.

44 formed the basis of the post-war generation of T-54, T-55 and T-62 tanks.

SU-85

The SU-85 was designed to counter German Tiger and Panther tanks introduced in 1943 that had out-ranged the T-34 with their 8.8cm (3.34in) and 7.5cm (2.95in) guns. It was based on a T-34 chassis with a V-12 373kW (500bhp) engine but with a simple superstructure mounting an 85mm (3.34in) D-5S gun. It was put together as a prototype very quickly and production was underway at the Uralmashzavod and Kirov plants in mid–1943. The SU-85 was 6.58m long (21ft 7in), 2.99m (9ft 10in) wide and 2.54m (8ft 4in) high. It weighed 29,600kg (29.13 tons) and had a crew of four. The vehicle had a road speed of 48km/h (30mph) and range of 320km (200 miles). Production halted when the T-34/85, armed with the D-5S gun, entered service.

SU-100

When the T-34/85 entered service, the Uralmashzavod factory took the chassis of the SU-85 and mounted the M1944 100mm (3.9in) D-10S naval gun. With muzzle velocity of 895m/s (2936ft/s), it fired a 15.88kg (35lb) shell to a maximum range of 20,650m (22,580yd).

The SU-100, which had 34 rounds stowed on board, was more than capable of destroying the heaviest German tanks. Its all-up weight was 32,515kg (320 tons); it was 5.92m (19ft 5in) long, 3m (9ft 10in) wide and 2.54m (8ft 4in) high. The V-12 diesel gave 373kW (500bhp) and a road speed of 56km/h (35mph) and a range of 300km (186 miles). Armour protection for the hull front was 75mm (3in) and for the gun mantlet 110mm (4.3in).

BELOW: On the brink of victory in May 1945, a column of SU-100s enter the central districts of Berlin. As the SU-100 did not have a point defence machine gun armament, and could not traverse its gun more than a few degrees, it relied on its escorting infantry to defend it from a *Panzerfaust* antitank rocket attack. Despite the proximity of the war's end, individual snipers and fanatics could still launch surprise attacks on unwary Soviet forces.

CHAPTER SIX

HEAVY TANKS

Heavy and even 'super heavy' tanks appealed to Soviet engineers and soldiers in the 1930s, even though the multi-turreted vehicles proved to be impractical. However the large KV-1 would be an ideal chassis for a generation of powerful, heavily armed, well-protected tanks such as the Iosef Stalin, IS-2 and IS-3.

World War I had confronted modern armies with the problems of breaking through strongly fortified and deep opposing defences. Solutions had been found by late 1917, largely through skilled coordination of infantry and artillery forces, whose individual capabilities were enhanced by new technologies and tactics. Tanks had also assisted Allied infantry attacks by crushing barbed wire and destroying enemy strongpoints. The close integration of various combat arms in action, especially the role of tanks, had a major impact upon the development of the Red Army's tactics and organization in the inter-war period. The value of tank support to the infantry for achieving a swift breakthrough of the enemy's tactical defences had a strong influence on Soviet tactics and tank design, leading to the creation of a series of NPP (Direct Infantry Support) and DPP (Distant (Remote)

LEFT: A battered KV-1 in the gutted remains of a Soviet city. The KV-1 had proved its worth in Finland, surviving multiple hits from Finnish antitank guns during the breakthrough operations on the Mannerheim Line. The inscription on the turret's side reads, 'For the Motherland!'.

ABOVE: The T-35 *Tyazholy Tank* (Heavy Tank) was, some western historians argue, based on the idea of the British Independent Tank, while Soviet historians argue that it was a pure Soviet design. By 1941 the tank was totally obsolete. At this point, it was vulnerable to the faster and better-armed German tanks. However, many of the original 61 vehicles were still in service with the Soviet armoured forces and they fought their last battles in front on Moscow in the winter of 1941. With all the turrets fitted and manned, the T-35 had a crew of 11.

Infantry Support) heavy tanks in the interwar years.

INITIAL HEAVY TANK DESIGNS

The stimulus to the actual development of heavy tanks for the NPP and DPP roles envisaged in the Red Army's Field Regulations of 1929 (PU-29) was the massive industrialization of the Soviet Union, begun in the First Five Year Plan (1929). This promised to provide the factories and technology capable of building the advanced weapons required to implement the Red Army's sophisticated doctrine of Deep Battle. Initial designs had to be abandoned because of technical problems.

The first heavy tank project was ordered in December 1930 by the Directorate of Mechanization and Motorization (UMM), in cooperation with the General Design Bureau of the Artillery Department. Classified as T-30, this project demonstrated many of the problems faced by a nation embarking on a rapid course of industrialization with only limited technical expertise. Initial

plans were for a 50.8 tonne (50 ton) vehicle armed with a 76.2mm (3in) gun and five machine guns were ambitious, and although a prototype was constructed in 1932, it was cancelled because of problems with its running gear design.

At the Bolshevik Factory in Leningrad the Experimental Design Mechanical Section (OKMO) designers, assisted by a team of German engineers, initially developed the TG-1 (or T-22) design, sometimes called the Grotte tank after the chief German engineer. The TG-1/T-22 was a sophisticated 30.4 tonnes (30 ton) design, utilizing pneumatic steering and suspension and armed with one 76.2mm (3in) gun, two 7.62mm (0.3in) machine guns, and 35mm (1.3in) armour. The Grotte team continued to experiment with other models characterized by multiple turrets. The TG-3/T-29 weighed 30.4 tonnes (30 tons), and had one 76.2mm (3in) gun, two 37mm (1.45in) guns and two machine guns.

The most ambitious concept was the massive TG-5/T-42, reputedly 101.60 tonnes (100 tons), armed with one

107mm (4.21in) gun and a mixture of other weapons in numerous sub-turrets. However, none of these designs were accepted for production on the grounds that they were either too complex for a youthful and inexperienced Soviet industry or, as in the case of the TG-5, they were simply impractical. It is also arguable that such over-ambitious projects were primarily intended to give Soviet engineers greater experience in tank design, rather than delivering actual production models. Creative freedom in weapons design was one of the hallmarks – and paradoxes – of a totalitarian Soviet régime notorious for its rigid control.

At the same time, the more successful T-35 heavy tank was developed by a second team at OKMO, led by N. Tsiets. Two prototypes of the T-35 were completed between 1932 and 1933. The first, the T-35-1, weighed 50.8 tonnes (50 tons), and had a main armament of a 76.2mm (3in) PS-3 gun based on the model 27/32 howitzer, surrounded by four sub-turrets, two with 37mm (1.45in) guns and two with machine guns. The number of guns required a crew of 10. Included in the design were

ideas developed from the TG prototypes, most notably the transmission of the M6 petrol engine, gearbox and clutches.

However, problems revealed in trials, the complexity of some parts, and the cost made the T-35-1 unsuitable for mass production. The second prototype was the T-35-2, powered by the more powerful M-17 engine with a re-built suspension, less turrets and consequently a crew of only seven. Its armour was slightly stronger, with 35mm (1.3in) frontal, and 25mm (0.9in) side, adequate for withstanding small-arms fire and shell splinters. Based on the experience of these prototypes, the STO Work Defence Council (STO) authorized production of the T-35A on 11 August 1933. Work already in hand at the Bolshevik Leningrad Factory meant that its production engineering was moved to the Kharkov Locomotive Factory (KhPZ).

A number of refinements were made to the T-35's basic design between 1933 and 1939. The 1935 model was longer, and equipped with the new turret designed for the T-28 medium tank, fitted with a L-10 76.2mm (3in) gun. Two 45mm (1.77in) guns, designed for

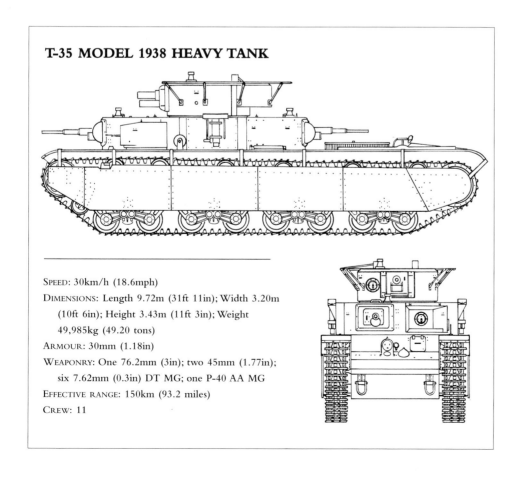

T-35 MODEL 1938 HEAVY TANK

SPEED: 30km/h (18.6mph)

DIMENSIONS: Length 9.72m (31ft 11in); Width 3.20m (10ft 6in); Height 3.43m (11ft 3in); Weight 49,985kg (49.20 tons)

ARMOUR: 30mm (1.18in)

WEAPONRY: One 76.2mm (3in); two 45mm (1.77in); six 7.62mm (0.3in) DT MG; one P-40 AA MG

EFFECTIVE RANGE: 150km (93.2 miles)

CREW: 11

the T-26 and BT-5, replaced the 37mm (1.4in) guns in sub-turrets. In 1938 the increasing threat from more powerful and numerous antitank guns saw a final batch of six tanks receive turrets with sloped armour for improved protection.

The inspiration for the T-35's design has caused disagreement between western and Russian historians. The former argue it was copied from the British Vickers A-6 Independent tank, but this is rejected by many Russian specialists. It is impossible to know the truth for certain, but there is strong evidence to support western claims, not least failed Soviet attempts to purchase the A-6. At the same time, the influence of German engineers developing similar designs in the late 1920s at their Kama base in the Soviet Union cannot be discounted. What is clear is that borrowing military technology and ideas from other nations was common to the majority of armed forces in the interwar years. The Red Army, with its purchase of British Vickers Carden-Loyd tankettes, Vickers-Armstrong E-Light and Mk II Medium tanks, and the American Christie suspension, was clearly one of the leading exponents of this practice.

Although intended for mass production, only around 61 T-35s were built

between 1933 and 1939. Delays were caused by the problems which had been experienced with the BT Fast Tank and T-26: poor quality control and assembly, and poorly processed parts. The performance of the tank suffered from a number of problems. Its large size and inadequate steering made it difficult to manoeuvre, particularly over obstacles; one officer exclaimed that it couldn't cross as much as a large puddle. The crew compartment was confined, and unless the tank was stationary it was difficult to coordinate and accurately fire its guns. With each tank costing as much as nine BT tanks, the Soviets sensibly concentrated resources on building other, more versatile, models.

During their service lives, the T-35s served in three battalions of the 5th Separate Heavy Tank Brigade in the Supreme Command Reserve. With less than 60 of the 94 tanks listed on the brigade's inventory, T-28 tanks had to be used to increase its combat effectiveness. The T-35 saw no action in the Russo–Finish War (1939–40); its main purpose seems to have been to appear in the May Day and November parades as a celebration of the apparent achievements and might of the Soviet Union. Such a

BELOW: A T-35 Model 1938 fitted with a radio antenna. The standard production model had sub-turrets with 45mm (1.77in) guns derived from those on the T-26 and BT-5. The T-35 was a star in many of the pre-war May Day Parades, making its début in 1933. The bulk of the tanks were built at the Kharkov Locomotive Works because of the overflow of work on the T-26 at the Bolshevik Factory.

representation was false. Advances in weaponry had made the T-35 unsuitable for front-line service, and in 1940 a conference of armoured specialists recommended re-assigning it to training duties at Russia's military academies. In the end it was decided to run them down in service, but this was pre-empted by the outbreak of war with Germany in June 1941. Little is known about its fate during the opening year of the war with Germany in 1941. A few were used as fixed strongpoints during the defence of Moscow in December. The majority were probably lost through mechanical failure during the summer battles in the Ukraine, serving with the 67th and 68th Tank Regiments of the 34th Tank Division of VIII Mechanized Corps.

DEVELOPMENT OF THE KV-1

The employment of Soviet tanks in support of Republican forces in the Spanish Civil War (1936–39)

ABOVE: Two *Luftwaffe* NCOs are dwarfed by a T-35 knocked out early in Operation Barbarossa. The tank looked impressive, but with a maximum armour thickness of 30mm (1.18in), it was vulnerable to most antitank guns. The multi-turret design would have been hard for the commander to control.

ABOVE: Snow covers an SMK knocked out during the Russo–Finnish War. The tank had detonated a large mine and when this photograph appeared in the West, the Germans erroneously designated the tank the T-35C. It was a completely different vehicle named after Sergius Mironovitch Kirov and designed in 1938 by the team headed by Z. Kotin. The prototypes were tested against the Finns in 1940 but were found to be too bulky and complicated.

demonstrated the weakness of their armour in the face of new 37mm (1.46in) antitank guns and large-calibre artillery guns. Although actual losses to this direct fire were light, and no T-35 heavy tanks were sent to Spain, it was clear that specifications for tank armour to withstand machine-gun fire and artillery splinters were becoming obsolete.

Consequently, in November 1937 the Directorate of Armed Forces (ABTU) laid down new requirements for a new heavy tank specification. The new tank was to be able to withstand fire from a 76.2mm (3in) gun up to 1200m (3937ft) and be powered by a diesel engine; petrol, unlike diesel, exploded in a fireball if the vehicle was fatally hit. Continuing from the T-35, it was initially suggested that the tank have five turrets, but on the appeal of the design teams involved, this was subsequently revised to three, mounting one 76.2mm (3in) and two 45mm (1.77in) guns. The new design was to be capable of performing the dual roles of supporting a breakthrough and destroying enemy armour.

Initial work was begun at the KhPZ, but the lack of resources and loss of

engineers caused by Stalin's ruthless purges of Russian society led to the work being re-assigned to two competing teams in Leningrad. These were the OKMO team under N. Barykov, and the Zirovskiy Factory led by Lieutenant-Colonel Zh. Kotin. Kotin was to prove one of the most imaginative and resourceful Soviet tank designers of the World War II period, and he was responsible for the powerful IS (Iosef Stalin) series of tanks.

On 4 May 1938 both teams presented their initial designs to a joint committee of the Politburo and Defence Council. Barykov's T-100, and Kotin's SMK (named after the deceased Bolshevik leader S. M. Kirov) were similar in configuration, with an upper main turret mounting a 76.2mm (3in) gun and two lower front sub-turrets with 45mm (1.77in) guns. A new innovation was the use of a torsion bar suspension for the chassis, instead of the T-35's older and less effective spring suspension. A wide cast track was also used on both vehicles, lowering ground pressure and improving the tanks' cross-country capability, which was essential, considering both the T-100's

58.9 tonne (58 ton) and SMK's 45.9 tonne (45 ton) weights.

The committee was generally impressed by the designs, and approval was granted to construct prototypes. However, there had been several tense and heated moments during the meeting. Kotin had bravely (or arguably foolishly) remonstrated to Stalin over the value of including so many turrets because of the increase weight they created. This, he argued, undermined the mobility of the heavier tanks under consideration. Several engineers risked their necks by arguing against Stalin's ignorant, spiteful crony, G. Kulik, head of the artillery, who wanted to use laminated armour.

The designers eventually won both arguments, retaining the 60mm (2.4in) steel armour, and removing one of the sub-turrets. Stalin's frequent willingness to accept the opinions of his technicians and field commanders on matters of tank design is worthy of note, especially in light of the standard historical view that he was totally ignorant of military affairs and unwilling to compromise his ideas. At times his interference in military affairs proved disastrous, but he was intelligent enough to grasp the essentials of weapon design and the conduct of war.

The prototype of the T-100 was completed in May 1939, and the first SMK was ready at the start of August. Both vehicles began testing at the Kubinka testing grounds outside Moscow. The test crews included a number of engineers from the two Leningrad factories who received special training in the skills needed to drive the vehicles and operate their armaments. Leading Communist Party and military officials attended the tests, most notably Marshal K. Voroshilov, who witnessed the trial of another new heavy tank, named the KV after him.

The KV tank was the result of frustration on the part of Kotin and his assistant chief engineer A. Yermolayev. They still disliked the weight problems and cramped crew compartment which was created by having two turrets. In typical fashion, in February 1939, Kotin, acting without higher approval, set his team the task of designing a single-turret variant of the SMK. In August 1939 Kotin showed the plans to Stalin and again managed to win him over. Official approval was given to construct a KV prototype and then

BELOW: The SMK, like the T-100, was originally designed with three turrets. When Kotin criticized this concept, Stalin simply broke off a turret from the presentation model with the quip 'Why make a tank into a department store?' and the Kotin and OKMO teams worked on a two-turret design. The SMK had a 76.2mm (3in) main gun with a 45mm (1.77in) in the secondary turret.

test it alongside the two dual-turret heavy vehicles. Apart from a new single turret, the KV inherited many features from the SMK; hull, transmission, optics and the torsion bar suspension. During the Kubinka trials, the KV proved superior in mobility to the SMK and T-100. However, the sternest test of the three new tank types came in December 1939, when they were deployed to take part in the Russo–Finnish War.

THE RUSSO–FINNISH WAR, 1939–40

On 30 November 1939 the Soviet Union attacked Finland with the intention of making a number of limited territorial gains along their mutual border. The sheer size of Soviet forces in comparison to the Finns, and their superiority in tanks, artillery and aircraft, made the Soviets confident of a swift victory. In the end, this was not to prove the case. Fierce and skillful Finnish resistance, and an initially risible Soviet performance saw the war drag on until mid–February 1940 when, with their reserves simply running out under constant Soviet attacks, the Finns were forced to capitulate to Soviet territorial demands.

The SMK, T-100 and KV prototypes saw action in the war, taking part in a number of skirmishes as part of the 91st Tank Battalion of the 20th Heavy Tank Brigade. Their first action took place near Summa between 17 and 19 December, and was one of mixed fortunes for the experimental tanks. In general, the KV performed well. During attacks on 18 December, although the Finns did manage to shoot off one of the KV's barrels, forcing it to be withdrawn, the tank proved to be mechanically reliable, and its thick armour was invulnerable to enemy direct-fire weapons.

BELOW: The SMK serving with the 20th Heavy Tank Brigade on the move in Finland. This picture shows clearly the slightly larger roadwheels and wide tracks that would be incorporated into the KV-1 design and prove very effective on snow and soft going. Following requests for a tank with armament capable of knocking out Finnish bunkers, work was under way to build an SMK-2.

The other two prototypes were less effective, nearly causing a major embarrassment for the Soviet Union in one engagement. On 19 December the SMK and T-100, accompanied by five T-28s, supported Soviet infantry as they again tried to penetrate Finnish defences at Summa. Invulnerable to Finnish light weapons, the tanks advanced deep into the enemy's defences until one of the SMK's tracks was disabled by a mine. The SMK's crew repaired the track whilst its own gunners and supporting vehicles provided them with covering fire. The situation worsened when it was discovered that the engine would no longer start. Attempts by the T-100 to tow the SMK were frustrated by icy conditions

ABOVE: A KV-1 crosses a timber bridge over a frozen river; the ice could take the tank's weight as long as the timber tresses distributed it evenly. It would eventually have the ZiS-5 76.2mm (3in) gun with 111 rounds and 3 DT machine guns.

115

ABOVE: A clear impression of the low ground-pressure of the wide tracks on the KV-1 can be seen in this picture of KV-1 at the Aberdeen Proving Ground in the USA. The tank was named after Klimenti, or Klim Voroshilov, the Soviet General of the People's Commissar for Defence, but was originally destined to be named the Kotin-Stalin. Like the T-34, it was an uncluttered design, but it had less well-angled armour to deflect enemy antitank rounds.

that prevented its tracks from acquiring sufficient grip. As ammunition ran low, the crew had no choice but to withdraw, abandoning the SMK. Desperate not to lose one of his valuable experimental tanks, D.G. Pavlov, head of the Directorate of Armed Forces, mounted an ineffective and costly rescue mission with elements of the 167th Motorized Battalion. Eventually the SMK was recovered in February when Soviet forces finally broke through Finnish defences along the Mannerheim Line.

In general the performance of the experimental heavy tanks in the Finnish War simply confirmed the decision made by the Red Army on 19 December 1939 to approve the KV-1 for general production and discontinue the SMK and T-100; a brief flirtation with a modified SMK (SMK-2) came to nothing. On another note, the war revealed certain deficiencies in the technical capabilities

of Soviet tanks when operating in winter conditions! Amongst a number of improvements adopted to overcome this bizarre situation was the introduction of compressed air tanks and separate reserve batteries for the ignition.

STRENGTHS AND WEAKNESSES

When it first appeared, the KV-1's combination of mobility, strong armour and firepower made it one of the most powerful tanks in the world, probably only rivalled or surpassed by the Soviet medium T-34. Its frontal hull and turret armour were 75mm (2.95in) and 90mm (3.5in) thick respectively, making it invulnerable to many existing antitank guns, other than at point blank range. Although weighing 43.6 tonnes (43 tons), a series of factors meant that it was relatively fast and mobile, capable of achieving 35km/h (21.8mph) on roads, and approximately 13km/h (8.1mph)

across country. This was achieved by a refined version of the SMK suspension which mounted the 12 wheels independently on torsion bars, and using wide tracks to lower ground pressure. Adequate power was provided by a 373kW (500bhp) model V-2K, V-12 diesel engine. Combined with a range of 160km (99 miles) by road, and 100km (62 miles) across country, the KV-1, in conjunction with the even more mobile T-34, seemed to give the Red Army the tools it required to implement the theory of Deep Operations.

Initially it was intended to arm the KV-1 with the F-32 76.2mm gun (3in) developed by the Grabin team, but delays in supply meant that the short L-11 76.2mm (3in) was used instead. Secondary armament comprised three DT machine guns, one co-axial, one in the front hull, and one in the rear of the turret. A crew of five was required to operate the tank.

Impressive as it was, the KV-1 did suffer from a number of problems, and not all had been solved by the time production ended in 1943. Initial models had major clutch and transmission problems, seriously impeding its mobility. Changing gear involved halting the tank, preventing it from ever attaining high speed. US Army tests on the transmission

at their Aberdeen Armoured Testing ground in 1942 noted that it was years out of date and had been rejected by the US Army because it was painfully hard for the driver to work. Engine performance was further reduced by inefficient air filters. Overall, these factors made the tank hard to steer.

The crew compartment was far from ideal and hampered performance in combat. When the hatches were closed, the driver and commander had severely restricted vision, making it difficult for them to carry out their tasks effectively. The driver's periscope had a limited traverse, and the laminated glass in his forward slit visor was often of such poor manufacture that it was difficult to see through. The commander had two periscopes of a reasonable standard mounted in the top of the turret, but his ability to direct the driver, radio operator and gunner were significantly hampered by having to double up as gun loader. All of this resulted in poor tactical mobility and coordination on the battlefield.

During the course of the war, refinements were made to the basic KV-1 design in order to iron out its flaws and extend its service life. In 1940 the KV-1 model 1940 appeared, armed with the higher velocity F-32 76.2mm (3in) gun firing a longer round and a new, more

ABOVE: The KV-1 chassis was used for 13,500 vehicles, tanks and SP guns during the war. In 1943, as work was being carried out on the new IS tank, a turret with a M1943 85mm (3.34in) gun with 71 rounds was fitted to a KV hull and the stop-gap vehicle was designated the KV-85. The KV-1-S was a lighter version of the original tank with maximum armour of 82mm (3.2in).

powerful 447kW (600bhp) V-2 engine. Parts of the turret and hull armour were increased by the crude and unpopular technique of bolting 35mm (1.3in) armour plates to them. This was caused by G. Kulik's bizarre belief that German tanks were armed with massive-calibre guns, and with the short-term inability of Soviet industry to produce thicker armour, he and Stalin wanted to counter this phantom threat. The turret plates were replaced later in the year when stronger welded turrets were produced.

In 1941 the ZiS-5 76.2mm (3in) gun was fitted for the first time to the KV-1. Similar to the F-34 76.2m (3in) gun mounted on the T-34/76 medium tank, it was significantly more powerful than the KV's existing F-32 76.2mm (3in). This was the result of another successful appeal by Kotin's team to Stalin and the Main Defence Committee (GKO). Upgrading the KV with the F-34 ended the illogical situation of the Red Army's medium tank being armed with a more powerful gun than its heavy tank. The earlier model's angular and weaker welded turret was replaced with a stronger cast version that was also easier to manufacture. The rear turret overhang was also eliminated.

A unique development of the KV-1 was its adaptation to a flamethrower role, designated KV-8. Work began on this project after the Russo–Finnish War

showed that light tanks adapted to being flamethrowers were too vulnerable to antitank fire. The KVS 76.2mm (3in) gun was replaced with a 45mm (1.77in) gun in order to make room for the ATO-41 flamethrower. A special gun jacket was added to camouflage the thin barrel of the weapon and prevent it being knocked out immediately by the enemy. The ATO-41 fired 3 shots every 10 seconds, and the KV-8 carried enough fuel for 107 shots. Later on the KV-8S was developed by re-equipping the KV-1-S.

KV-2 DREADNOUGHT

The Russo–Finnish war was an essential catalyst, not just in confirming the soundness of the decision to manufacture the KV-1, but in providing the stimulus for the development of an artillery support variant, designated KV-2. Combat in the Finnish war had revealed that existing Soviet tanks were under-armed for dealing effectively with reinforced enemy bunkers and other fortifications. The North-West Front Headquarters, and in particular the commander of the Seventh Army, K. Meretskov, made forceful requests that a heavy tank with a large gun be developed for bunker-busting tasks. Three projects were immediately undertaken. In one of its last projects before disbandment, the OKMO team revived its T-100 hull, mounting a B-13 130mm (5.1in) naval gun. Designated the

LEFT: The KV-1 production line was located at the Kirov Factory in Leningrad, but once the city had been cut off by the German siege, this obviously became impractical, and thereafter work was transferred to Chelyabinsk. A plan to build a KV-3 mounting a huge 107mm (4.2in) gun at Kirov was shelved and the chassis mounting a 85mm (3.34in) naval gun was used in the defence of Leningrad.

KV-1 HEAVY TANK

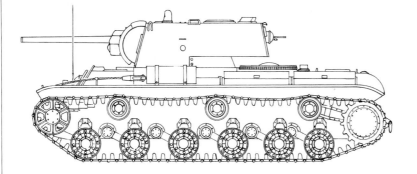

SPEED: 35km/h (21.8mph)

DIMENSIONS: Length 7.41m (24ft 3in); Width 3.49m (11ft 5in); Height 2.87m (9ft 5in); Weight 42,910kg (42.23 tons)

ARMOUR: 106mm (4.17in)

WEAPONRY: One 76.2mm (3in); three 7.62mm (0.3in) MG

EFFECTIVE RANGE: 225km (140 miles)

CREW: 5

ABOVE: Up-armouring work on the KV-1, the Model 1942, was undertaken by Kotin's TsKB-2 (Central Design Bureau) and hull protection was increased from 75mm (2.9in) to 90mm (3.54in). A new and thicker cast turret with 120mm (4.72in) at the front was introduced. However, the thicker armour degraded the vehicle's automotive performance and as a result of this, the KV-1 Model 1942 was looked upon as a mixed blessing by its crews.

T-100U, it was not accepted for production. Rejection of the design may have been a result of the army's lack of access to barrels and the naval semi-armour piercing round at a time when the Soviet Navy was beginning a massive expansion programme to create a powerful, ocean-going fleet. More pragmatically, the development of a design by Kotin's team based on the proven KV chassis made more sense in terms of streamlining production and saving costs.

An initial attempt to mount a 152mm (5.9in) BR-2 and a 203mm (7.9in) B-4 howitzer on a lengthened KV hull was never completed. It was the expediency of the third design – completed in two weeks by mounting a standard 152mm (5.9in) howitzer with two machine guns on an unmodified KV chassis – that was accepted for production as the KV-2. The first trials of the KV-2 were conducted on 10 February 1940, and soon afterwards two prototypes were sent to the front on the Karelian Isthmus. There is some debate whether these tanks were involved in actual combat in 1940. Recent evidence seems to suggest that Meretskov's and others' reports about the

excellent results achieved by the KV-2 against fortified positions and pillboxes were referring to tests conducted against captured enemy positions.

The KV-2 possessed one of the most unique silhouettes of any tank of World War II. The hull was that of the KV-1 series, but in order to mount the power-ful 152mm (5.9in) 1938/1940 L20 howitzer, a large box-shaped 12.19 tonne (12 ton) turret was required. This gave the vehicle a silhouette of 4.9m (16ft) compared to 3.1m (10ft) for the KV-1. The visibility of the KV-2 on the battle-field was compensated for by the turret's armour; frontal 110mm (4.3in), side 75mm (2.9in) thick.

In the opening years of the war, when the KV-2 was operational in significant numbers, it was virtually invulnerable to direct fire from all but high-velocity weapons at uncomfortably close range. The best the enemy could hope to achieve was to force the crew to abandon their KV-2 by disabling the tank with hits against its tracks and wheels. In light of the KV-2's size and armoured strength, its six-man crews gave it the nickname the 'Dreadnought'.

Nonetheless, the KV-2 did pay a high price for its massive gun and strong impenetrable armour. Its mobility between engagements and during battle was restricted by many of the initial gear, transmission and crew problems inherited from the KV-1. This situation was compounded by its increased weight which went up to 53.8–57.9 tonnes (53–57 tons) depending on the model, as well as by the use of an unimproved 373kW (500bhp) V-2 diesel engine.

The road speed of the KV-2 could only ever reach a maximum of 25km/h (15.62mph), and cross-country it reached at best 12km/h (7.4mph). Problems encountered in traversing the heavy turret if the tank was not on relatively flat ground also limited its flexibility in combat. The KV-2 was a formidable opponent in a static position, but it lacked the speed and mobility that were shown to be vital in the opening year of the war on the Eastern Front.

KV-1 AND KV-2 IN COMBAT

The German attack on 22 June 1941 caught the Red Army by surprise: it was badly deployed and in the midst of a major re-organization of its armed forces. During the course of the 1941 campaign, the Red Army suffered enormous losses in men and matériel, including the bulk of its vast tank park. In spite of the overall poor performance of Soviet forces, the resilience of the KV-1 and KV-2 came as a shock to the Germans. They had no comparable tanks in strength and armament, and few antitank guns to destroy them. In his memoirs, *A Soldier's Duty*, Marshal K.K. Rokossovsky recalled:

The KV tanks literally stunned the enemy. They withstood the fire of every type of gun that the German tanks were armed with. But what a sight they were returning from combat. Their armour was pocked-marked all over and sometimes even their barrels were pierced.

BELOW: The production line at Chelyabinsk Tractor Factory (ChTZ). When the line was set up, the design was simplified in much the same way as the T-34 programme. A new cast turret that was easier to manufacture than the welded design was introduced, along with a simpler roadwheel. Hull appliqué armour was simplified and standardized.

BELOW: Workers meet the crews of a KV-1B regiment. The tank, introduced in 1941, had the thicker cast turret with its distinctive curved bustle. These tanks in winter camouflage and painted with slogans have spare fuel drums stowed on their rear decks. The KV-1B had a hull machine gun added to its armament.

Typical of the problems which were faced by the German armed forces when engaging the Soviet KV-2 was the experience of the 1st Panzer Division on 23 June 1941 in Lithuania, which was recorded thus:

Our companies opened fire from 700 metres [2296ft]. We got closer and closer ... Soon we were only about 50–100 metres [164–328ft] from each other. A fantastic engagement opened up – without any German progress. The

Soviet tanks continued their advance and our armour-piercing projectiles simply bounced off. The Soviet tanks withstood point-blank fire from both our 50mm [1.9in] and 75mm [2.9in] guns. A KV-2 was hit more than 70 times and not a single round penetrated. A very few Soviet tanks were immobilized and eventually destroyed as we managed to shoot at their tracks, and then brought up artillery to hammer them at close range. It was then attacked on foot with satchel charges.

BELOW: Workers meet the crews of a KV-1B regiment. The tank, introduced in 1941, had the thicker cast turret with its distinctive curved bustle. These tanks in winter camouflage and painted with slogans have spare fuel drums stowed on their rear decks. The KV-1B had a hull machine gun added to its armament.

The majority of KV-2 losses in 1941 were to breakdowns or lack of fuel, which subsequently forced them to be abandoned. The 41st Tank Division lost two-thirds of its 33 KV-2s, but only five of these were as a result of enemy action. They were too few in number to decisively effect the collapse of the Red Army's positions in western Russia.

By July 1941 only 500 KV-1s and 2s were left. In October 1941, KV-2 manufacture was halted as Russian factories were moved eastwards away from the Germans; by this point only 334 had been built. An increasingly small number continued to see service as strongpoints in positional battles such as the defence of Moscow in winter 1941, and at Stalingrad in 1942 with Major-General V. Chuikov's Sixty-Second Army.

KV-1-S

Constant increases in the armour of the KV-1 between 1941 and 1942, resulting in greater weight and lower speed, began to have a serious impact on the ability of Soviet armoured formations to operate the KV-1 alongside the T-34. Grouping the KV-1 into separate armoured brigades for purely assault and infantry support roles in October 1942 solved part of the problem. However, it left open the need for heavy-tank support for the mobile units now facing increasingly more effective German tanks and antitanks guns, armed with more sophisticated and lethal munitions. Ultimately the dilemma was only resolved in late 1943 when the T-34 was up-gunned with the DT-5 85mm (3.3in) and the heavier Iosef Stalin models introduced.

ABOVE: The huge turret of a KV-2 looms over a BA-10 armoured car during fighting in 1941. The KV-2 had a crew of six and was armed with a 152mm (5.98in) M1938/40 howitzer – which had 36 rounds – as well as two machine guns. It was intended for direct fire support, a need identified during the war against the Finns, but proved unsatisfactory in this role, so that when production of the KV tank moved from Leningrad, it was discontinued.

RIGHT: A view of the
massive KV-2 showing its
152mm (5.9in) gun off to
good effect. Although
difficult to manoeuvre, the
KV-2 could absorb a great
deal of punishment, and
there are a number of
recorded incidents where
KV-2s continued fighting
despite a number of hits
from antitank and tank guns.

RIGHT: A view of the
massive KV-2 showing its
152mm (5.9in) gun off to
good effect. Although
difficult to manoeuvre, the
KV-2 could absorb a great
deal of punishment, and
there are a number of
recorded incidents where
KV-2s continued fighting
despite a number of hits
from antitank and tank guns.

During 1940, Kotin and his team had in fact already developed two prototypes for a KV-3 based on modifications to the KV-1 that would have fitted the new heavy-tank requirements in 1942. Object 220 had a longer hull, larger turret, and a 107mm (4.2in) gun. Object 222 retained the basic external design of the KV-1 with an enhanced turret layout. It was their need for a new powerplant, which would have disrupted tank production in the critical period 1941–42, which led the GKO to reject the KV-3 models.

An attempt was made to solve the Red Army's field requirements and demands of production with the KV-1-S (S: *skorostnoy*, or speed). To achieve a road speed of 40km/h (25mph), the weight of the tank was reduced by thinning its armour; for example 60mm (2.3in) at the front. It had a smaller, thinner turret and lighter road wheels. A new gearbox, main

KV-2A HEAVY TANK

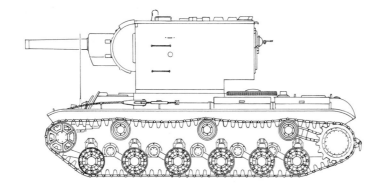

SPEED: 26km/h (16.2mph)

DIMENSIONS: Length 7.31m (23ft 11in); Height 3.93m
(12ft 11in); Weight 53,850kg (53 tons)

ARMOUR: 110mm (4.3mm)

WEAPONRY: One 152mm (5.9in) howitzer; two 7.62mm (0.3in) MG

EFFECTIVE RANGE: 200km (125 miles)

CREW: 6

clutch and improvements in engine-cooling and lubrication also assisted in enhancing its speed and mobility. Production began in August 1942, but after 1370 vehicles had been built, it was discontinued in late 1943 as improved designs began to appear. The design was not especially liked by tank officers such as General M.E. Katukov who, in late 1942, told Stalin that if the KV had a more potent gun or one of greater calibre than the T-34, he might excuse its weight and other shortcomings.

LATE WAR YEARS

KV-1 and KV-1-S production ended in favour of new, more powerful models capable of surviving an increasingly lethal battlefield. However, the role of the KV series in the Great Patriotic War did not end altogether. At Kursk in 1943, KV-1-S tanks of the 53rd Guards and Fifty-Seventh Army Heavy Tank Brigades took part in the vicious fighting of 12–14 July that broke the impetus of the German offensive. KV-1 tanks supported infantry of the 3rd Byelorussian Front in East Prussia in late 1944. Some KV-1 and KV-1-S are alleged to have taken part in the Berlin operation of April–May 1945. By the war's later stages, many had been allocated to support duties, such as command tanks for the ISU-152 tank-destroyer regiments. What is certain is that after 1943, the basic hull design and chassis of the KV influenced a series of late-war Soviet tanks that were amongst the best designs of any nation during the war.

ABOVE: German technical intelligence staff watch as a captured KV-2A manoeuvres in the hands of its new crew. Though the main armament was very powerful, the tank was slow and unwieldy, and more agile and better-handled German tanks could get in close enough to inflict serious damage. The turret could not be traversed unless the tank was on level ground, and its original role as a bunker buster was irrelevant in 1941–42.

CHAPTER SEVEN

LATE WAR TANKS

The lessons of the fighting in Russia and Eastern Europe generated late war designs that would serve into the 1960s. Tanks were produced with an emphasis on firepower and protection rather than crew comfort. For their German opponents, they were a source of amazement.

In 1943 the course of World War II underwent a decisive shift in favour of the Allied powers in both Europe and the Pacific. Primarily this change was caused by two factors. Firstly, the maturing of Allied economic plans began to deliver weapons and matériel in an abundance, far greater than Germany and Japan could manage. Winning the war of production gave the Allies a numerical superiority that doomed their opponents to eventual defeat. Critically related to production was the second factor: the emergence of British, American and Soviet military formations which were capable of using the new and vast amounts of resources to defeat enemy forces in combat.

On the Eastern Front the production and military tides of war turned in late 1942, with the defeat of 250,000 German troops at Stalingrad and the destruction of another three German army groups during subsequent operations in the winter of 1942–3. In July 1943 at

LEFT: Soviet infantry of the 1st Ukrainian Front in Poland, dressed in *shinel* (greatcoats) and *shapka-ushanka* fur caps with ear flaps, on the warm rear deck of ISU-152 heavy assault guns, where the heat rises from the 447kW (600bhp) engine in the winter cold of January 1945.

ABOVE: A *Samochodnaya Ustanovka* (Self Propelled) SU-122 Assault Howitzer – drives carefully across a pontoon bridge over the River Dniepr. The SU-122 was fitted with angled 20mm (0.78in) to 45mm (1.77in) armour, and the same engine and chassis fitted to the T-34/76. Its role was to provide direct gunfire support. Firing high explosive anti-tank (HEAT) rounds, it was capable of penetrating 200mm (0.78in) of armour at a range of 630m (688yd), while with a high explosive (HE) round, it could reach out to 11,800m (12,904yd).

the Battle of Kursk, Soviet armoured forces met and defeated the German panzer forces in one of the largest tank operations in history. But the real significance of the Battle of Kursk was twofold. First, the Red Army seized the initiative from the Germans. Second, despite what is often claimed, Kursk did not destroy the German panzer arm as an effective fighting force. Rather, what began at Kursk was the erosion of German strength by a series of Soviet offensives that rippled across the whole Front throughout 1943, inflicting continual heavy losses on the Germans.

The ability of the Soviets to organize and carry out large-scale offensive operations from late 1942 onwards relied upon the re-organization of the Red Army's command cadres, the re-introduction of its pre-war concepts of deep battle and operations, and the creation of armoured forces capable of carrying out these theories. In the initial phases of the 1943 summer campaign, Soviet armoured formations were equipped with a mixture of KV heavy, T-34 medium and T-60 and T-70 light tanks. Over the course of the year, several of these classes were modified or phased out and replaced by new

designs. The spur to these changes in the Soviet tank inventory were essentially twofold. First was the continued innovation and creativity of Soviet tank designers, who sought to create improved designs with which to equip the Red Army. This natural desire to advance technology was driven by the second and more pragmatic realities of combat conditions which had changed dramatically with the appearance of several new and powerful German tank designs.

War is a clash of two competing sides who constantly strive to acquire some form of advantage over each other, and this is especially true of their weapons. The shock administered to the German armed forces when they encountered the much more powerful Soviet KV and T-34 tanks during Operation Barbarossa in 1941 forced them to initiate the development of their own medium and heavy tanks capable of overturning the Red Army's tactical advantage. Based upon an assessment of the T-34 delivered on 25 November 1941, it was decided to develop the medium Panther tank, incorporating design features where the T-34 outmatched existing German tanks; a long-barrelled 75mm (2.95in) KwK

L/70 high-velocity gun; sloped armour (80mm/3.14in frontal, 45mm/1.77in side); and large road wheels and wide tracks for speed and mobility. The Germans also developed the heavy Tiger tank with thick, slab-sided armour (100mm/2.54in frontal, 80mm/3.14in side) and the powerful 88mm (3.46in) KwK 43 L/56 gun. The Tiger entered operational service on the Eastern Front in August 1942, inflicting heavy losses on Soviet armoured forces. The Panther's début at Kursk in July 1943 was more muted because of technical troubles, but once these problems were resolved, it proved to be an effective tank-killer.

The Soviet response to the shift in advantage to the Germans was swift and typically pragmatic. Unlike the Germans, they did not design completely new tank types. Instead, they increased the protection of the T-34, replacing its 76mm (2.99in) gun with the more powerful 85mm (3.34in) DT-5S. The T-34 Christie and KV vehicle chassis were adapted to form the basis of a series of strongly armoured and heavily armed self-propelled guns, such as the SU-122/152, ISU-122/152, intended to carry out the dual roles of infantry support and anti-tank. This series of vehicles was complemented by the introduction of the KV-85 and IS (Iosef Stalin) class of tanks. These new armoured fighting vehicles furnished the Red Army with the capability to engage and defeat the new German tanks and to decisively win the war in the east.

SELF-PROPELLED GUNS

Within the First Five Year Plan (1929–34) the Red Army had identified the need for self-propelled artillery guns to support tank and infantry forces. The self-propelled weapons were known by the designation SU (*Samakhodnaya Ustanovka*). Initial designs, such as the SU-2, mounted a 76.2mm (3in) gun on the chassis of a Kommunar tractor, while a number of T-27 tankettes were equipped with a 37mm (1.46in) gun for use in an antitank role.

Despite considerable interest and effort, the Red Army did not possess an effective assault/antitank self-propelled vehicle on the outbreak of war with Germany in June 1941. Adoption of the self-propelled weapons had been hampered by the increasingly excessive size and complexity of designs (the SU-7 was over 102.6 tonnes/106 tons with a 203mm/8in howitzer) that raised serious doubts about their utility in combat and suitability for mass production. The manufacture of more realistic designs based on proven models like the T-26 was not undertaken on a large scale because of the Red Army High Command's preference for concentrating resources on tank construction. Experimental work did

SU-122 MODEL 1943 MEDIUM SELF-PROPELLED HOWITZER

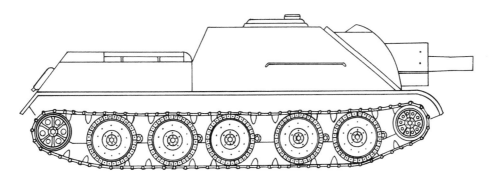

SPEED: 55km/h (34mph)

DIMENSIONS: Length 6.95m (22ft 8in); Width 3m (9ft 8in); Height 2.3m (7ft 5in); Weight 30,900kg (34 tons)

ARMOUR: 45mm (1.77in)

WEAPONRY: One 122mm (4.8in) howitzer

EFFECTIVE RANGE: 300km (186.4 miles)

CREW: 5

Rising like primeval monsters from a swamp, two ISU-152s ford a river. The ISU-152K with external stowage and engine improvements remained in production until as late as 1952. The assault gun was armed with the powerful 152mm (5.9in) gun-howitzer ML-20S with 25 rounds. The ISU-152 and ISU-122 series of assault guns were normally grouped in independent heavy assault gun regiments and brigades.

continue with SU models in the initial phase of the Great Patriotic War, but the pressing need to replace the huge losses in tanks and to re-locate industry meant that production of SU vehicles had to be forgone in 1941 and for much of 1942.

By late 1942 the demands of Red Army tank, mechanized and cavalry forces or armoured vehicles were being satisfied by a revitalized industrial base. In light of this, on 23 October 1942 the Chief Defence Commissariat decided that there was now sufficient industrial capacity to order the design and production of self-propelled guns. The decision was spurred on by three other factors.

First, the success of the German StuG III assault gun had demonstrated the utility of self-propelled guns. Secondly, Soviet rifle and armoured formations reported an urgent tactical requirement for greater and more mobile direct artillery and antitank support than was currently provided by towed weapons. Third, the absence of a turret and its complex working parts meant they were cheaper and quicker to produce. This advantage was increased by the Chief Defence Commissariat emphasizing that designers use existing tank components

as much as possible. Consequently, the chassis of the T-70 was used as the basis for the light SU-76 series, while medium and heavy self-propelled weapons used the T-34 and KV chassis respectively.

SU-122

In April 1942 the Central Artillery Directorate (GAU) instructed several teams to begin work on a medium mechanized self-propelled vehicle capable of mounting the powerful 122mm (4.8in) gun. The work of the Uralsky Heavy Machine Tool Factory (UZTM) and Zavod Nr 592 was overseen by a special team from the Commissariat for Tank Production (NKTP).

UZTM based its U-35 (subsequently known as the SU-122) vehicle on the chassis and hull of the T-34, placing the M-30 12mm (0.47in) gun in a fully armoured casemate with 45mm (1.77in) frontal armour. The increased size of the crew compartment, in comparison to a turreted vehicle, allowed a crew of five (commander, gunner, driver, and two loaders) to operate the large gun with relative ease. To increase production and also to keep costs low, the engine and transmission of the T-34 were retained.

LEFT: Trailing exhaust smoke from its diesel, an ISU-152 of the 2nd Baltic Front thunders through a wood with what appears to be a KV-1 tank following behind. When it entered service at the Battle of Kursk in 1943, the big SP gun was one of the few Soviet armoured vehicles that could take on German Tigers, Panthers and Elephants on even terms, and so earned itself the nickname *Zvierboy* (Animal Hunter). The 43.4kg (95lb 11oz) shells had a muzzle velocity of 655m/sec (2150 ft/sec).

With an overall weight just over 30.5 tonnes (30 tons), the SU-122 had a road speed of 55km/h (34mph) and with added fuel tanks, a range of 300km (186 miles), making it more than capable of keeping up with rapidly advancing Soviet tank forces. Production of the SU-122 began in late December 1942 after receiving approval from GKO.

Although the SU-122 was capable of engaging enemy armour, the heavy weight of its shell reduced the muzzle velocity, making it a poor antitank weapon. Attempts to improve its firepower with the BP-460A HEAT (High Explosive Anti-Tank) round proved less successful than hoped and, like most Soviet self-propelled guns, its primary role was direct fire support of infantry against enemy strongpoints. Even so, at short range the SU-122, with its low profile and large gun, was capable of dealing with heavy German armour, although results could be mixed.

In August 1943 the Red Army followed up its victory at Kursk with a powerful drive on the city of Kharkov in Operation Polkovodets Rumnyantsev. Attempting to halt the Soviet thrust, the German High Command mounted a series of counterattacks against the centre and eastern flank of Soviet tank forces. The Panzergrenadier Division *Grossdeutschland* spearheaded the eastern attack against Twenty-Seventh Army and the flank of the First Tank Army.

As the Front Commander General N. F. Vatutin threw in reserves, initially to stabilize the front and then counterattack, a vicious melée erupted, lasting from 18 to 21 August. At one point on 21 August, Tiger tanks of the *Grossdeutschland*, 3rd Panzer Regiment were roughly handled by SU-122 guns of III Guards Tank Corps. One Tiger of the 10th Company suffered six hits to its turret, but none of the rounds penetrated; instead they either dented, or

SU-152 MODEL 1944 SELF-PROPELLED GUN

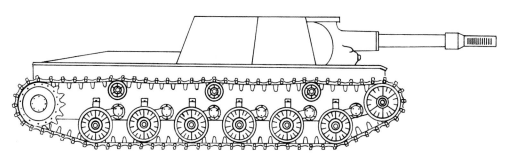

SPEED: 43km/h (27mph)

DIMENSIONS: Length 8.95m (29ft 4in); Width 3.25m (10ft 8in); Height 2.45m (8ft); Weight 45,500kg (50.1 tons)

ARMOUR: 75mm (2.95in)

WEAPONRY: One 152mm (5.9in)

EFFECTIVE RANGE: 240km (150 miles)

CREW: 5

BELOW: A Soviet GAZ-MM 4 x 2 cargo truck drives past a line of ISU-152 assault guns in Lvov, in the Ukraine, in July 1944. The photograph gives a good view of the chassis' running gear, with KV-1's spoked wheels rather than the disc wheels used on the T-34 and its variants.

chipped small pieces off, the armour. One round did slice off a large chink of armour that ricocheted into the fighting compartment, killing or wounding the crew. A hit on the hull's side armour would open up weld seams, leaving the inside of the Tiger exposed and also disabling the main armament.

The SU-122's mixed performance against enemy armour led to an abortive attempt in 1943 to develop a tank destroyer variant, named the SU-122P, armed with a long-barrelled gun. No serious production was undertaken

because the weight of the weapon proved too large for the chassis. Similar problems dogged the SU-122M and SU-122-3. One improvement on the first production batches was the adoption of a new ball mount for the gun, which improved its traverse and the vehicle's frontal protection. The advent of the more powerful SU-152 self-propelled gun, as well as the highly effective SU-100 tank destroyer in mid–1943, led to the decision in November 1943 to discontinue production of the SU-122, just 11 months after it had first begun.

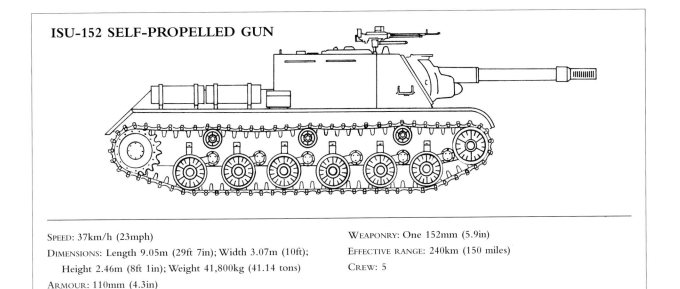

ISU-152 SELF-PROPELLED GUN

SPEED: 37km/h (23mph)

DIMENSIONS: Length 9.05m (29ft 7in); Width 3.07m (10ft);
    Height 2.46m (8ft 1in); Weight 41,800kg (41.14 tons)

ARMOUR: 110mm (4.3in)

WEAPONRY: One 152mm (5.9in)

EFFECTIVE RANGE: 240km (150 miles)

CREW: 5

SG-122 AND SU-76I

The Zavod Nr 592 design, designated SG-122, proved less successful than the UZTM SU-122. The vehicle was a mix-and-match design, placing a Soviet-designed hull and gun atop a captured German Panzer III chassis. This attempt to graft native technology onto foreign proved imperfect; the SG-122 was difficult to maintain in forward army depots because of lack of spares for the Panzer III chassis, whilst its performance was far below the rival UZTM design. These handicaps meant that although it was accepted for service in July 1942, the SG-122 was quickly withdrawn.

However, the desperate need for self-propelled artillery in the opening months of 1943 led Soviet designers to revive the idea of using over 300 Panzer III and StuG chassis which had been captured at Stalingrad. This move was intended as a stop-gap to make up for a shortage in self-propelled artillery when large numbers of the recently introduced SU-76s had to be temporarily withdrawn in order to iron out mechanical failures. Zavod Nr 38's proposal was to take the basic design of the SG-122 and re-arm it with the 76.2mm (3in) ZiS-5 gun. Problems in installing the gun led to the adoption of the 76.2mm (3in) S-1 gun, which was specifically designed for self-propelled guns and which was easily mounted onto the front armour. After gruelling trials at Sverdlovsk, it was accepted for service as SU-76i ('i' denot-

ing 'inostrannaya', or foreign) in March 1943, and they were deployed to front-line units from May onwards, just in time to see service with Colonel-General K. K. Rokossovsky's Central Front and General N. F. Vatutin's Voronezh Front at the Battle of Kursk in July that year.

Although available in only limited numbers, the SU-76i served widely in Soviet operations throughout the summer and winter of 1943, until the Chief of Armoured Forces, Marshal Ya. N. Federenko, ordered all remaining vehicles to be transferred to training duties at the start of 1944. Despite its *ad hoc* nature, the vehicle seems to have proved popular with crews, who developed the dangerous habit of removing the bolted armour plate roof to increase their comfort! Modifications to the vehicle prevented this practice on later models. In all, just over 200 SU-76is were built, but they illustrate the resourcefulness, ingenuity and occasional desperation of the USSR's total war effort.

SU-152

The development of a larger assault gun-tank destroyer which mounted the 152mm (5.98in) ML-20 gun was a direct reaction to the appearance of the German Tiger tank during fighting near the besieged city of Leningrad in January 1943. During 1942 the Central Design Bureau's two teams (TsKB-2), led by veteran designer Lieutenant-Colonel Z. Kotin (responsible for the KV tank), had

ABOVE: Under the cover of a smoke-screen, an ISU-122 belonging to the Third Guards Tank Army of the 1st Ukrainian Front crosses a pontoon bridge which has been erected over the River Spree near Cottbus in April 1945. After their drive across the Spree, the tanks of the 1st Ukrainian Front pushed north and west, before eventually managing to link up with the 1st Byelorussian Front. The combined Soviet forces then proceeded to cut off Berlin to the west of the German city.

been developing a new heavy tank to replace the increasingly obsolete KV-1. This vehicle was termed KV-13 and was based extensively on the original chassis, but with a new hull and turret.

In late 1943, Kotin's team's new design would be the basis for the KV-85 and IS series of heavy tanks that would serve the Red Army to the end of the war. In early 1943 these new designs were still some way from completion, which was unacceptable to the GKO and the Army High Command, who saw the desperate need for quickly deploying an armoured vehicle capable of countering the Tiger. Rising to the occasion in just 25 days from receiving orders to proceed on 4 January 1943, Kotin and L. Troyanov completed two designs for self-propelled gun-tank destroyers.

The KV-12 mounted the massive 203mm (8in) B-4 Model 1931 howitzer, but lacking the range to engage the Tiger's 88mm (3.46in) gun, the design was rejected. Instead the KV-14, built on a KV-1's chassis and equipped with the longer-range 152mm (5.98in) ML-20 gun-howitzer, was accepted for production on 14 February 1943 as the SU-152. With a muzzle velocity of 655m/s (2149ft/s), the SU-152's gun was a formidable weapon, and was capable of penetrating 110mm (4.3in) of armour

plate at a distance of 2000m (2187yd). The effectiveness of the gun was diminished by the need for a multi-component round that restricted fire to two shots a minute, while like most Soviet armoured vehicles, the ability to actually engage targets at stated textbook ranges was restricted by the limited capability of the telescopic sights and quality of the crew. It is, however, important to note that in the long term, once the new heavy tanks entered service, the SU-152's principal role was envisaged as being to serve as infantry support.

The first regiment to be equipped with the SU-152 was formed in May 1943 and, like the smaller SU-76i, was rushed to take part in the fighting at Kursk. Only 12 vehicles were available but they later claimed to have killed 12 Tigers and 7 Elephants (a heavily armoured self-propelled gun also making its début at Kursk). These claims are difficult to substantiate; throughout the war, crews on both sides had a tendency to report any kill as the strongest tank which their opponents possessed in his arsenal. What is clear is that the SU-152 proved devastatingly effective in combat, quickly earning itself the nickname *Zvierboy*, (Animal Hunter), after its reputed ability to kill the entire German zoo of Tigers, Panthers and Elephants.

ISU-122/152 GUNS

The success of the SU-152, coupled with the development of the IS (Iosef Stalin) heavy tank hull, led the NKTP to order design teams at Chelyabinsk, in cooperation the Mechanized Artillery Bureau (BAS) and General F. Petrov, to design two new heavy assault guns based on the IS-2 tank's hull and chassis. The initial vehicle, designated Object 241, or ISU-249, was similar to the SU-152, except for a higher superstructure and more rectangular with less sloped side armour.

Thicker frontal and side armour (90mm/3.54in compared to 60mm/2.36in on the SU-152) meant that the internal area of both vehicles was the same, with storage for only 20 rounds each for the 152mm (5.98in) ML-20 howitzer gun. The main difference between the SU-152 and ISU series of vehicles was a lower suspension and a new, heavy two-piece gun mantlet bolted onto the right-hand side of the hull. Re-classified as ISU-152, production began at the end of 1943.

Problems with the availability of the 152mm (5.98in) gun type because of a lack of available manufacturing capacity in Soviet artillery factories led to orders to the TsKB-2 team to explore the possibility of mounting the more abundant 122mm (4.8in) A-19 gun on the ISU hull. This proved a relatively easy task, because both calibres of gun had the same gun carriage, meaning that no radical re-design of the hull or vehicle interior was required. The new assault gun entered service in December 1943 as the ISU-122. In 1944 its firepower was improved with the introduction of the 122mm (4.8in) D-25S gun designed for the IS-2 tank. This modified design, termed ISU-122-2, also had an new gun mantlet and improved crew space. In external appearance both gun types were identical, except for the ISU-152's shorter gun barrel with a muzzle brake.

The appearance of the immensely powerful *Panzerkampfwagen* VIb Royal Tiger in fighting south of Warsaw in August 1944 led to a number of plans to up-gun both types of ISU with the new 122mm (4.8in) BR-7 and 152mm (5.98in) BR-8 long-barrelled guns, but the realization that the Germans could not deploy the Royal Tiger in significant numbers caused production of these prototypes to be abandoned. Another reason was the conclusion of Soviet technicians, based on combat results, that the IS-2 tank could deal with this new threat.

Post-war changes were made to the final production run of ISU-152Ks by using the IS-2m chassis and the IS-3 engine deck. A total of 4075 ISU-152s were produced during the war, and a further 2450 manufactured between 1945 and 1955, when production ceased. Despite a brief break in manufacture between 1945 and 1947, 3130 ISU-122s were produced up to 1952. The chassis of many of these vehicles were adapted for special purposes in the 1960s. The Oka was armed with a 406mm (15.98in) gun

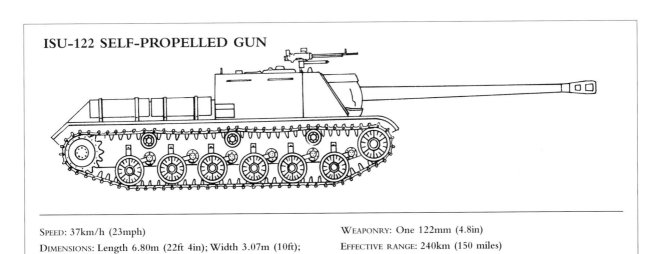

ISU-122 SELF-PROPELLED GUN

SPEED: 37km/h (23mph)

DIMENSIONS: Length 6.80m (22ft 4in); Width 3.07m (10ft);
Height 2.46m (8ft 1in); Weight 46,000kg (50.7 tons)

ARMOUR: 90mm (3.54in)

WEAPONRY: One 122mm (4.8in)

EFFECTIVE RANGE: 240km (150 miles)

CREW: 5

ABOVE: An ISU-122 heavy assault gun from the Soviet armoured forces enters the Berlin suburbs in May 1945. The ISU-122 had a crew of five and the same gun as that which was fitted to the IS-2 tank. This ISU-122 is passing a grocery shop, the wall to the right of the shop bearing a slogan which reads 'Berlin remains German', coined by Dr Josef Goebbels shortly before the German defeat. As the Soviet and Allied forces closed in on Germany in 1945, slogans exhorting or challenging the population were painted in public places by the SS and Nazi Party functionaries.

designed to fire tactical nuclear shells to break up NATO front-line and reserve units. The ISU mounted the first FROG medium-range missiles, armed with either conventional, chemical, or nuclear warheads. Outside of these special roles in the Warsaw Pact armed forces, the ISU-152 saw service in its original role with the Egyptian Army in the 1967 and 1973 Arab–Israeli wars.

ISU ASSAULT GUNS IN ACTION

The ISU-122 and ISU-152 were used in Independent Heavy Self-Propelled Artillery Regiments, which were awarded the Guards honorific after December 1944. By the end of the war there were 56 such units. Generally attached to the tank corps, they were deployed in the second echelon of an assault, providing long-range direct, and on occasion indirect, fire support to tanks in the first echelon, targeting German strongpoints and armoured vehicles. They were also vital in providing defensive antitank and artillery support for infantry.

The dual role of the ISU-152 is demonstrated by fighting on 15–16 January 1945 in the area of the Polish village of Borowe. Elements of Marshal K. K. Rokossovsky's 2nd Byelorussian

Front were vigorously counterattacked by the Panzergrenadier Division *Grossdeutschland*. The initial German assault proved very effective, driving the Soviets back. As elements of the spearhead 2nd Fusilier Battalion consolidated their gains, the 3rd Fusilier Battalion moved through them towards Soviet positions around Borowe. Both battalions soon came under high explosive and armour-piercing fire from SU-152s of the 390th Guards Independent Heavy Artillery Regiment. The 3rd Fusilier Battalion and its supporting armour did manage to secure the town on 16 January under intense antitank fire from SU-152 guns supported by rocket artillery. But success was shortlived, as Soviet success in other areas collapsed the front, forcing a withdrawal. Even so, as one soldier of the 2nd Battalion starkly described, being under fire from 'Black Pigs' was harrowing:

Black detonations in front of us, behind us, beside us – and we lay on the frozen ground with no possibility of crawling into it ... Now and then someone raised his face a little beneath his steel helmet to see if the other was alive. For an hour there was nothing but the sound of incoming and exploding shells.

During the 1st Ukrainian Front's breakout from the Sandomierz bridgehead over the river Vistula in central Poland, Marshal I. S. Konev used several ISU-equipped regiments to enhance the devastating opening barrage of 450 medium- and heavy field guns per kilometre of front. When the assault troops moved forwards, poor weather and lack of visibility in the harsh winter conditions made it difficult to operate with air and artillery support.

However, the momentum of the attack was maintained through the close fire support provided by ISU-122 and ISU-152s operating alongside the infantry. The result was an advance of 12km (7.45 miles) on the first day, carrying Soviet forces through the forward German tactical defences and creating the conditions for the release of the second echelon tank armies with their fast medium T-34s to exploit deep into the enemy's operational rear. This pattern of attack was a thorough vindication of pre-war Soviet ideas about the interaction of heavy and medium armour in carrying out the deep battle and deep operation respectively.

KV-85 AND IS-85/1 HEAVY TANKS

Concurrent to the development of the new self-propelled gun series in 1943, Soviet design teams completed longer-term projects for a new generation of heavy tanks to replace the ageing KV-1 types. By the start of 1943, 21 heavy tank designs had been created, but at one

point, work was threatened when Josef Stalin decided to cancel heavy tank production after scathing reports about the poor mobility and armament of the KV-1 from experienced commanders such as General P. A. Rotmistrov. Fortunately Stalin relented under the combined impact of lobbying from the NKTP, and the more immediate need to counter new German medium and heavy tanks.

The need to hasten the deployment of heavy tanks to counter the German threat led Lieutenant-Colonel Kotin to divide his TsKB-2 bureau to form two teams, each with their own design specifications. One team was instructed to undertake a modernization of the KV beyond the KV-1-S, which was being introduced in mid–1943 as a stop-gap for the new heavy tank. This project was eventually designated the KV-85.

The vehicle was essentially a re-worked KV-1-S hull, which increased frontal armour from 82mm (3.2in) to 110mm (4.3in). The second team, headed by N. V. Tseits (recently released from a forced labour camp), began work on the KV-13 which had a heavily re-designed hull and chassis. This vehicle, designated IS-85 (IS – Iosef Stalin), was superior in mobility and had better all-round armour protection than the KV-85.

Technical delays in completing the IS-85, compounded by urgent requests from the front for tanks with more powerful armament, led to 148 KV-85s being produced as a temporary expedient in the autumn of 1943 by placing the IS-85

BELOW: The KV-85 was a stopgap solution to the problem of replacing the ageing KV-1 heavy tank. A new turret, intended for the IS-85 (later redesignated the IS-1) and armed with the same 85mm (3.34in) gun as the T-34/85, was mounted on the KV-1-S chassis.

KV-85 HEAVY TANK

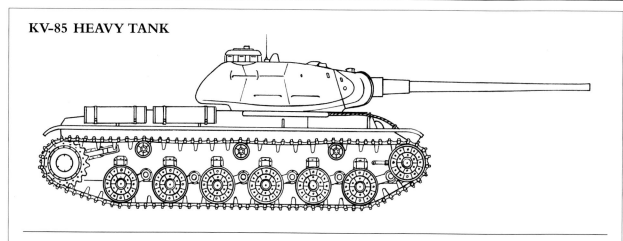

SPEED: 35km/h (22mph)

DIMENSIONS: Length 8.49m (27ft 10in); Width 3.25m (10ft 8in);

    Height 2.8m (9ft 2in); Weight 46,000kg (50.7 tons)

ARMOUR: 100mm (3.94in)

WEAPONRY: One 85mm (3.35in); three 7.62mm (0.3in) MG

EFFECTIVE RANGE: 160km (100 miles)

CREW: 4

turret mounting a 85mm (3.34in) D-5T gun on the KV-85's hull. The larger turret mounting of the KV-85 increased the size of the under turret box which could only be accommodated by modification of the hull's width. The fifth crewmember was also lost because of the demands for ammunition racks containing 70 rounds each, as well as because of the size of the gun's breech.

The IS-85 was based on the KV-13 prototype. Although the development process received a significant increase in resources in 1943, the vehicle was in fact the fruition of a much longer process of evolution than the hasty KV-85 design. The first KV-13 prototype was tested by the Experimental Tank Factory at Chelyabinsk as early as May 1942. One of the most notable features was the extensive use of casting in the manufacture of the turret and large sections of the hull. The initial trials revealed flaws in the vehicle's transmission, as well as a tendency to damage and throw tracks.

Despite remedying many of these defects through adopting parts of the KV-1-S chassis and transmission, further work was slowed by the previously noted reticence of Stalin and many military personnel about heavy tanks. Even so, the drive and self-belief that had characterized Kotin's earlier work on heavy tank design saw him instruct the design team to re-develop the internal workings of the experimental vehicle. This was accomplished by the start of 1943 with

only the hull, torsion bar suspension and chassis of the first prototype retained. Within a few months, Kotin's initiative was justified when the demand for new heavy tanks was realized by the GKO. Whilst the KV-85 was rushed into service, work continued on the IS-85, which was subsequently renamed IS-1. In August the completed model was demonstrated to Stalin to great approval, and production was authorized.

The design of both KV-85 and IS-1 were strongly influenced by the need to mount a more powerful gun than the standard issue 76.2mm (3in) gun, which was relatively ineffective against the Tiger and Panther. Test-firing of various gun calibres against a captured Tiger at the Kubinka testing grounds showed that the 85mm (3.34in) 52-K model 1939 AA gun could penetrate the vehicle's 100mm (3.93in) frontal armour at up to 1000m (9144yd), although the low quality of Soviet telescopic sights meant that in practice, these long-distance ranges were rarely achieved by the Soviet crews with any real consistency.

Under orders from the GKO, the Central Artillery Design Bureau tested the S-31 and D-5T gun variants. The latter proved the more effective weapon and was accepted for production. The installation of an 85mm (3.34in) gun affected the construction of the turret designed for the KV-85 and IS-1, requiring an increase in size to avoid greatly degrading the crew's workspace and the vehicle's combat effectiveness. This increased the hull size and weight of both of these heavy tanks.

KV-85 AND IS-1 IN COMBAT

The combat performance of the KV-85 and IS-1 series was chequered. In one engagement in the Ukraine in November 1943 the 34th Guards Heavy Tank Breakthrough Regiment was repulsed with the loss of one-third of its 20 KV-85s by fire from Panzer IVs and Marder II self-propelled guns. Naturally, tactical factors could influence the level of loss, and it is worth noting that on the following day, a German counterattack was beaten off with no Soviet casualties.

However, after-action reports collected by the GBTU highlighted the need for better protection and a larger gun in order to engage German tanks at longer ranges. Similar comments were recorded about the IS-1 after it entered service in September 1943. A major problem was the need for greater protection against long-range enemy fire. Whilst enemy rounds at long ranges did not always penetrate the IS-1's armour, their impact created splintering inside the turret, and wounded the crew.

That said, as the engagement of 4 March 1944 at Staro-Konstantinov, which involved 1st Guards Heavy Breakthrough Regiment, would prove, the IS-1 was more than capable of standing up to the might of the Tiger; it was the gun that was the real issue with both of the new heavy tanks. The production of the KV-85 was therefore terminated at the end of 1943, and following that, the IS-1 was re-armed in early 1944.

IS-2 HEAVY TANK

The need for a larger gun for the IS-1 had in fact been identified by Kotin's team and designers at Zavod Nr 9 in the wake of the Battle of Kursk in July 1943. This realization had two effects. First, production of the IS-1 with an 85mm (3.34in) gun was restricted until it could be equipped with a more powerful gun. Second, the 100mm (3.93in) BS-3 and 122mm (4.8in) A-19 guns were adapted for the IS-1 and put through firing tests during November 1943.

The smaller gun proved to have the more effective armour penetration, although the larger one showed its potency by ripping the frontal armour off a captured Panther. Ultimately the 122mm (4.8in) gun was selected because there was a surplus of manufacturing resources for the gun and its ammunition, whilst the 100mm (3.93in) was in short supply. The barrel was initially fitted with a single chamber muzzle brake, but

BELOW: A German soldier examines one of three IS-1s knocked out in fighting in East Prussia. The IS-1 originally entered service with a 85mm (3.34in) gun in September 1943, but it was upgunned in early 1944 to mount the powerful 122mm (4.8in) A-19 gun. This example has been destroyed by internal explosions following a hit by a German antitank gun.

RIGHT: A Soviet officer, standing on the road, directs a column of IS-2 heavy tanks along the streets of the suburbs of Berlin in May 1945. Tank *desant* troops shown in this picture are seated on the rear deck of the tank. These infantrymen would be absolutely invaluable during the street-fighting, since they would be capable of neutralizing enemy antitank guns. In the meantime, the IS-2 tanks could provide powerful, long-range support to an attack. Soviet tank commanders would direct the 12.7mm (0.5in) Dsh K1938 heavy AA machine gun – which was mounted in the turret – to pound the German enemy with the maximum effect. This machine gun, with its optical sight, was well-equipped to engage German positions.

this was changed to two chambers after one of the guns exploded during testing and narrowly avoided fatally wounding Marshal K. E. Voroshilov.

Not content with up-gunning the IS-1 design, Kotin developed the IS-2 with improved armour and mobility. The stepped armour glacis plate of the earlier design was replaced by a flat sloping type, giving better protection, but avoiding the need for thicker armour that would increase the vehicle's weight. The new hull could withstand a direct shot from a German 8.8cm (3.46in) armour-piercing round at over 1000m (9144yd), whilst its own gun could penetrate 160mm (6.29in) of armour at the same range, if its gunners could hit the target. Attempts to improve the turret's protection had to be cancelled because the weight of the 122mm (4.8in) gun would have made it unbalanced. The possibility of re-designing the turret was turned down because of the cost and a lack of time.

In reality, the IS-2 had several major shortcomings. The designers were aware that the IS-2's effectiveness in combat was restricted by a slow rate of fire (just 2 or 3 rounds per minute) and stowage room for only 28 rounds. The former factor was partially solved in 1944, when an improved D-25T gun was introduced with a more efficient breech. Combat experience also revealed that the 122mm

(4.8in) gun could not penetrate the Panther's sloped armour above 600m (656yd), whilst splintering remained a problem for the IS-2's own armour. Tempering the frontal armour to very strong hardness proved too complex and costly to introduce, and the deficiency was allowed to remain. Ironically, in late 1944 the difficulty in dealing with the Panther was partially, though unintentionally, solved by the Germans. Shortage of manganese led to a switch to using high-carbon steel alloyed with nickel for armour plate, which made it more brittle, in particular along weld seams.

IS-2 IN ACTION

The IS-2 was issued to Guards Heavy Tank Regiments from the start of 1944. The first unit equipped with them to see action was the 11th Guards Independent Heavy Tank Brigade in April in operations in the southern Ukraine, following the successful encirclement and destruction of German forces in the Korsun-Shevchenkiovsky area. In 20 days of fighting, the 72nd Independent Guards Tank Regiment lost only eight IS-2s, whilst inflicting great loss on the enemy, although Soviet claims of 41 Tigers and Elephants is excessive and probably the result of mistaken identity. During this period of action, one IS-2 withstood five direct hits from the 8.8cm (3.46in) gun

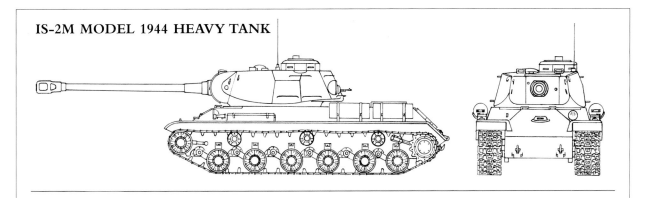

IS-2M MODEL 1944 HEAVY TANK

SPEED: 37km/h (23mph)

DIMENSIONS: Length 10.33m (33ft 6in); Width 3.36m (11ft); Height 2.92m (9ft 6in); Weight 45,000kg (49.6 tons)

ARMOUR: 120mm (4.72in)

WEAPONRY: One 122mm (4.8in) gun; one 12.7mm (0.5in) AA MG; three 7.62mm (0.3in) MG

EFFECTIVE RANGE: 240km (149 miles)

CREW: 4

of an Elephant fired from 1500–2000m (1640–2187yd). The vehicle was eventually knocked out by another of these vehicles at 700m (765yd). The loss of other vehicles to fire and engine damage serves to highlight the point that even the most heavily armoured tank still has areas of vulnerability.

One of the IS-2's most notable engagements took place during the fighting in August 1944 to establish a bridgehead across the river Vistula around the town of Sandomierz. This was the first time that the IS-2 had come up against the fearsome Royal Tiger. During the engagement on 13 August, the 71st Independent Heavy Tank Regiment's 11 IS-2s blocked an attack by 14 Royal Tigers of the 501st Heavy Panzer Regiment. Engaging at 600m (656yd) coupled with skilled tactical handling saw four Royal Tigers destroyed and seven damaged, for the loss of three IS-2s and seven damaged. This was a very creditable performance, although post-battle analysis again revealed that the IS-2's armour was vulnerable up to 1000m (9144yd) because of faulty casting.

LEFT: Refugees emerge from the cellars of gutted buildings and trudge past the IS-2 tanks of the 1st Byelorussian Front in the rubble-clogged streets of Berlin in April 1945. The tanks have a white band painted around their turrets as an air identification marking in order to prevent RAF and USAAF fighter-bombers attacking them in error. As the Allies and Soviet forces closed in on Germany, there were encounters in the air, and finally on the ground at Torgau on April 25, between the US First Army and 1st Ukrainian Front.

IS-3 HEAVY TANK

Continued analysis of the combat performance of tanks, in particular the location and type of damage inflicted on them, led to the development of the IS-3 tank. This was to be the last Soviet heavy tank produced during the war. The vehicle's design was drawn from ideas which were developed by two separate teams.

One under Kotin developed an unusual frontal armour glacis. This consisted of two plates welded together at an angle, sloping down to the vehicle's front, termed a Pike nose by its creators. The design reduced the tank's weight but, it was hoped, increased the strength of the hull and its resistance to enemy fire. The other team under N. L. Dukhov developed a radical rounded-bowl shaped turret, housing a 122mm (4.8in) gun. This radical shape increased protection by deflecting the kinetic energy of incoming shells, whilst improving the internal layout of the turret and consequently the tank's fighting efficiency.

The decision to combine the two teams' novel ideas into a single model was taken by the Minister of Tank Industry, V. A. Malyshev. The first prototype was shown to Marshals G. K. Zhukov and A. M. Vasilevsky in October 1944, and received a strong recommendation for production. The first production models appeared in the early months of 1945, and it is reported that some saw action towards the end of the fighting in Berlin. Production of the vehicle was continued until mid–1946, by which time a total of 2311 tanks had been produced.

The IS-3 continued in service with Red Army front-line forces until as late as the 1960s. During this time it underwent a series of modifications in order to remedy serious design faults; unreliable engine and gearbox, and a defective hull in areas. However, these modifications proved only a partial success, and by this stage, Soviet tank design and doctrine was focusing on the medium tank as the main armoured vehicle which would be the most effective during every stage of the deep battle and deep operation.

CONCLUSION

Throughout World War II, Soviet tank designers repeatedly demonstrated their creativity and pragmatism. Consistently they made maximum use of their limited resources by asking if a specific design was adequate for the task required, rather than squandering extra time and resources – as their German counterparts did – on creating totally new components, or striving for total perfection and

BELOW: IS-3 tanks roll through Berlin in the Allied victory parade in 1945. The superb angled armour and 'frying pan' turret was a surprise to western observers. The suspension was slightly lowered and mechanically improved compared to the IS-2, and this gave the tank an excellent low silhouette. The power-to-weight ratio for the tank was 11:42.

LEFT: Soviet guards stand at regular 20-pace intervals along a platform in Germany as IS-3 tanks on flat cars are readied for the return journey back to the USSR. The IS-3 was first shown as a prototype in 1944 and as the most powerful tank of World War II, was the last Soviet tank produced during that period. By mid-1946, 2311 had been made. Into the 1950s its capabilities would present Western tank designers with a huge challenge, as the pointed glacis plate and rounded turret proved to have excellent shot-deflection surfaces.

accepting only the best. This meant that Soviet tanks lacked the exterior and interior refinements of German and western vehicles, but as the bottom line was how the vehicle performed during operations, these shortcomings were acceptable. As a result, the British and American designs lagged behind those of the Red Army throughout the war in what they could achieve on the battlefield. The whole Soviet approach to war was summed up by a British Army platoon sergeant called John Erickson (later a Professor of Modern History and one of the leading pioneers in research on the history of the Soviet armed forces) who commented on a Red Army parade in Berlin after the war was finally over:

an army of unwashed, uncouth little Ukrainians, squat riflemen from the Central Asian Republics, combat medals a-jingle, cradling superb self-loading rifles – but above all, the tanks in their fungal green colouring, the paint just slapped over those powerful turreted guns. It was also an army that won.

IS-3 HEAVY TANK

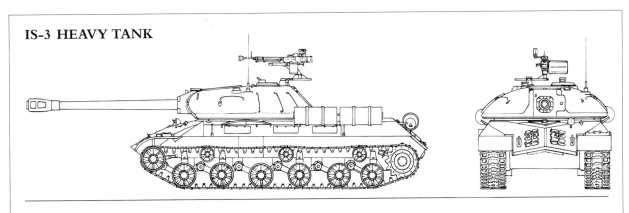

SPEED: 37km/h (23mph)
DIMENSIONS: Length 10.74m (35ft 3in); Width 3.44m (11ft 3in); Height 2.92m (9ft 6in); Weight 46,500kg (51.2 tons)
ARMOUR: 230mm (9in)

WEAPONRY: One 122mm (4.8in); one 12.7mm (0.5in) AA MG; one or two 7.62mm (0.3in) MG
EFFECTIVE RANGE: 208km (192.3 miles)
CREW: 4

CHAPTER EIGHT

FOREIGN TANKS IN SOVIET SERVICE

After the severe tank losses of 1941, the Red Army relied heavily on captured enemy vehicles and tanks supplied by Britain and the USA. Most Western tanks were seen as inferior, but were vital until new Soviet tanks arrived.

The USA, Britain and Canada supplied 22,800 armoured vehicles to the USSR during World War II. Of these, 1981 were lost at sea on the hazardous Arctic convoys to Murmansk. The shipments that did arrive were the equivalent of 16 per cent of Soviet tank production, 12 per cent of self-propelled gun production, and all of the armoured personnel carrier (APC) production. The first shipment in 1941 totalled 487 Matildas, Valentines and Tetrachs from Britain, and 182 M3A1 Light Tanks and M3 Medium Tanks from the USA. A year later, these figures had risen to 2487 from Britain and 3023 from the USA.

LEFT: Soviet soldiers of the South-Western Front sit on a captured StuG III Ausf. B bis D SdKfz 142 assault gun. The assault gun had 50mm (1.9in) frontal and 30mm (1.18in) hull armour and a short 7.5cm (2.9in) StuK L/24 or L/33 gun, but initially no hull-mounted machine gun. In the F to G marks, this was rectified.

Despite being pressed in North Africa, Britain committed 14 per cent of her tank production to Lend-Lease supplies. Though Lend-Lease tanks helped the USSR while it was under serious pressure between 1941 and 1942 after it had suffered huge tank losses, in the long run, US trucks were the real war winners. The USA supplied 501,660 tactical wheeled- and tracked vehicles: 77,972 Jeeps, 151,053 1.01 tonne (1 ton) trucks and 200,662 2.03 tonne (2 ton) trucks. These gave the infantry and logistic troops working with them a tactical mobility. The initials 'USA' stencilled on these vehicles were in the USSR taken to stand for the slogan '*Ubiyat Sukinsyna Adolfa*' – 'Kill that son of a whore Adolf'.

In the Cold War period, it was common for Soviet historians to denigrate the quality of the Lend-Lease tanks supplied by Britain and the USA. It is true that their medium tanks did not compare well against the T-34. However, the M3A1 light tank was comparable or superior to the T-60 and T-70 light tanks, and the M4A2 Sherman was more durable and reliable than the T-34. Interestingly, in post-war encounters between the Sherman and T-34 in Korea and the Middle East, the M4 often came off the winner, even though it was theoretically an inferior design. The first unit to go into action with Lend-Lease armour was in the Staraya Russa and Valdai areas, fielding Valentines, Matildas and captured German tanks.

THE VICKERS-ARMSTRONG VALENTINE
The Russians admired the robust and simple automotive design of the 1940 British Mk III Valentine, but were merely polite about the tank's main armament, which fell well below Eastern Front requirements. Some tanks had their main armament replaced by 76.2mm (3in) guns in factories in the USSR. The narrow tracks were also reported to be a problem in winter, first clogging with snow, then freezing, and immobilizing the vehicle.

Designed by Vickers-Armstrong in 1938, the Valentine was a private venture project drawing on their experience with the A9 and A10 Cruiser designs. Rather quaintly, the Valentine took its name from the fact that its plans were submitted to the War Office close to the date of St Valentine's Day in February. The War Office took over a year to make up its mind, since there were some reservations about the two-man turret, which was thought to be too small to be up-gunned. However, when they committed to the project, they requested that Vickers-Armstrong make the first delivery in the shortest time possible.

Production ceased in 1944 after a total of 8275 tanks had been built by three companies, representing a quarter of British tank output. There had been plans to stop production in 1943 on grounds of obsolescence, but it had continued for the extra year to satisfy Soviet requirements. The Valentine was produced in Britain by Metropolitan-Cammell and Birmingham Carriage & Wagon, as well as Vickers, and in Canada by Canadian Pacific of Montreal; here, of the 1420 Mk VI tanks produced, all but the 30 retained for training went to the Soviet Army.

The Valentine was originally armed with a 2pdr (40mm (1.57in)) gun, but this was upgraded to a 6pdr (57mm (2.24in)) gun in the Mark VIII, IX and

BELOW: The Soviet Union was no stranger to foreign equipment, being adept at purchasing new technology from the West in the 1920s and 1930s. Here a Vickers Medium MkII (left) is parked next to a A6E1 Medium III (right). Fifteen Vickers Medium Mk II tanks were bought between 1930 and 1932, and were used in the joint German-Russian training grounds near Kazan. Remarkably a few survivors were captured by the Finns in 1941 near Vitele.

LEFT: A shell explodes near to a Vickers Valentine or Infantry Tank Mk III, throwing debris high into the air. The tank was manufactured both in the UK and in Canada. Canada sent the bulk of its production of 1388 Valentine VI and VII to the USSR, keeping back a small number for training purposes, while Britain provided some 2394 tanks. The Valentine was popular in Soviet service because of its mobility. Due to its popularity, production of the tank would continue right into 1944, solely in order to meet the Soviet requirement.

X. The Mark XI, fitted with a 75mm (2.95in) gun, was the final production type. Reliability and performance was improved when a GMC two-stroke diesel was installed, replacing the AEC petrol or diesel engines. Production speeded up when all-welded construction replaced all-riveted.

THE MATILDA INFANTRY SUPPORT TANK
The British Matilda II (A12) has the distinction of being the only British tank to serve throughout the whole of World War II, a rare feat for any tank. The British sent 1084 to the USSR, where it was second only to the Valentine as the most common type of British tank in Soviet service. Proposals by the British Mechanization Board to produce a tank with the same level of protection as the Matilda I, but armed with either a 2pdr (40mm (1.57in)) gun or twin machine guns, produced the Matilda Senior or Matilda II.

The Matilda II was originally built at the Vulcan Foundry at Warrington, where

work had begun to build 165 vehicles in 1937. However, as the pace of re-armament increased, contracts for further vehicles were placed a year later with

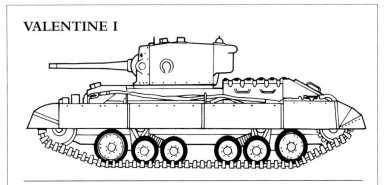

VALENTINE I

SPEED: 24km/h (15mph)
DIMENSIONS: Length 5.41m (17ft 9in); Width 2.63m (8ft 7in); Height 2.28m (7ft 5in); Weight 16,260kg (16 tons)
ARMOUR: 65mm (2.5in)
WEAPONRY: One 2pdr (40mm (1.57in)); one 7.92mm (0.31in) MG
EFFECTIVE RANGE: 145km (90 miles)
CREW: 3

ABOVE: A Matilda II tank in the Ukraine in 1944, with a small tree trunk as an unditching beam and a fuel drum tied to the hull.

Fowler and Ruston & Hornby under Vulcan's parentage, and later with LMS, Harland & Wolff and North British Locomotive. When production ceased, a total of 2987 Matilda IIs had been built.

Though the armour protection was excellent, it was produced using a time-consuming and expensive casting process, and later, when there were attempts to up-gun the tank, the turret ring was found to be too small to take a larger-calibre weapon. In Soviet service, sections of steel bar were welded to the tracks to give better traction in snow and mud. The Matilda was more heavily armoured than the T-60 and T-70, and so was used as an infantry support tank.

THE TETRACH LIGHT TANK

Twenty British Tetrach (A17) Light Tanks were also sent to the Soviet Union overland via Iran, but were not popular with their Russian crews. Privately developed by Vickers in 1937, the Tetrach, originally known by the company by the project name 'Purdah', was accepted for service by the British Army in 1938 as the Light Tank Mk VII. Production of the vehicle started in 1940, but this was soon halted when it was realized that light tanks were becoming increasingly vulnerable on the modern battlefield.

Unlike earlier vehicles in this class, the Tetrach used a modified Christie suspension in which the front wheels could be steered in order to bend the track for

MATILDA II

SPEED: 24km/h (15mph)

DIMENSIONS: Length 5.61m (18ft 5in); Width 2.59m (8ft 6in); Height 2.51m (8ft 3in); Weight 26,950kg (26.5 tons)

ARMOUR: 78mm (3in)

WEAPONRY: One 2pdr (40mm (1.57in)); one 7.92mm (0.31in) MG

EFFECTIVE RANGE: 257km (160 miles)

CREW: 4

gentle turns. This method overcame the problem of loss of power which was found with steering a vehicle by skidding the tracks on the ground. If a tighter manoeuvre was necessary, the controls automatically braked one track in order to allow the tank to make a conventional skid turn. The suspension was pneumatic shock absorbers on each of the four road wheels and it was necessary to maintain the correct pressure with a foot-pump. In the USSR the tanks were often the subject of many photographs which would be used for propaganda purposes.

DEVELOPING THE CHURCHILL

Some 301 Mk I, II and IIIs Churchills (A-22) were sent to the Soviet Union in Arctic convoys, and it was related that Soviet forces liked the thick armour but felt that the tanks were too lightly armed. Forty-three were lost at sea and none were supplied after 1942.

The Churchill grew out of British pre-war perceptions that a heavy infantry tank would be required to fight in a future war. It was assumed that this would be a re-run of World War I, with its slow trench warfare. The first work on this vehicle, the A-20, was done by the Superintendent of Tank Design, Woolwich and Harland & Wolff. It was found to be under-powered, and so Vauxhall Motors was tasked with the production of the A-22 and gave it a new Vauxhall-Bedford engine. Until then, the biggest engine Vauxhall had produced was the 53.6kW (72bhp) Bedford truck engine, but in 89 days they designed and built a test-bed engine with 261.1kW (350bhp) to power the A-22.

The final prototype tank was a much lighter vehicle than had first been envisaged. With the threat of a German invasion in 1940, work was pushed ahead. The first production model vehicle, the Churchill I, produced in 1941, had a cast turret with a 2pdr (40mm) gun and 75mm (2.95in) howitzer mounted in the hull, but this was soon dropped and replaced with a machine gun. At the Battle of Prokhorovka at Kursk in 1943,

BELOW: A small number of Light Tank Mk VII 'Tetrach' were sent to the Soviet Union. They were not popular due to their thin armour and modest armament, and were used for patrols in the Caucasus. In British service, they were transported by glider and used at Normandy in June 1944 and the Rhine Crossings in March 1945.

TETRACH LIGHT TANK

SPEED: 64km/h (40mph)

DIMENSIONS: Length 4.11m (13ft 6in);
Width 2.31m (7ft 7in); Height 2.12m
(6ft 11in); Weight 7620kg (7.5 tons)

ARMOUR: 14mm (0.55in)

WEAPONRY: One 2pdr (40mm (1.57in));
one 7.92mm (0.31in) MG

EFFECTIVE RANGE: 225km (140 miles)

CREW: 3

the only heavy tanks available to the Fifth Guards Tank Army were 35 Churchills.

THE BREN GUN CARRIER

Widely known as the Bren Gun Carrier, the Carden-Loyd Universal carrier evolved in 1939 from the vehicles that were based on the Carden-Loyd series of light vehicles developed in the 1930s. A total of 2656 were supplied to the USSR. They were not popular because their narrow tracks performed badly in snow. Britain also delivered to the USSR a total of 25 Valentine bridgelayers, as well as 6 Cromwells.

THE US M3 SERIES

From the USA the Soviet Union received 1386 M3 Medium tanks of various models. They were not widely liked, being inferior to the T-34. A number were captured by the Germans, who then used them against Soviet forces.

Events in Europe after mid-1940 when 1000 M2A1 Mediums were ordered demonstrated that a 37mm (1.46in) gun was an inadequate main armament for a battle tank. German tanks with 75mm (2.95in) cannon were sweeping all European tanks – mostly armed with 37mm (1.46in) or 6pdr

(57mm (2.24in)) guns – before them. The US Ordnance Department wanted to fit a 75mm (2.95in) to the M2A1 Medium, but there was no turret available that was able to take this gun and fit into the limited space atop the barbette.

As a stop-gap measure based upon experience with the earlier T5E2, an installation was devised whereby an M2 75mm (2.95in) gun was mounted in the right side of the hull of a modified M2A1. The M2 gun was developed from the standard French-designed US Army howitzer and could penetrate 60mm (2.36in) armour sloped at 30 degrees at a range of 500m (547yd), making it a better weapon than contemporary German tank guns. The main gun had only limited traverse, 30 degrees in azimuth and 29 degrees in elevation. The 37mm (1.45in) was rotatable by hand, a 360-degree sweep taking 20 seconds.

A wooden mock-up of the new interim tank was completed in August 1940. Configuration was basically that of the M2A1, with the 75mm (2.95in) in the place of the right machine-gun sponsons and with a new 37mm (1.45in) turret on top. The mock-up board ordered several changes, including removal of the remaining machine-gun sponsons, and the lowering of the turret.

The M3A1 was built by the American Locomotive Company with a cast upper hull, rather than a riveted construction with large rivets that would fly about inside when the tank was struck. In total, 300 were built. Only 12 M3A2s with a welded hull and petrol engine were built before production switched to the similar M3A3 with a twinned GMC 6046 diesel truck engine. This offered better economy, range and combat safety, but required many changes at the rear, including armoured radiators, and raised the weight by 1179kg (1.16 tons). The M3A5 was a version (332 built) with riveted hull and diesel powerplant.

The M3 was built by several US companies, including Alco, Baldwin, Detroit, Pressed Steel Car and Pullman-Standard, and it became the first US medium tank to go into volume production. Factories in Canada also built 1100 M3s. At first, the M3 had a seven-man crew, with a loader and gunner for each main weapon and a radio operator. This latter position was soon deleted and the radio given to

the driver. The suspension inherited from the M2 turned out to be inadequate for the heavier M3, and was re-designed with heavier springs. Ammunition stowage was 46 rounds of 75mm (2.95in), 178 of 37mm (1.46in), and 9200 rounds of machine-gun ammunition. The USSR received M3A3 and M3A5 tanks but, with high silhouettes and archaic configuration, were unpopular, and nicknamed the 'Grave for Seven Brothers'.

Although the US Army Armored Force would have preferred to develop a new light tank with a gun of up to 75mm (2.95in) calibre, its pressing need was to re-arm before the United States became embroiled in the European war. As a result, the next development was an

ABOVE: Churchill III tanks went to the Soviet Union from May 1942 with the 6pdr (57mm (2.24in)) gun and a new type of welded turret, full track covers and new air intakes. They were used during the fighting around Kursk in 1943.

CHURCHILL TANK III

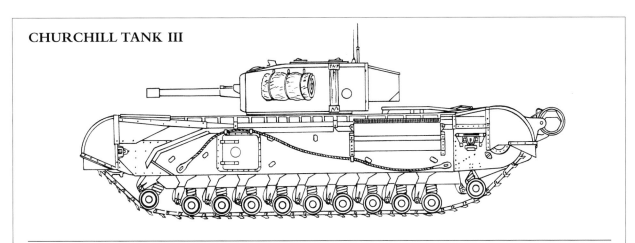

SPEED: 24.9km/h (8mph)

DIMENSIONS: Length 7.47m (24ft 6in); Width 2.74m (9ft); Height 2.97m (9ft 9in); Weight 39,620kg (39 tons)

ARMOUR: 101mm (3.98in)

WEAPONRY: One 6pdr (57mm (2.24in)); two 7.92mm (0.31in) MG

EFFECTIVE RANGE: 145km (90 miles)

CREW: 5

ABOVE: These Soviet tank crew could easily be mistaken for GIs in their US crew crash-helmets, armed with Thompson submachine guns or Browning machine guns and sitting on M3A1 Stuart Light Tanks. The Soviet Union received a total of 1676 M3s from the US during the war. The bulk of them were powered by diesel engines. Although the Stuart tanks were not popular with their crews, they were superior to the T-70 Light Tank.

evolutionary step, rather than a revolutionary leap in tank design.

The US Army chose to modernize the M2A4. The major change was to increase the armour thickness on the upper surfaces and replace the brittle, face-hardened steel with homogenous rolled plate. The extra weight required a beefed-up suspension, specifically a new idler wheel mounted at ground level. Standardized in July 1940, production of the M3 Light Tank began in March 1941, directly after the last M2 was rolled out. During production, the M2's turret with its large rivets was replaced by a welded unit with reduced weight and afforded better ballistic characteristics. Jettisonable external fuel tanks were added to increase range, and a simple gyro-stabilizer was fitted to the 37mm (1.46in) gun. This last addition was a major advance. Based on a system for naval guns, the gyroscopes held

the gun in elevation even as the tank moved across undulating terrain. This allowed the tank to fire without stopping first, and was a major tactical advantage, as no Axis (or other Allied) nation developed such a system during World War II.

The M3A1 version eliminated the remotely operated sponson machine guns and introduced an all-welded hull during production. Other improvements were made to the sights, vision equipment, radio and crew intercom. A gyro-stabilizer was fitted to the 37mm (1.46in) gun, the first such equipment to enter service. The turret cupola was removed to lower the vehicle's silhouette. The M3A3 had a redesigned all-welded hull with longer side sponsons, and it entered production in 1943. The Soviet Union received 1676 Guiberson diesel-powered M3A1 Light Tanks under Lend-Lease. A small number were shipped from British stocks, but the bulk came from the USA. Soviet crews criticized the high silhouette of the tank and also ridiculed the hull machine guns.

The M3 Medium was always regarded as an interim solution to US tank needs while a turret could be produced to mount a 75mm (2.95in) gun. Improvements in casting technology and success with the 37mm (1.46in) turret on the M3 encouraged development of a compact, curved unit, which was drawn up by March 1941. The Armored Force Board was offered five options based on this turret and, in April 1941, selected the simplest, which involved fitting it to a modified M3 hull and chassis. The T-6 Medium mock-up was approved in May, and the pilot model delivered to Aberdeen in September 1941. One change was the elimination of a machine-gun cupola. The T-6 hull was of welded construction, as in later M3s, and its prominent side hatch was deleted in the production model.

THE M4 SERIES

Production was authorized when the T-6 was standardized as the M4 Medium in October 1941. Schedules called for 1000 deliveries per month during 1942, from no fewer than 11 car- and locomotive plants and engineering works. A second

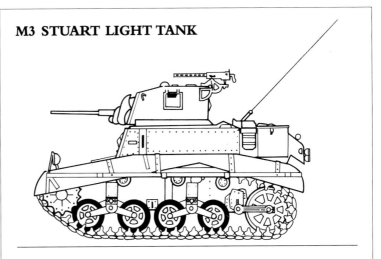

M3 STUART LIGHT TANK

SPEED: 58km/h (36mph)

DIMENSIONS: Length 4.54m (14ft 1in); Width 2.24m (7ft 4in); Height 2.51m (8ft 3in); Weight 13,680kg (13.46 tons)

ARMOUR: 51mm (2in)

WEAPONRY: One 37mm (1.45in); five 7.62mm (0.3in) MG

EFFECTIVE RANGE: 113km (70 miles)

CREW: 4

government tank arsenal, which was run by Fisher, was built at Grand Blanc, Michigan, in 1942. The initial production models utilized a Wright radial engine, but the aircraft industry had a far greater

BELOW: M3 Stuarts and M3 Grants during a training exercise. US tanks were unpopular due to their thin armour and high silhouettes.

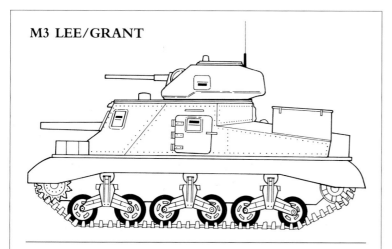

M3 LEE/GRANT

SPEED: 42km/h (26mph)

DIMENSIONS: Length 5.64m (18ft 6in); Width 2.72m (8ft 11in); Height 3.12m (10ft 3in); Weight 29,930kg (29.46 tons)

ARMOUR: 37mm (1.46in)

WEAPONRY: One 75mm (2.95in); one 37mm (1.46in); three or four 7.62mm (0.3in) MG

EFFECTIVE RANGE: 193km (120 miles)

CREW: 6

In combat, 25mm (0.98in) appliqué armour was added to the side of the upper hull to protect the ammunition stowage. The tendency for the M4 Sherman's internally stowed ammunition to catch fire when the tank was hit led to the introduction of wet stowage for ammunition. 'W' was used to indicate this, as in M4A3(75)W. Thirty-eight gallons of water mixed with antifreeze and an anti-corrosion product called 'ammudamp' were needed for 100 shells

The GMC diesel-powered M4A2 medium tank went to the USSR. It was similar to the M4A1; 8053 were armed with 75mm (2.95in) guns and 3230 with 76mm (2.99in) guns. Of these, the USSR received 2007 75mm (2.95in) armed tanks and 2095 76mm (2.99in) M4A2s. The Soviet crews disliked the M4A2 with its thin armour and high silhouette. The M4A3 was the most produced version, and many of these were supplied to the British (as the Sherman IV), while 1386 went to Soviet forces.

demand for this engine and for the manufacturing plant's production capacity, and so alternate powerplants were sought. These included both the petrol and the diesel car/truck engines.

THE WHITE MOTOR CAR COMPANY

The White Motor Company was an important American truck manufacturer before the war. To meet the Army's requirement for a high-speed scouting

M4 SHERMAN

SPEED: 42km/h (26mph)

DIMENSIONS: Length 5.89m (19ft 4in); Width 2.62m (8ft 7in); Height 2.74m (9ft); Weight 33,180kg (32.66 tons)

ARMOUR: 75mm (2.95in)

WEAPONRY: One 75mm (2.9in); two 7.62mm (0.303in) MG; one 12.7mm (0.5in) MG

EFFECTIVE RANGE: 193km (120 miles)

CREW: 5

vehicle, the company offered an armoured version of one of its commercial truck chassis designs. This was tested as the T-7, accepted in 1938, and standardized as the M3 Scout Car in June 1939. Nearly 21,000 were built and 3340 of the M3s, widely known as the White Scout Car, were supplied to the USSR.

The White Motor Company was also responsible for producing the first US-designed half-track used during the war. Based on a White commercial truck chassis, it had the body of the M3 Scout Car. This was tested as the T-14 in 1939 and standardized as the Half-Track Car M2 and the Half-Track Personnel Carrier M3 in September 1940.

The USSR would eventually receive 342 M2 Half-tracks, 2 M3s, 421 M5s, and 413 M9s. The most popular of these was the M17 Multiple Gun Motor Carriage, which was armed with quad 0.50 calibre (12.7mm) Brownings, and the M15A1 armed with a 37mm (1.46in) automatic

cannon and twin Brownings. The USSR was sent 1000 M17s and 100 M15A1s. These vehicles were very popular during World War II because they had no indigenous armoured self-propelled anti-aircraft gun. The United States also supplied 5 M5 Light Tanks, 2 M24 Light Tanks, 1 M25 Heavy Tank, and 115 M31 ARVs. In addition to the receiving the half-track based mechanized guns, the USSR was sent 650 T48 Tank Destroyers (TD), 5 M18 TDs and 52 M10 TDs.

The Soviet Army pressed into service many captured enemy vehicles. These included StuG III assault guns, which were used as a replacement for either the SU-76 or SU-122. An interesting modification of the PzKpfw III, many of which were captured at Stalingrad, was as an SU-76 assault gun. A total of 200 of these vehicles were fielded by the Red Army during the war. By the end of the war, so many PzKpfw V Panther tanks had been captured that they equipped entire Soviet tank units.

ABOVE: A Don Cossack cavalry officer stands with a group of Soviet soldiers next to a captured and slightly battered PzKpfw IV Ausf. F1. As far as Soviet tank crews were concerned, when compared to their Soviet manufactured tanks, the German PzKpfw III and IV which had been the mainstay of the German tank arm – *Panzerwaffe* – seemed slab-sided vehicles that were much more vulnerable to hits by solid shot antitank rounds. In contrast, the Soviet T-34 had a lower silhouette and its angled armour would often deflect oncoming shot.

CHAPTER NINE

STALIN'S LEGACY

Tank design that had been honed in combat in World War II improved in the post-war years. With new, more powerful AFVs came a return to the Deep Penetration tactics of the 1930s; however, war in Europe would now be fought with terrifying weapons of mass destruction.

Prior to World War I, armour had virtually disappeared from the European battlefield. Some of the field guns were equipped with armoured shields, and the Belgians and British both equipped a few cars with steel or iron plates for reconnaissance. However, following World War I, all the participants began to develop tanks and to work on theories of armoured warfare. In the newly established Union of Soviet Socialist Republics (USSR), Red Army officers – most notably Boris Shaposhnikov, V.K. Triandafillov and Mikhail Nikolaevich Tukachevsky – began to develop new tactics for a tank arm that, at the time, was virtually non-existent. Simultaneously, in France, Germany and Britain, theoreticians such as colonels Charles de Gaulle and J.B. Estienne, Colonel Heinz Guderian, Captain G. Le Q. Martel and Colonel J.F.C. Fuller offered concepts which broke away from the conventional idea of land forces which were composed of the three elements of cavalry, artillery and infantry.

LEFT: With black exhaust smoke choking an unhappy Soviet bridging engineer, this T-55 crosses a PMP pontoon bridge during Warsaw Pact exercises. The T-55 substantially resembled the T-54 but included various enhancements; however, for recognition, the two tanks were often grouped as T-54/55.

ABOVE: A battered T-10M heavy tank, with its distinctive 122mm (4.8in) gun with multi-baffle muzzle brake. It was the standard heavy tank of Soviet Ground forces during the 1950s and 1960s and was exported to Warsaw Pact allies and friendly nations. According to US estimates, the total post-war production of heavy tanks was about 9000 vehicles; about 1000 were IS-3M and IS-4, and the remainder were T-10 and T-10M.

Tanks were a unique arm that combined mobility, firepower and protection for their crew. Normally the vehicle sacrificed one or two of these features if it emphasized the third; however, with the T-34 and later marks of the Panther, the Russians and Germans produced tanks in World War II that struck an equal balance.

The anti-Bolshevik White Russians had been supplied with 67 British Mk V tanks and 19 Whippets and 100 French Renault FTs during the Civil War following World War I. In January 1920, when the Whites finally gave up the fight, the tanks were captured and formed into the first Soviet tank unit, or *Avotanki*. The captured FT was copied, and the vehicle that was the first Russian-built tank in service was known variously as the *Krasno-Sormovo* (KS), *Russkiy-Renault* or, more clumsily, the 'Freedom Fighter Comrade Lenin'.

On 29 June 1919 during the Civil War four White Russian Mk Vs, led by a British-crewed vehicle, put in an attack on the Volga river town of Tsaritsin, a city that would later be renamed Stalingrad and which, 23 years later, would survive a far more intense and prolonged armoured assault.

In the late 1920s the Russians attempted to build an engineering and industrial base that would allow them to construct tanks and heavy tractors, and they looked to the West for ideas and tactical concepts. The British Experimental Armoured Force, an all-arms grouping that manoeuvred across Salisbury Plain in 1927, was a pointer to future tank developments. The use of radio for battlefield communications between vehicles made their reaction times far faster and also increased their tactical flexibility.

In the USSR, Red Army officers were not required to think defensively, but rather to think offensively: the Marxist Revolution was to be exported and unbelievers converted, if necessary, by the sword. In 1929 Triandafillov wrote *The Character of Operations of Modern Armies* which predicated that a tank arm could, working in conjunction with existing arms, extend operations deep into the enemy interior. It was Blitzkrieg by another name. Under Stalin's leadership, the 1928 Five Year Plan initiated the process of industrialization that would establish the main Soviet factories. These factories would manufacture the most effective tanks like the T-34 and KV.

Following Triandafillov's paper, the *Polevoi Ustav Krasnoi Armii* (PU-29), or 1929 Field Service Regulation, spelled out the concept of manoeuvre warfare with tanks and assault troops. Through the USA, the USSR acquired the Christie suspension that would be used on the *Bystrokhodnii Tank* (BT), or Fast Tank, series, and it now had the vehicle with which to test the theories. The Soviet forces were plagued by a lack of radios that prevented them from exploring the techniques of command and control. Flag signals were used; this technique remained in use into the 1970s as a way of ensuring radio silence on the move.

A MODERN TANK PROGRAMME

It was not until 1933 that the USSR reached the stage where it could announce that it had embarked on a modern tank programme, building versions of British and US designs and improving on them constantly. It was this year that I.K. Khalepsky – a Red Army officer who had been instrumental in acquiring the Christie vehicles and pushing for a modern tank arm – proposed that the army should not have just a tank

brigade, but rather an independent mechanized corps, *Tankovyy Korpus*. It would have about 500 tanks and 200 armoured cars. Tank battalions would provide infantry support and a special Supreme Command Tank Reserve would be used for breakthroughs, either in cooperation with infantry or horsed cavalry, or independently. The idea found favour with the chief of staff of the Red Army, Alexsandr Yegorov who, in February 1933, published 'Provisional Instructions on the Organization of Deep Battle' (*Gluboki Boi*).

By the beginning of 1934 the Soviet industrial and engineering base under the Director of Armaments, Tukachevsky, and the Director of Mechanization and Motorization, Khalepsky, was in a position to meet the requirements of the Red Army for its deep penetration operations. Light tanks like the T-27 and amphibious T-37 would conduct reconnaissance, while the T-26 and T-35, backed by artillery and air attacks, would make the breakthrough that the fast BTs and T-26s would exploit.

The tactics were tested at the large-scale combined arms manoeuvres at Kiev in 1935, and were observed by both

BELOW: A T-10M showing its Iosef Stalin parentage. The tank had a crew of four and the gun mantlet an armour thickness of 250mm (9.8in). The big rifled D-49T gun had 30 rounds, of which 20 were HE and the remainder one of three types of antitank round. The size of the rounds meant that the crew could only achieve a rate of fire of two to three rounds a minute.

British and French officers, who were impressed by the high technical ability of the Red Army. However, the British tank expert Lieutenant-Colonel Giffard Martel noted that in both the 1935 and 1936 manoeuvres, the unsophisticated Russian soldiers were still grappling with the new weapons and technology.

STALIN'S PURGES

However, just as the officers and soldiers of the Red Army were reaching the level of technical and command competence to make this deep penetration effective, Stalin struck. In a rage of paranoia, between 1937 and 1938, Stalin purged 45 per cent of the command and political staff of the armed forces: 3 of the 5 marshals of the Soviet Union; all 11 deputy commissars for defence; 75 of the 80 military council members; 57 of the 85 corps commanders; 110 of the 195 divisional commanders; and 186 of the 406 brigade commanders. Some were exe-

cuted and others banished to the Gulag prison camps of Siberia. Khalepsky was arrested and died in prison in 1938, and Tukachevsky and Uborevich were 'cleansed' in 1937 and Griaznov in 1938. The soldiers, engineers and political officers who survived were cowed and terrified, trying to anticipate the moves that would least offend Stalin.

The 'brains' of the armoured forces had been destroyed, and in the Spanish Civil War of 1936–39 the Soviet T-26s and BT-5s employed in deep-penetration tactics suffered badly. The tanks in Spain were commanded by General Dmitrii Grigorevich Pavlov. After 1938 he reported that tanks should be used in more traditional infantry-support operations. At the Eighteenth Party Congress in 1939, the Defence Commissar Klimenti Voroshilov, crony of Stalin and former cavalryman, stated that horse cavalry could 'carry out great missions'. The day of the Deep Battle seemed to be over.

BELOW: T-62 tanks on the move during a winter exercise. The T-62 is armed with a 115mm (4.5in) smoothbore gun with 40 rounds. It entered production in the USSR and Czechoslovakia in 1961 and ceased in 1975. It is still in service in Mongolia, Vietnam and Algeria, while Israel holds stocks which were captured during fighting with Egypt and Syria.

On 22 June 1941, when German tanks crossed the Soviet border, the Red Army was in no fit state to resist effectively. Though the T-34 was entering service, the army was still largely equipped with BTs and other obsolescent types. This meant that it would be the huge distances, poor weather and roads, and the grossly over-extended German logistic chain, plus Hitler's interference at even tactical level, that would save the USSR from being totally overwhelmed.

However, by May 1942 the USSR had formed the first of six tank armies and re-discovered the doctrines of Deep Battle. At Moscow (1941–42) they had held the enemy and counterattacked. At Stalingrad (1942–43) they showed how they had mastered these techniques, as four tank corps – the formation favoured by Khalepsky – struck in November 1942. I, IV, and XXVI tank corps hit the northern shoulder of the German line and IV Tank Corps to the south. When they linked up at Kalach on the Don, the fate of the German Sixth Army at Stalingrad was sealed and a total of 300,000 men were killed or captured.

Stalin, who originally had not been a believer in Deep Battle, nor in its effectiveness, was now a true convert. He wanted Soviet forces to cut off those elements of the German Army Group A that were buried deep in the Caucasus, before driving for the Sea of Azov and creating an enormous pocket.

However, the German troops were able to withdraw, and in the summer of 1943 at Kursk, Hitler attempted a counterattack against the shoulders of a salient which had been formed in the fighting of February 1943. It was not an example of the deep armoured thrusts that had characterized the two summer offensives of 1941 and 1942. The Germans faced five fronts or army groups that had already been alerted to the date and direction of the attack. On this occasion, the German attack was stopped for the loss of 500,000 men, 1500 tanks, 3000 artillery pieces and over 3700 aircraft. The Soviet West, Bryansk, Voronezh and South-Western Fronts then proceeded to swing onto the offensive.

A defining feature of all subsequent Soviet attacks was the intensity of the preliminary bombardments: the weight of high explosive that crashed onto the German positions would not have been imagined by Tukachevsky or any of the armoured theorists of the mid–1930s. The autumn offensive broke through the German 'East Wall' or 'Panther' line and, halted only by local counterattacks, rolled on to the old pre-war borders of Poland. The Soviet forces were equipped with

ABOVE: A T-54/55 held by the US Army in Germany during the Cold War. Weapons and vehicles captured by the Israelis in 1967 and 1973 were passed to the US for evaluation and later used in training. The T-55 had a significantly larger ammunition load: 43 rounds compared to the 34 of the T-54. Though the technique of tank *desants* was by then obsolete, Soviet tanks continued to be produced with grab rails on the turret.

RIGHT: T-62s move in line abreast. Although by now the Soviet Union had excellent radios, tank crews were nonetheless trained in the use of flags like their fathers and grandfathers had been before them. This might seem quaint, but it did have the advantage that radio silence could be maintained during an advance to the forward edge of the battle area. The T-62 with its smoothbore 115mm (4.5in) gun marked the move away from rifled tank guns by the Soviet Union, a move which was later copied in the West.

formidable tanks like the T-34/85 and backed up by numerous US-supplied trucks that gave them tactical mobility.

Writing after the war, *Generaloberst* Erhard Rauss asserted, 'The German could never assume that the Russian would be held back by terrain normally considered impassable. It was in just such places that his appearance, and frequently his attack, had to be expected.'

The Soviet winter offensive of 1944 saw the 1st Ukrainian Front under General Vatutin advance over 400km (250 miles) in two months against stiff opposition from Army Group South. Consolidating on these gains in the spring offensive, the western Ukraine was

liberated, and in this fighting the First Panzer Army was trapped in a huge pocket to the east of the Dniestr on 28 March by the 1st Ukrainian Front under Zhukov, and Konev's 2nd Ukrainian Front. It only began to break free on 30 March and it reached safety on 7 April. Konev was a survivor of Stalin's purges.

OPERATION 'BAGRATION'

The climax of the Red Army's armoured campaigns in the west was the 1944 summer offensive, Operation 'Bagration'. Between 22 June and 31 August, the attacks destroyed Army Group Centre and took the Soviet forces to the borders of the Third Reich and, in the south, the

LEFT: A T-54/55 flame-throwing tank opens fire on a night range with a huge and intimidating burst of flame. The ATO-200 flamethrower has the capacity for 460 litres (101 imperial gallons) of fuel, and this can be fired in bursts of 35 litres (7.6 imp. gallons). The weapon can fire a total of seven bursts in one minute. Flamethrowers are a terrifying weapon that can induce panic in infantry, even though conventional gunfire may actually be more effective at causing casualties than a raw flame.

key Romanian oilfields of Ploesti. In this campaign, Hitler's intransigence caused German forces to be trapped in pockets all along the front; this was Deep Battle with a vengeance.

The autumn offensive of 1944 reached Warsaw and Budapest, and in the spring of 1945, Zhukov, Rokossovsky (another purge survivor) and Konev drove west to Berlin. Berlin was encircled on 25 April 1945 and fell on 2 May. In the Allied victory parade British and American officers saw for the first time the awesome Iosef Stalin IS-3 *Shchuka* or 'Pike'. The superbly angled armour and 122mm (4.8in) gun made it a formidable vehicle. The IS heavy tank series would develop through the IS-4 and end with the T-10, or IS-8.

The final demonstration of Deep Battle took place in Manchuria in August

1945. Veteran Soviet troops were transferred to the Far East and moved up to the border of Japanese-held Manchuria. Their old enemies, the 600,000-strong Kwantung Army, under General Yawada, were attacked by the Trans-Baikal Front under General Rodion Malinovsky, the 1st Far East Front under General Kiril Meretskov, and the 2nd Far East Front under General Purkayev.

At dawn on 9 August, the well-equipped and experienced Soviet forces – with a three to two superiority in men, five to one in guns and tanks, and two to one in aircraft – punched across the border. They reached Harbin on 20 August and had pushed on to Port Arthur by 22 August. The Sixth Guards Tank Army, of the Trans-Baikal Front, had taken the Japanese by surprise by

RIGHT: The rifling can be seen clearly on the barrel of the gun of this T-54/55. The T-54/55 proved a very versatile tank that was modified and improved. The East German Army actually favoured it over the T-62 and accordingly did not adopt the more modern tank when it became available. The soldiers shown in this picture are jumping well clear of this T-54/55, like tank *desants* of World War II would have done – but the difference here is that this is merely an exercise, and not a T-34 crashing into a German trench line.

crossing two major obstacles: the Greater Khingan Mountains and 435km (270 miles) of desert, and was now in position to cross the plains of central Manchuria.

The aftermath of this campaign was a divided Korea: the north in the Communist orbit, and the south with the United States, split at the 38th Parallel. In the war of 1950–53, the North Koreans attacked with the weapons and tactics that had been honed in World War II. In Vietnam, Deep Battle tactics appeared again when North Vietnamese T-54 and T-55 tanks, under General Dung, rolled south between 1974 and 1975, and captured Saigon on 30 April 1975.

On 5 March 1946, speaking at Fulton, Missouri, Winston Churchill had used a phrase that defined the split between the Communist East and Capitalist West. 'From Stettin in the Baltic to Trieste in the Adriatic, an iron curtain has descended across the continent.' Three years later the North Atlantic Treaty Organization (NATO) was established to bring together the countries of western Europe and Iceland, Canada and the United States in a defensive treaty in the face of Soviet pressure. In September 1949 the USSR exploded its first atomic bomb; some asserted that the days of conventional war were over. Massed armour backed by mobile infantry and artillery would not be used in action again.

Stalin died in 1953 and the military leaders like Marshal Zhukov who he had feared as potential rivals were recalled from exile in remote commands. From 1955 onwards Zhukov pressed to upgrade the equipment for the ground forces, including new APCs.

When in 1955 West Germany, with its own independent army, joined NATO, Moscow countered by establishing the Warsaw Pact. This treaty group included the USSR, Bulgaria, Czechoslovakia, East Germany, Hungary, Poland and Romania. The lines were now drawn for nearly 35 years of tension in Europe and plans for attack and defence. During this time, Warsaw Pact- or Soviet tanks and infantry were deployed, but to suppress outbreaks of anti-Russian nationalism in East Germany, Hungary in 1956, and Czechoslovakia in 1968.

The main purpose of the Warsaw Pact and notably the Group of Soviet Forces in Germany (GSFG) was as an offensive force that could be used to bring political pressure to bear on the West. If the West appeared so weak and demoralized and the USA had become isolationist, the opportunity might present itself to GSFG and its Warsaw Pact allies to make a swift attack combining the tactics of Deep Battle with weapons of mass destruction: nuclear and chemical weapons. The experience of Operation Barbarossa had convinced the USSR that it would never be caught on the defensive again and that from now on, attack would be the best form of defence.

SOVIET INVASION PLAN

An attack on West Germany had three obvious axes, with a secondary through Austria. The main objective would be the federal capital of Bonn on the Rhine. To the north, the Second Guards Army, Third Shock Army and Third East German Army would drive across the North German Plain against British forces. In the centre, the Eighth Guards Army would drive through the Fulda Gap into US forces, while to the south, the First and Fourth Czech armies would be responsible for attacks against Nuremberg in the US-defended areas.

If they were committed to attack, Soviet commanders identified three types of action based on their experience in World War II: the meeting engagement; engagement of defence; pursuit. In the meeting engagement, both forces were moving, and by careful use of reconnaissance, the Soviet force attacking off the march aimed to hit their opponent in the flank or rear. The engagement of defence was an attack against a hasty or prepared defensive position, and in these circumstances Soviet forces aimed to have a local superiority and go for the classic Deep Battle penetration, with attacks on the flanks and rear. With the tactics of pursuit, the Warsaw Pact nations aimed to give their fleeing enemy not a moment's rest. By maintaining continuous contact, they would ensure a complete defeat and thus prevent a new line of defence from being established.

From their wartime experience Soviet forces had developed a system of echelons for all their major elements. The first echelon, the main attacking force charged with seizing or destroying the primary objectives, had about two-thirds of the strength of the force committed. The second echelon, following up, concentrated on the subsequent objectives and other tasks. This was known as leapfrogging and allowed the second echelon to continue the offensive.

Replacement of casualties in the attack was achieved by units 'passing through' other formations. It was essential to use this method to maintain the

BELOW: T-54/55 tanks ford a shallow river during an exercise. The Soviet Union was expert at staging dramatic exercises in the Cold War as it had been in the 1930s. Some river-crossing operations were carefully rehearsed for the benefit of visitors or TV crews, and did not correspond to the reality of a war in Europe.

RIGHT: The commander of a T-64 of a Guards Regiment gives a smart 'eyes right' as he leads a column of tanks in a parade. The T-64 was armed with a D-18T 125mm (4.9in) smoothbore gun with 40 rounds, and this weapon was capable of six to eight rounds a minute. Significantly, the T-64 tank served only with Soviet forces, and as such, its presence on the battlefield would constitute an intelligence 'signature'. The tanks would have been deployed as part of the Motor Rifle Division of the Group of Soviet Forces in Germany (GSFG).

momentum of attack. Against organized defences and without recourse to nuclear weapons, Soviet planners predicated a rate of 30km (18 miles) a day, and if nuclear weapons were used, this rate went up to 60km (36 miles) a day.

The echelon concept was peculiarly Soviet and was employed to break through German defences. These defences were normally in two layers. The second line was intended to hold a penetration long enough for a counterattack to restore the front line.

24-HOUR BATTLE

Soviet doctrine also emphasized continuity of operations: the 24-hour battle in all weather and conditions. Ironically the most impressive demonstration of this was during Operation Desert Sabre, the brief land campaign by Coalition forces (largely US and British) in the Gulf War of 1991. Soviet infantry were trained to fight from the armoured personnel carriers (APCs) and not to dismount if at all possible. Engineers were forward to clear minefields and bridge gaps.

Firepower included tactical nuclear weapons as well as persistent and non-persistent chemical agents, the latter including nerve agents. The planning for the release of nuclear weapons, which would normally be air-burst, would be conducted at Front level, but the decision to use them would have been made at higher levels. Chemical agents, depending on their nature, would either be ground-burst or air-burst, and one of the most

favoured delivery systems would be the truck-mounted BM-21 122mm (4.8in) multiple rocket launcher.

Soviet doctrine favoured the use of armour in massed multiple formations, and since it offered protection to its crews against radiation and chemical contamination, it was the ideal arm with which to exploit gaps in defences caused by chemical or tactical nuclear attack.

Faced by a defensive position that was still able to offer resistance, Soviet doctrine stated that it should either be penetrated or bypassed. Given that forces as small as a Motor Rifle Regiment had a frontage of about 5–10km (3.1–6.2 miles) in which to manoeuvre, tactical circumstances would often have obliged them to make a frontal attack. However, if they could manoeuvre, they had a choice of deep or close envelopment.

Deep envelopment drew on the old Deep Battle principles, and it would have been executed at Front level. Areas where defences were light, like mountain or arctic regions, were the most favourable terrain for executing a deep envelopment manoeuvre. Close envelopment could be used against one (Okhrat) or both flanks (Obkhod) and would be supported by fire from the attacking troops' rocket or artillery batteries. These types of close-envelopment manoeuvres might also be launched in conjunction with a frontal spoiling attack.

To undertake these missions, the GSFG had two formations: the Motor Rifle Division (MRD) and the Tank

Division (TD). A combined-arms army would have had two to four MRD, and two TD backed by artillery, engineers and signals. The most obvious distinguishing feature between them was the number and type of tanks and APCs. The MRD, with a Tank Regiment (TR) with 95 tanks, and three Motor Rifle Regiments (MRR) with 31 tanks, also deployed the eight-wheeled BTR60P APC and the T-64 or T-72. The TD was the opposite: with three TR and one MRR, it had 316 medium and 17 light amphibious tanks, and 190 APCs. The MRR had the BMP tracked amphibious APC.

Just as the T-34 became the model by which medium tanks were assessed in the 1940s, so the BMP – developed in the 1960s and first seen in public in 1967 – set a new standard in APC design. In fact, it was not an APC, a 'battle taxi' that would carry an infantry section into battle, but a whole new concept: a Mechanized Infantry Combat Vehicle (MICV). With a 73mm (2.9in) turret-mounted gun and a 9M14 *Malyutka* (AT-3 'Sagger'), the BMP-1 had the gun and ATGW combination that would only enter service with the West when the US Army accepted the Bradley and the British the Warrior MICV in the 1980s.

The BMP had its drawbacks: it was cramped and the suspension could give a nauseous ride at speed cross-country. However, in 1970 it was years ahead of other designs. Since then the USSR, and now Russia, have continued to improve on the original concept with new armament and ATGW and a two-man turret in the BMP-2. The armament could be used either for self-defence, or for shooting in the infantry squad if it had dismounted to attack an objective.

Like earlier Soviet designs, both the less sophisticated BTR and the BMP are vehicles that have been updated and modernized: the BMP-1 has now gone through three marks and is currently fielded as the BMP-3. The BTR60P, a design that dates back to the 1950s, has

ABOVE: Tanks on parade in the October Revolution Parade in Red Square in November 1981, an activity that is now only a memory. Here T-72 Main Battle Tanks (MBT) roll past the crowds. Entering production in 1967, the T-72 was first seen in public in 1977. It was widely exported and is built under licence in Czechoslovakia, India, Poland and the former Yugoslavia. The tank had a 125mm (4.9in) smoothbore gun with 45 rounds.

RIGHT: A young Soviet tank driver of a Guard Regiment looks out of the hatch of a T-72. The T-72 was developed using the Christie suspension, and Red Army officers would have recognized the characteristic big wheels on this later vehicle. The distinctive Guards Regiment insignia can be seen on the cover of the tank's infrared searchlight behind him. The status of Guards was assigned during World War II to units which had performed heroically. In modern reference, it is seen as a title for well-trained and motivated formations.

grown through to the BTR-80, a chassis that is used as an APC, and for armoured recovery, chemical reconnaissance and as a 120mm (4.7in) armed SP gun.

The proponents of Deep Battle would also have been delighted to discover that the Tank and Motor Rifle Regiments now had their own mechanized artillery: the SO-152 *Akatsiya* 152mm (5.9in) self-propelled gun and the SO-122 *Gvozdika* 122mm (4.8in) self-propelled gun. As antiaircraft defence, there were wheeled and tracked surface-to-air missile launchers, and the formidable ZSU-23-4 *Shilka* radar-controlled quad 23mm (0.9in) tracked AA gun. These vehicles were new, but Red Army officers would have noticed that the new generation of medium tanks that entered service in the 1950s and 1960s looked familiar.

Though the T-54, T-55 and T-62 had a turret and hull as well as main armament that was unrecognizable from the mid–1930s, they had Christie suspension with characteristic big wheels. Even later vehicles like the T-72 and T-90 have a similar suspension, though they have idlers to ensure better track tension. However, this similarity is not surprising, since the T-54

grew out of the T-44, a modification of the T-34/85. The first prototype T-54 was completed in 1946 and production followed at Kharkov in 1947. For a design that is over 50 years old, it is still extremely successful, with large numbers still in service around the world and numerous updates and modifications. Taking a good basic design and improving on it meant that the tank was to develop through the T-55 up to the later T-62.

THE END OF AN ERA

Even as late as the mid–1980s, the tough old veteran of World War II, the infamous T-34/85, was still soldiering on. The largest users were North Korea with 250, followed by Syria with 200, while Cuba, Egypt and Iraq had 100, and Israel had a similar number which had been captured from her Arab neighbours. Besides being manufactured in factories in the USSR, the T-34/85 was also made in Poland from 1953, and in Czechoslovakia from 1951. The Czechs built 3000 tanks, some of which were supplied to Egypt in 1956. It is only appropriate that the famous, war-winning T-34 should have had such a lasting effect on tank warfare.

Annual Allied and Axis Crude Steel Production 1939–45 (metric tons (imperial tons))

DATE	USA	USSR	UK	CANADA	TOTAL	GERMANY	ITALY	HUNGARY	RUMANIA	JAPAN	TOTAL
1939	—	—	13.2 (12.99)	1.4 (1.38)	**14.6** (14.37)	23.7 (23.33)	—	—	—	—	**23.7** (23.33)
1940	—	—	13.0 (12.79)	1.7 (1.67)	**14.7** (14.46)	21.5 (21.16)	2.1 (2.07)	0.7 (0.69)	0.3 (0.29)	—	**24.6** (24.21)
1941	—	17.9 (17.62)	12.3 (12.11)	2.5 (2.46)	**32.7** (32.19)	28.2 (27.75)	2.1 (2.07)	0.8 (0.79)	?	—	**31.1** (30.61)
1942	80.6 (79.33)	8.1 (7.97)	12.8 (12.60)	2.8 (2.76)	**104.3** (102.66)	28.7 (28.25)	1.9 (1.87)	0.8 (0.79)	0.3 (0.29)	8.0 (7.87)	**40.5** (39.07)
1943	82.2 (80.90)	8.5 (8.37)	13.3 (13.09)	2.7 (2.66)	**106.7** (105.02)	30.6 (30.12)	1.7 (1.67)	0.8 (0.79)	0.3 (0.29)	8.8 (8.66)	**42.2** (41.53)
1944	85.1 (83.76)	10.9 (10.73)	12.1 (11.91)	2.7 (2.66)	**110.8** (109.06)	25.8 (25.39)	—	0.7 (0.69)	?	6.5 (6.40)	**33.0** (32.48)
1945	86.6 (85.23)	12.3 (12.11)	11.8 (11.61)	2.6 (2.56)	**113.3** (111.51)	1.4 (1.38)	—	?	?	0.8 (0.79)	**2.2** (2.17)
TOTAL	**334.5** (329.22)	**57.7** (56.80)	**88.5** (87.10)	**16.4** (16.15)	**497.1** (489.27)	**159.9** (157.38)	**7.8** (7.68)	**3.8** (3.75)	**0.9** (0.87)	**24.1** (23.72)	**196.5** (193.40)

Soviet Tank Production by Type and Year

	1941	1942	1943	1944	1945	TOTAL
Light Tanks						
T-40	41	181				222
T-50	48	15				63
T-60	1,818	4,474				6,292
T-70		4,883	3,343			8,226
T-80		120				120
Sub-total	1,907	9,553	3,463			14,923
Medium Tanks						
T-34	3,014	12,553	15,529	2,995		34,091
T-34-85			283	11,778	7,230	23,661
T-44					200	200
Sub-total	3,014	12,553	15,812	14,773	7,430	53,582
Heavy Tanks						
KV-1	1,121	1,753				2,874
KV-2	232					232
KV-1S		780	452			1,232
KV-85			130			130
IS-2			102	2,252	1,500	3,854
Sub-total	1,353	2,533	684	2,252	1,500	8,322
Total Tanks	**6,274**	**24,639**	**19,959**	**17,025**	**8,930**	**76,827**
Assault Guns						
SU-76		26	1,928	7,155	3,562	12,671
SU-122		25	630	493		1,148
SU-85			750	1,300		2,050
SU-100				500	1,175	1,675
SU-152			704			704
ISU-122/ISU-152			35	2,510	1,530	4,075
Sub-total		51	4,047	11,958	6,267	22,323
Total AFVs	**6,274**	**24,690**	**24,006**	**28,983**	**15,197**	**99,150**

Annual Allied and Axis Tank and Self-propelled Gun Production 1939-45 (units)

DATE	USA	USSR	UK	CANADA	TOTAL	GERMANY	ITALY*	HUNGARY	JAPAN*	TOTAL
1939	—	2,950	969	?	**3,919**	247	40	—	—	**287**
1940	331	2,794	1,399	?	**4,524**	1,643	250	—	315	**2,208**
1941	4,052	6,590	4,841	?	**15,483**	3,790	595	—	595	**4,980**
1942	24,997	24,446	8,611	?	**58,054**	6,180	1,252	?	557	**7,989**
1943	29,497	24,089	7,476	?	**61,062**	12,063	336	c. 500	558	**12,957**
1944	17,565	28,963	4,600	?	**51,128**	19,002	—	?	353	**19,355**
1945	11,968	15,419	?	?	**27,387**	3,932	—	—	137	**4,069**
TOTAL	**88,410**	**105,251**	**27,896**	**5,678**	**227,235**	**46,857**	**2,473**	**c. 500**	**2,515**	**c. 52,345**

* Figures exclude light tanks and tankettes.

Soviet Tank Strength in September 1939

		T-37	T-26	BT	T-28	ARMOURED CARS
Belorussian Front	15th Tank Corps	—	—	461	—	122
	6th Tank Brigade	—	—	248	—	—
	21st Tank Brigade	—	—	29	105	19
	22nd Tank Brigade	—	219	—	—	3
	25th Tank Brigade	—	251	—	—	27
	29th Tank Brigade	—	188	—	—	3
	32nd Tank Brigade	—	220	—	—	5
Ukrainian Front	25th Tank Corps	—	27	435	—	74
	10th Tank Brigade	—	10	30	98	19
	23rd Tank Brigade	—	8	209	—	5
	24th Tank Brigade	—	8	205	—	28
	26th Tank Brigade	—	228	—	—	22
	36th Tank Brigade	—	301	—	—	24
	38th Tank Brigade	4	141	—	—	4

The Eastern Front Tank Balance 1941–45

	1941	1942	1943	1944	1945	TOTAL
Soviet tank production	6,274	24,639	19,959	16,975	4,384	72,231
German tank production	3,256	4,278	5,966	9,161	1,098	23,759
Production ratio	1:2	1:5.6	1:3.3	1:1.85	1:4	1:3

	1941	1942	1943	1944	1945	TOTAL
Soviet tank losses	20,500	15,000	22,400	16,900	8,700	83,500
German tank losses	2,758	2,648	6,362	6,434	7,382	·25,584
Tank exchange ratio* (German:Soviet)	1:7	1:6	1:4	1:4	1:1.2	1:4.4

*German tank losses here include all fronts; the tank exchange ratio shown is an estimate of the Soviet-German loss ratio.

Soviet and German Armoured Fighting Vehicle Strengths on the Eastern Front 1941-45

DATE	June 41	March 42	May 42	Nov 42	March 43	Aug 43	June 44	Sept 44	Oct 44	Nov 44	Dec 44	Jan 45
SOVIET	28,800	4,690	6,190	4,940	7,200	6,200	11,600	11,200	11,900	14,000	15,000	14,200
GERMAN	3,671	1,503	3,981	3,133	2,374	2,555	4,470	4,186	4,917	5,202	4,785	4,881

These figures include tanks and all kinds of self-propelled guns, but the number of serviceable vehicles on both sides was less than the figures shown. The Russian figures do not include the permanent armoured force held on the Manchurian Front.

German and Soviet Armoured Fighting Vehicle Strengths at the Beginning of Selected Major Offensives 1944–45

DATE	SECTOR	FORMATIONS GERMAN	SOVIET	TANKS AND SELF-PROPELLED GUNS GERMAN	SOVIET
14 Jan 44	Leningrad	18 Army	Leningrad Fr.; Volkov Fr.	200	1,200
30 Jan 44	Krivoi Rog/Nikopol	6 Army	3 Ukrainian Fr.; 4 Ukrainian Fr.	250	1,400
4 Mar 44	R. Pripet/Nikolaev	1 Pz Army; 4 Pz Army; 6 Army; 8 Army	1 Ukrainian Fr.; 2 Ukrainian Fr.3 Ukrainian Fr.	1,300	6,400
5 Mar 44	Uman/Kirovgrad	8 Army	2 Ukrainian Fr.	310	2,400
8 April 44	Crimea	17 Army	4 Ukrainian Fr.; Ind. Cst. Army	70	900
22 Jun 44	Vitebsk/R. Pripet	Army Group Centre	1 Baltic Fr.; 1 Byelo. Fr.2 Byelo. Fr.; 3 Byelo. Fr.	800	4,100
12 July 44	Kovel/Tarnopol	A. Group N. Ukraine	1 Ukrainian Fr.	700	2,040
18 July 44	Chelm/Rava Russkaya	4 Pz Army	3 Gds Army; 13 Army; 1 Gds Tk Army	174	550
19 July 44	Mariampol/Daugavpils	3 Pz Army	1 Baltic Fr.; 3 Byelo. Fr. (parts)	95	1,100
20 Aug 44	Bendory/Chernovitsy	A. Group S. Ukraine	2 Ukrainian Fr.; 3 Ukrainian Fr.	400	1,880
14 Sep 44	Narva	Army Group North	Leningrad Fr.; 1 Baltic Fr.; 2 Baltic Fr.; 3 Baltic Fr.	400	3,000
12 Jan 45	Warsaw/Tarnow	Army Group A	1 Byelo. Fr.; 1 Ukrainian Fr.	770	6,460
13 Jan 45	E. Prussia	Army Group Centre	2 Byelo. Fr.; 3 Byelo. Fr.	750	3,300
1 Mar 45	Pomerania	3 Pz Army	1 Byelo. Fr. (part)	70	1,600
16 Apr 45	Oder/Neisse confluence to Stettin	A. Group Vistula	1 Byelo. Fr.; 2 Byelo. Fr.	750	4,100
16 Apr 45	R. Neisse	4 Pz Army	1 Ukrainian Fr.	200	2,150

Soviet Tank Technical Details

Type	T-60	T-70	T-34	T-34	T-34-85	KV-1	KV-1S	IS-2M
Variant	Model 42	Model 42	Model 41	Model 43	Model 44	Model 42	Model 43	Model 45
Road range (km(miles))	450 (280)	360 (224)	400 (249)	465 (289)	360 (224)	250 (155)	250 (155)	240 (149)
Terrain range (km(miles))	250 (155)	180 (112)	260 (162)	365 (227)	310 (193)	180 (112)	160 (99)	210 (130)
Armour (mm(in))								
turret front	25 (0.98)	60 (2.36)	52 (2.05)	70 (2.76)	90 (3.54)	120 (4.72)	82 (3.23)	160 (6.30)
turret side	15 (0.59)	35 (1.38)	52 (2.05)	52 (2.05)	75 (2.95)	120 (4.72)	82 (3.23)	110 (4.33)
turret rear	15 (0.59)	35 (1.38)	45 (1.77)	52 (2.05)	60 (2.36)	90 (3.54)	82 (3.23)	100 (3.93)
turret roof	7 (0.28)	10 (0.39)	20 (0.79)	20 (0.79)	20 (0.79)	40 (1.57)	30 (1.18)	30 (1.18)
hull glacis	35 (1.38)	45 (1.77)	45 (1.77)	47 (1.85)	47 (1.85)	110 (4.33)	75 (2.95)	120 (4.72)
hull side	25 (0.98)	45 (1.77)	45 (1.77)	60 (2.36)	60 (2.36)	90-130 (3.5-5.1)	60 (2.36)	95 (3.74)
hull rear	25 (0.98)	35 (1.38)	47 (1.85)	47 (1.85)	47 (1.85)	60-75 (2.36-2.95)	40-75 (1.57-2.95)	60 (2.36)
hull top	13 (0.51)	10 (0.39)	20 (0.79)	20 (0.79)	20 (0.79)	30 (1.18)	30 (1.18)	30 (1.18)
hull floor	13 (0.51)	10 (0.39)	20 (0.79)	20 (0.79)	20 (0.79)	30 (1.18)	30 (1.18)	30 (1.18)

Tanks and S.P. Guns with 75mm (2.95in) guns and above

DATE	USA	USSR	UK	GERMANY
1939	—	—	—	—
1940	—	—	—	—
1941	—	3,135	—	1,028
1942	?	14,589	?	2,841
1943	?	20,091	?	11,349
1944	?	28,483	?	18,576
1945	?	26,297	?	c. 4,000
TOTAL	71,067	92,595	?	37,794

Soviet Assault Gun and Tank Destroyer Technical Details

Type	SU-76M	SU-85	SU-100	SU-122	SU-152	ISU-122	ISU-152
Crew	4	4	4	5	5	5	5
Weight (tonnes(tons))	10.2 (10.04)	29.2 (28.74)	31.6 (31.10)	30.9 (30.41)	45.5 (44.78)	45.5 (44.78)	46 (45.27)
Length (m(yds))	5 (5.47)	8.15 (8.91)	9.45 (10.33)	6.95 (7.60)	8.95 (9.79)	9.85 (10.77)	9.18 (10.04)
Width (m(yds))	2.7 (2.95)	3 (3.28)	3 (3.28)	3 (3.28)	3.25 (3.55)	3.07 (3.36)	3.07 (3.36)
Height (m(yds))	2.1 (2.30)	2.45 (2.68)	2.25 (2.46)	2.32 (2.54)	2.45 (2.68)	2.48 (2.71)	2.48 (2.71)
Armament	ZiS-3	D-5S	D-10S	M-30S	ML-20S	A-19S	ML-20S
Calibre (mm(in))	76.2 (3)	85 (3.35)	100 (3.93)	122 (4.8)	152 (5.98)	122 (4.8)	152 (5.98)
Ammo stowed	60	48	34	40	20	30	20
Engine	GAZ-203	V-2	V-2	V-2	V-2	V-2	V-2
Kilowatts (horsepower)	127 (170)	373 (500)	373 (500)	373 (500)	373 (500)	447 (600)	447 (600)
Fuel (litres(gallons))	420 (92)	810 (178)	770 (169)	810 (178)	975 (214)	860 (189)	860 (189)
Max. road speed (km/h(mph))	45 (28)	47 (29)	48 (30)	55 (34)	43 (27)	37 (23)	37 (23)
Road range (km(miles))	320 (199)	400 (249)	320 (199)	300 (186)	330 (205)	220 (137)	220 (137)
Terrain range (km(miles))	190 (118)	200 (124)	180 (112)	150 (93)	120 (75)	80 (50)	80 (50)
Armour (mm(in))							
hull front	35 (1.37)	45 (1.77)	45 (1.77)	45 (1.77)	60 (2.36)	90 (3.54)	90 (3.54)
hull side	16 (0.63)	45 (1.77)	45 (1.77)	45 (1.77)	60 (2.36)	90 (3.54)	90 (3.54)
hull rear	16 (0.63)	45 (1.77)	45 (1.77)	45 (1.77)	60 (2.36)	60 (2.36)	60 (2.36)
hull roof	0-10 (0-0.39)	20 (0.79)	20 (0.79)	20 (0.79)	30 (1.18)	30 (1.18)	30 (1.18)
hull floor	10 (0.39)	20 (0.79)	20 (0.79)	20 (0.79)	30 (1.18)	30 (1.18)	30 (1.18)

Causes of T-34 Tank Losses During World War II (per cent)

	20mm (0.79in)	37mm (1.45in)	short 50mm (1.97in)	long 50mm (1.97in)	75mm (2.95in)	88mm (3.45in)	105mm (4.13in)	128mm (5.04)	AT rocket	Unknown
Up to September 1942	4.7	10.0	7.5	54.3	10.1	3.4	2.9	0	0	7.1
Stalingrad operation Central Front,	0	0	25.6	26.5	12.1	7.8	0	0	0	28.0
Orel operation 1943	0	0	10.5	23.0	40.5	26.0	0	0	0	0
First Belorussian Front, June-September 1944	0	0	0	0	39.0	38.0	—	—	9.0	14.0
First Belorussian Front, January-March 1945	0	0	0	0	29.0	64.0	0	1.0	5.5	0.5
First Ukrainian Front, January-March 1945	0	0	0	0.5	19.0	71.0	0.6	0	8.9	0
Fourth Ukrainian Front, January-March 1945	0	0	0	0	25.3	51.5	0.9	—	9.0	13.3
First Belorussian Front, Oder-Berlin 1945	0	0	0	1.4	69.2	16.7	—	—	10.5	2.2
2nd Guards Tank Army, Berlin 1945	0	5.4	0	0	36.0	29.0	6.6	0	22.8	

Soviet Tank Guns

GUN	Thickness of armour (mm (in)) penetrated at: m(yards)					
	229 (250)	457 (500)	686 (750)	914(1000)	1372 (1500)	1829 (2000)
37mm (1.45in)	?	38 (1.49) (at 366m (400yd))	?	?	—	—
45mm (1.77in)	all	80 (3.15)	?	50 (1.97)	?	—
57mm (2.24in)	all	140 (5.51)	?	?	?	?
76mm (3in)F-34 firing DS a.p.	all	92 (3.62)	?	60 (2.36)	?	?
85mm (3.35in) D-5	all	138 (5.43)	?	100 (3.94)	?	?
100mm (3.94in) D-10 firing HE a.p.	all	195 (7.68)	?	185 (7.28)	?	?
122mm (4.8in) M-30 firing HE a.p.	all	145 (5.71)	145 (5.71)	145 (5.71)	?	?

Combat Ranges of Armoured Vehicle Engagements 1943–44

Distance in metres (yards)	75mm (2.95in) gun	88mm (3.45in) gun
100-200 (109-219)	10.0*	4.0
200-400 (219-437)	26.1	14.0
400-600 (437-656)	33.5	18.0
800-1000 (875-1094)	7.0	13.5
1000-1200 (1094-1312)	4.5	8.5
1200-1400 (1312-1531)	3.6	7.6
1400-1600 (1531-1750)	0.4	2.0
1600-1800 (1750-1968)	0.4	0.7
1800-2000 (1968-2187)	0	0.5

* Percentage of Soviet tanks and assault guns knocked out by range.

Soviet Self-propelled Guns

Designation	Function	Gun	Carriage/Chassis
SU-76M	SP	76.2mm (3in) Zis-3	T-70M
SU-85	TD	85mm (3.35in) D-5S	T-34
SU-100	TD	100mm (3.94in) D-10S	T-34
SU-122	AG	122mm (4.8in) M30-S	T-34
SU-152	TD/SP	152mm (6in) ML-20	KV-1S
ISU-122	TD/SP	122mm (4.8in) A-195		IS-1
ISU-152	TD/SP	152mm (6in) ML-20	IS-1

Soviet Guards Tank Corps

Guards Tank Corps were honorific redesignations of existing line tank corps.

Guards Tank Corps	Original Line Corps	Year Redesignated
1	26	1942
2	24	1942
3	7	1943
4	17	1943
5	4	1943
6	12	1943
7	15	1943
8	2	1943
9	3	1944
10	30	1943
11	6	1943
12	16	1943

Guards Mechanized Corps

Guards Mechanised Corps were created by redesignating existing line corps or by amalgamating smaller units.

Guards Mech Corps	Original Corps	Year Formed	How formed Redesignated	Amalgamated
1	—	1942	✓	—
2	—	1942	✓	—
3	4	1942	—	✓
4	13 Tk.	1943	—	✓
5	6	1943	—	✓
6	—	1943	✓	—
7	2	1943	—	✓
8	3	1943	—	✓
9	—	1944	✓	—

Soviet Line Tanks Corps

Tank Corps	Year Formed	Year Destroyed	Year* Reformed	IF REDESIGNATED Year	New Designation†	Year Original Reformed
1	1942	—	—	—	—	—
2	1942	—	—	1943	8 Gds. Tk. Corps	—
3	1942	—	—	1944	9 Gds. Tk. Corps	—
4	1942	—	—	1943	5 Gds. Tk. Corps	1943
5	1940	—	—	1942	5 Mech. Corps	1942
6	1942	—	—	1943	11 Gds. Tk. Corps	1943
7	1942	—	—	1943	3 Gds. Tk. Corps	1943
8	1942	—	—	—	—	—
9	1942	—	—	—	—	—
10	1942	—	—	—	—	—
11	1942	—	—	—	—	—
12	1942	—	—	1943	6 Gds. Tk. Corps	—
13	1942	—	—	1943	4 Gds. Mech. Corps	1943
14	1942	1942	1942	1942	6 Mech. Corps	—
15	1942	—	—	1943	7 Gds. Tk. Corps	—
16	1942	—	—	1943	12 Gds. Tk. Corps	—
17	1942	—	—	1943	4 Gds. Tk. Corps	1943
18	1942	—	—	—	—	—
19	1942	—	—	—	—	—
20	1942	—	—	—	—	—
21	1942	1942	—	—	—	—
22	1942	—	—	—	—	—
23	1942	—	—	—	—	—
24	1942	—	—	1942	2 Gds. Tk. Corps	1943
25	1942	—	—	—	—	—
26	1942	—	—	1942	1 Gds. Tk. Corps	1942
27	1942	—	—	—	—	—
28	1942	—	—	1942	4 Mech. Corps	1942
29	1943	—	—	—	—	—
30	1943	—	—	1943	10 Gds. Tk. Corps	1943
31	1943	—	—	—	—	—

* If not redesignated. † Fate of redesignated unit is given in appropriate table.

Separate Tank Battalion (November 1941)

	Officers	NCOs	Other ranks	Equipment
Battalion Headquarters	14	5	4	1 T-34, 2 m/c, 1 truck
Heavy Tank Company	7	19	0	5 KV tanks
Medium Tank Company	13	30	0	10 T-34 tanks
Two Light Tank Companies, each	7	16	0	10 T-40 or T-60 tanks
Trains elements	5	12	47	1 m/c, 1 car, 22 cargo trucks, 6 shop trucks, 4 tractors

Tank Division (June 1941)

Division HQ
Signal Battalion
Reconnaissance Battalion
  Armoured Car Co (15 Arm Cars)
  Light Tank Co (17 T-40)
  Motorcycle Rifle Co (12 LMG, 3x5cm (1.97in) Mort)
Two Tank Regiments, each
  Regiment HQ (1 T-34, 3 AAMG)
  Reconnaissance Co (13 Arm Cars)
  Heavy Tank Battalion
    Battalion HQ (1 KV, 3 Arm Cars)
    Three Cos, each (10 KV)
  Two Medium Battalions, each
    Battalion HQ (1 T-34, 3 Arm Cars)
    Three Cos, each (17 T-34)
  Flamethrower Battalion
    Battalion HQ (1 T-26, 3 Arm Cars)
    Three Cos, each (3 T-26, 9xflamethrower T-26)
  Maintenance Company
  Supply Company
Motorized Infantry Regiment
Artillery Regiment
  Regiment HQ (1 KV tank, 3 AAMG)
  Light Field Howitzer Battalion
    Three Batteries, each (2 LMG, 4x122mm (4.8in) How)
  Heavy Field Howitzer Battalion
    Three Batteries, each (2 LMG, 4x152mm (6in) How)
Anti-Aircraft Battalion
  Three Light Batteries, each (4x37mm (1.46in) AA)
Pioneer Battalion

Tank Brigade (December 1941)

	Men	Main Weapons
Brigade Headquarters	22	
Headquarters Company	170	2 light machine guns
Two Tank Battalions, each		
Battalion HQ	20	
Light Tank Company	17	8 T-60
Medium Tank Company	43	10 T-34
Heavy Tank Company	27	5 KV
Trains Platoon	40	
Motorized Rifle Battalion Battalion HQ	407	
Two Rifle Companies, each	108	9 light machine guns, 2 machine guns, 3 anti-tank rifles
Submachine Gun Company	79	
Mortar Company	42	6 x 82mm (3.23in)
Trains		
Anti-Aircraft Battery	47	3 heavy machine guns, 4 x 37mm (1.46in)
Trains & Medical	206	

Tank Brigade (July 1942)

	Men	Main Weapons
Brigade HQ & Company	147	1 T-34
Medium Tank Battalion	151	
Battalion HQ & Platoon	24	1 T-34
Three Medium Tank Companies, each	44	10 T-34
Supply & Trains Group	39	
Light Tank Battalion	146	
Battalion HQ & Platoon		1 T-60/70
Two Light Tank Companies, each		10 T-60/70
Supply & Trains Group		
Motorized Rifle Battalion	403	
Battalion HQ & Platoon		3 armoured cars
Two Rifle Companies, each	112	9 light machine gun, 2 machine gun, 3 anti-tank rifle
Submachine Gun Company	79	
Mortar Company	43	6 x 82mm (3.23in)
Trains Company		
Anti-Tank Battery	52	4 x 76mm (3in)
Trains Company	101	
Medical Platoon		

Tank Brigade (November 1943)

	Brigade Headquarters	Headquarters Company	Three Tank Battalions, each	Motorised Submachine Battalion	Anti-Air Machine Gun Company	Trains Company	Medical Platoon
Trucks	1	10	12	30	9	58	2
Field Cars	—	—	1	—	—	1	—
Motorcycles	3	9	—	—	—	—	—
Medium Tanks	2	—	21	—	—	—	—
Armored Cars	—	3	—	—	—	—	—
45mm (1.77in) AT Guns	—	—	—	4	—	—	—
82mm (3.23in) Mortars	—	—	—	6	—	—	—
AT Rifles	—	—	—	18	—	—	—
Heavy MGs	—	—	—	—	9	—	—
Medium MGs	—	—	—	4	—	—	—
Light MGs	—	4	—	18	—	—	—
Rifles & Carbines	8	97	43	50	37	113	14
Submachine Guns	—	41	30	280	1	10	—
Personnel	54	164	148	507	48	123	14

Tank Corps Authorized Strength 1942–45

		April 42	January 43	January 44	May 45
Personnel		5,603	7,853	12,010	11,788
Armour	T-60 Light	40	—	—	—
	T-70 Light	—	70	—	—
	T-34 Medium	40	98	208	207
	KV Heavy	20	—	1	—
	SU-76	—	—	21	21
	SU-85	—	—	16	21
	SU-152/ISU-152	—	—	12	21
Guns & Mortars	82mm (3.22in) Mortars	42	48	52	52
	120mm (4.72in) Mortars	4	4	42	42
	45mm (1.77in) AT Guns	12	12	12	12
	57mm (2.24in) AT Guns	—	—	16	16
	37mm (1.45in) AA Guns	20	2	18	16
	76mm (3in) Guns	20	24	12	36
	M-13 Rocket Launchers	—	8	8	8

Tank Corps (January 1945)

Corps Headquarters	32
Signal Battalion	253
Motorcycle Battalion	451
Three Tank Brigades, each	1,362
Motorized Rifle brigade	3,222
Heavy Assault Gun Regiment (SU-152)	374
Assault Gun Regiment (SU-85/100)	318
Light Assault Gun Regiment (SU-76)	225
Light Artillery Regiment	625
Rocket Launcher Battalion	203
Mortar Regiment	596
Anti-Aircraft Regiment	397
Pioneer Battalion	455
Trains elements	298

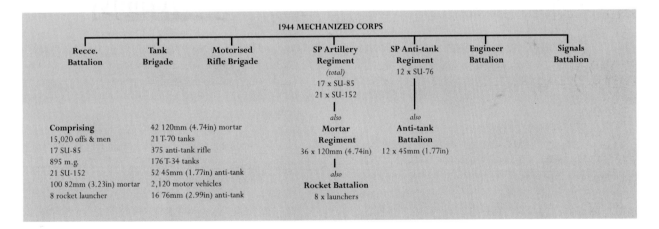

1944 MECHANIZED CORPS

Recce. Battalion — Tank Brigade — Motorised Rifle Brigade — SP Artillery Regiment *(total)* 17 x SU-85 21 x SU-152 — SP Anti-tank Regiment 12 x SU-76 — Engineer Battalion — Signals Battalion

also Mortar Regiment 36 x 120mm (4.74in) *also* Rocket Battalion 8 x launchers

also Anti-tank Battalion 12 x 45mm (1.77in)

Comprising
15,020 offs & men
17 SU-85
895 m.g.
21 SU-152
100 82mm (3.23in) mortar
8 rocket launcher

42 120mm (4.74in) mortar
21 T-70 tanks
375 anti-tank rifle
176 T-34 tanks
52 45mm (1.77in) anti-tank
2,120 motor vehicles
16 76mm (2.99in) anti-tank

PICTURE CREDITS

Aerospace: 6-7, 42, 44, 46, 47, 53 (b), 69, 111, 149, 160. **Amber Books:** 148 (b), 153 (t), 154 (t). **Ian V. Hogg:** 8, 11, 18, 65, 93, 116, 117, 142, 146, 147, 151. **Novosti:** 14, 22-23, 24, 31, 35, 82, 85, 86, 94, 95, 110, 122, 137, 152. **Popperfoto:** 27, 58. **Richard Stickland:** 17, 20, 38 (b), 62, 67, 68, 73, 77, 100, 113, 124, 159. **Tank Museum, Bovington**: 15, 21, 81, 112, 114, 121, 139, 158. **TRH Pictures:** front cover, endpapers, 9, 25, 28 (t), 29, 30, 36 (both), 38 (t), 40-41, 50, 54 (t), 55, 59, 60-61, 64, 72, 79, 92, 97, 101, 103, 104, 106-107, 108, 115, 118, 120, 123, 125, 130, 131, 143, 153 (b), 156-157, 161, 162, 163, 164, 165, 166, 167, 168, back cover. **Ukrainian Central State Archive**: 26, 28 (b), 32, 33, 34, 37, 39, 56, 57, 74-75, 78, 80, 83, 84, 87, 88, 89, 90, 91, 96, 99, 105, 126-127, 128, 132, 134, 136, 140, 141, 144-145, 148 (t), 155.

Illustrations by Steve Seymour

INDEX

Page numbers in **bold** indicate captions

A

Amtorg Trading Company 67, 68
Anglo–Soviet Trade Treaty (1922) 15
antitank guns **36**
armoured forces, origins 9–11
armoured trains 9, 10
assault guns
    ISU-152 **127**
    StuG III Ausf.B bis D SdKfz 142 **145**
    SU-85 **91, 102, 103, 104**, 105
    SU-100 **104, 105**
Astrov, N.A. 52, 54
atomic bomb 164
Autumn offensive (1944) 163

B

Baranov, Major **80**
Battle of Kursk 57–8, 128, 129
Berlin 7–9, **29, 141**, 163
Bolshevik Factory 11, 12, 108
Bolshevik Party 9, 14
Britain, supply of armoured vehicles to USSR 145, 146
British units
    Royal Artillery **8**
    Royal Tank Regiment **18**
Brusilov, General 27

C

camouflage **26**
Central Artillery Design Bureau 138
Central Artillery Directorate (GAU) 87, 130
Christie, J.W. 19, 66–8
Christie suspension 49, 61, 66–7, 100–101, 148, 159
Chuikov, General V.I. 9
Civil War, Russian (1919–21) 9, 10, 158
Cold War **165**
collectivization 17
Commissariat for Tank Production (NKTP) 130
Crimea **30, 80**

D

DD (long range exploitation) tanks 30, 31
'Deep Battle' 14, 26–7, 39, 108, 159, 161, 163, 164, 166
    tactics for 27–30
    testing 33–4
'Deep Operations' 26, 30–32, 39
    testing 33–4
deep penetration armoured tactics 23
Defence Council of the Soviet of People's Commissars (SNAKE) 76, **77**, 79
defensive operations 32–3
desanti echelons 31
diesel engines 72
    T-34 100–102

Directorate of Armoured Forces (ABTU) 75, 112
Directorate of Mechanization and Motorization (UMM) 108
DPP (long range infantry support tanks) 29, 31, 107, 108

E

Eastern Front 129
Experimental Design Mechanical Section (OKMO) 108, 109, 119

F

Far East (1938–39)
    BT-7 tank in 70–71
    T-18 tank in 12–13
    T-26 tank in 46, 47
Fedorenko, General 36
Field Regulations
    (PU-29) 27, 108, 159
    (PU-36) 30
    (PU-44) 30
Firsov, A. 76
First Five Year Plan (1929–34) 16–18, 23, 108, 129
Five Year Plans 16
flamethrowers
    OT-26 48
    OT-130 48
    OT-133 48
Ford Motor Company 17–18
foreign tanks 145–55
    purchase of 18
Frunze, Marshal M.V. 25

G

German Army 24
German units
    1st SS *Leibstandarte Adolf Hitler* Panzergrenadier Division 58
    501st Heavy Panzer Regiment 141
    Grossdeutschland Panzergrenadier Division 131
    Panzer Division 28
Germany
    crossing of Soviet border 161
    and the Red Army 33–4
    Soviet–German cooperation 19–21
    T-18 tanks in 13
    tank development 20
Great Patriotic War *see* World War II
Grotte tank 108
Group of Soviet Forces in Germany (GSFG) 164–5
Gulf War (1991) 166

H

half-track vehicles 155
heavy tank regiments 39
heavy tanks 106–25
    initial designs 108–11
Independent Heavy Self-Propelled Artillery Regiments 136

industrialization 16–17, 41
international relations 14–15
Izhorskiy Factory 11

J

Japan 163–4

K

Kalinovsky, K.B. 27, 28
Katukov, Major-General M.E. 56–7
Khalepsky, General I.A. 18, 19, 44, 67, 68
Khalepsky, I.K. 159, 160
Kharkov 131, 168
Kharkov design team 76–7
KhPZ (factory) 112
Kiev 33, **34**
Kirov, S.M. 112
Konev, Marshal I.V. 8, 162, 163
Korea 164
Koshkin, M. 76, 78, 80
Kotin, Lieutenant-Colonel Zh. 112, 113, 133, 134, 137, 138, 140, 142
Kruhlev, N. 10
Kucherenko, N. 76
Kulik, G.I. 34, 87, 113, 119
Kursk 32, **151**, 161
    Battle of 57–8, 128, 129
    T-70 tanks in 57–8

L

late war tanks 126–43
leapfrogging 165
Lend-Lease tanks 146, 152
Lenin, Vladimir Ilyich **9**
Leningrad 133
light amphibious scout tanks 49–52
light tanks 41–59
    production 42–3
    reconnaisance 43
    of World War II 52–8

M

Main Defence Committee (GKO) 37, 52
Main Military Council 35, 76, 78
Malyshev, V.A. 142
Manchuria 163–4
Marxist Revolution 158
maskirovka 27
Mechanization of the Red Army (UMM) 44
Mechanized Artillery Bureau (BAS) 135
mechanized corps, formation 37
Mechanized Infantry Combat Vehicles (MICV) 167
medium tanks 61–73
modern tank programme 159–60
modern war theory 26
Morozov, A. 76
Moscow 161

N

NATO (North Atlantic Treaty Organisation) 164

NPP (infantry support) tanks 28, 29, 31, 107, 108

O

Operation
    Bagration 162–5
    Barbarossa 92, **111**, 128
    Desert Sabre 166
    Polkovodets Rumnyantsev 131
    Uranus **87**
'operational shock' 31

P

Panzerfaust antitank weapon 8
Pavlov, General D.G. 75–6, 160
Persia **38**
Petrograd 9
Pilsudski, Marshal 16
Ploesti oilfields 163
Poland 16, 137
Politburo **27**
Provisional Armoured Board 10
Provisional Field Regulations (1925) 15

R

radios **44**, **73**, 84–5, **92**, **110**, 159, **162**
Red Army 128
    2nd Tank Squadron 9
    31st Tank Brigade 58
    armoured forces, origins 9–11
    development 13–14
    and Germany 33–4
    Guards tank armies 7–8
    interwar years 23, 24, 25–6
Red Guards 9
Revolutionary Military Council 10, 12
Revolutionary War Council (RVS) 43
Rokossovsky, Marshal K.K. 133, 136, 163
    A Soldier's Duty 121
Rotmistrov, General P.A. 137
Russian Revolution 9
Russian units
    1st Byelorussian Front **134**
    2nd Byelorussian Front 8, 136
    Eighth Guards Army 9
    1st Guards Heavy Tank Breakthrough Regiment 139
    34th Guards Heavy Tank Breakthrough Regiment 139
    11th Guards Independent Heavy Tank Brigade 140
    20th Heavy Tank Brigade **114**
    72nd Independent Guards Tank Regiment 140
    71st Independent Tank Regiment 141
    infantry **33**
    11th and 45th Mechanized Corps 27
    Southern Front **32**
    tank armies, formation 37
    91st Tank Battalion 114
    Third Guards Tank Army, 1st Ukrainian Front **89**, **96**

1st Ukrainian Front 8, **127**, **134**, 137, 162
2nd Ukrainian Front 8
see also Red Army
Russo–Finnish War (1939–40) 33, 35, 114–16
    T-26 tank 46, 47–8

S

Scientific Test Institute of Tank Technology (NIB) 78
Seaton, Colonel Albert 24
self-propelled guns 129–37
    Elephant (German) 134, 140–41
    ISU-122 30, **134**, 135–6, **136**
        in action 136–7
    ISU-152 8, **28**, **29**, 30, **130**, **131**, **132**, **133**, 135–6
        in action 136–7
        Model 1944 **25**, **28**
    SG-122 133
    SO-122 168
    SO-152 168
    SU-2 129
    SU-76 **37**
    SU-76i 133
    SU-76M **57**, **59**
    SU-122 **128**, 130–32
        Model 1943 **129**
        variants 132
    SU-122/152 30
    SU-152 133–4, **134**
        Model 1944 **132**
Soviet High Command (STAVKA) 24
Soviet industrial evacuation 92–3
Soviet invasion plan 165–6
Soviet–German cooperation 19–21
Spanish Civil War 34, 62, 75, 160
    T-26 tanks in 46–8
Stalin, Josef 16, 17, **27**, 52, 56, 76, 164
    purges of the military 26, 34, 160–61
Stalingrad 161
Supreme Command Tank Reserve 159
suspension
    Christie system 49, 61, 66–7, 100–101, 148, 159
    M1928 system 19

T

tank armies, formation 37
tank crew **39**
tank destroyers
    SU-85 **102**, **104**, 105
    SU-100 **104**, **105**
tank forces, organization 1938–45 34–9
tank regiments, size 35
tanks
    A6E1 Medium III (British) **146**
    A-20 **76**, **77**
        prototypes 77–9
        wheel/track problem 76, 77
    A-30 76
    A-32 (T-32) 76

up armouring 79
BMP series 167–8
Bren Gun Carrier (British) 150
BT series 66, 159
BT-1 69
BT-2 69–70, **69**, **70**
    armament 69–70
    Model 1932 **68**
BT-5 fast tank **30**, 70, **71**, **72**, **73**
BT-5 (V) **61**
BT-7 fast tank 70–72, **73**
    in the Far East 70–71
    variants 71
BT-7M 72
BT-8 72
BT-IS 72
Christie M1928 (US) **66**
Christie M1930 (US) **67**
Churchill (British) 149–50
    Churchill III **151**
DD (long range action/exploitation) 30
DPP (long range infacntry support) 29
IS-1 30
    in combat 139
IS-2 8, **23**, **26**, 30, 139–40, **141**
    in action 140–41
IS-2M Model 1944 **141**
IS-3 142, **143**, 163
IS-85/1 137–9
KV-1 8, **24**, 30, **107**, **115**, **116**, **117**, **119**, 125
    armament 119
    in combat 121–23
    development 111–14
    Model 1942 **120**
    production line **119**
    strengths and weaknesses 116–19
KV-1-S 123–5
KV-1B **122**
KV-2 30, 119–21, **123**, **124**
    armament 120, **124**
    in combat 121–23
    production line **121**
KV-2A **124**, **125**
KV-12 134
KV-13 134
    prototype 138
KV-85 30, 137–9, **137**, **138**
    in combat 139
light amphibious scout tanks 49–52
light tanks of World War II 52–8
M2 Light Tank (US) 152
M3 series (US) 150–53
    Grant Light Tank (US) **153**
    Lee/Grant (US) **154**
    Stuart Light Tank (US) 152, **153**
M3A1 (US) 146
M3A1 (US) Stuart Light Tank **152**, **153**
M4 Sherman series (US) 153–4, **154**
    M4A2 Sherman 146
Mark V (British) 10, **11**, **12**
Matilda II infantry support tank (British) 147–8, **148**

Medium B Whippet (British) 10, **11**, **13**
medium tanks 61–73
Motor Vessel Type AM 11
MS series 63
    MS-1 (later T-16/18) 11–15
    MS-3 **16**, **17**
NPP (infantry support) 28, 29
Panther (German) 128–9
PT-1 amphibious tank 72–3
PzKpfw IV Ausf.F1 (German) **155**
Renault FT-17 (French) **7**, **8**, **10**
Royal Tiger (German) 135, 141
Russkiy-Renault/Russkiy-Reno (Light
    Tank M) **14,** 158
SMK **112**, **113**, **114**, 115
T-3 66, 67
T-10M **159**
T-12 medium tank **62**, **63**
T-16/18 11–15
T-18 12–13, **15**
    in the Far East 12–13
T-22 62–3
T-24 63
T-26 30, **36**, 43–6
    in action 46–8
    armament 45–6
    engineering vehicles 48
    in the Far East 46, 47
    late model 48
    turrets 45
    weaknesses 47–8
    T-26B-2 Model 1933 **44**
    T-26S Model 1939 **38**, **43**
    T-26TU Model 1931 **42**
T-27 tankette 18–19, **20**, 43
    T-27A Model 1932 tankette **21**
T-28 30, 64–8, **65**
    armament 64–5
    model 1934 **64**
    modifications 65
    T-28A **64**
T-32, prototype 78
T-33 50
T-34 19, 30, **32**, 75–105, **88**, 128
    armament **81**, 88–90, **96**, 98, 99
    chassis and suspension 81
    commander and loader 85–7
    diesel engines 100–102
    driver and controls 82–3
    early versions 80
    engine 91–2
    gunner/radio operator 84–5
    hexagonal turret 87–8
    hull and armour 81–2
    M1941 **75**
    Model 1941 102
    Model 1942 **84**, 102
    optical devices 86

production 93–4, 95–7
production levels 94–5
production line **79**
secondary armament 90–91
turret 85
upgrading 97–8
variants 98, 99–100
T-34/76 **39**
T-34/76B **31**, **78**, **80**, **82**
T-34/76C Model 1943 **84**
T-34/76D **34**, **83**, **85**, **87**, **89**, **90**, **92**
T-34/76E 102–3
T-34/76F 103
T-34/85 **8**, **35**, **86**, **93**, **94**, **95**, **96**, **97**,
    98–9, **98**, **101**
T-34/85/1 **99**, 103
T-35 30, **108**, 109–11, **111**
    Model 1938 **109**, **110**
T-37 amphibious tank 19, 50–51
    Model 1934 **45**, **46**
T-37(V) **47**
T-38 amphibious tank 51
    Model 1937 **48**
T-40 amphibious tank, Model 1940 **49**
T-40 amphibius tank 51–2
T-41 50
T-44 **100**, **101**, 103–5
T-46 **38**, 49, **51**
T-50 49, **52**
T-54 168
T-54/55 **161**, **163**, **164**, **165**
T-55 **157**, 168
T-60 52–4
    in action 56–8
    armament 54
    Model 1942 **53**
    T-60A light tank **53**
T-62 **160**, **162**, 168
T-64 **166**
T-70 **50**, 54–6, **54**, **56**, **58**
    in action 56–8
    armament 55
    Model 1942 **54**
    weaknesses 55–6
    T-70A Model 1942 **55**
T-72 168
T-74 Main Battle Tank (MBT) **167**
T-80 56
T-90 168
T-100 115
    prototype 113
Tetrach light tank (British) 148–9, **149**,
    150
TG-1 (T-22) 108
TG-5/T-42 108
Tiger (German) 129, 131, 132
Vickers Carden-Loyd (VCL) Mk VI
    tankette (British) 18–19, **18**, **19**

Vickers Medium Mk II (British) **146**
Vickers-Armstrong Valentine (British)
    146–7, **147**
Tarshinov, M. 76
Technical Bureau for Tank Study 11
tracks **34**
Treaty of Rappallo (1924) 15
Triandafillov, Lieutenant-General V.K. 26
    'Fundamentals of the Deep Operations'
    30
    The Nature of Operations of Modern Armies
    27, 158
Trotsky, Leon 10, 14, 16
Troyanov, L. 134
24-hour battle 166–8

U
underwater crossings **101**
USA, supply of armoured vehicles to USSR
    145, 146

V
Vasihev, P. 76
Vasilevsky, A.M. 142
Vatutin, General N.F. 131, 133, 162
Vickers-Armstrong 44
Vietnam 164
Vistula river 137, 141
Voroshilov, Marshal K. 113, **116**, 140

W
War Industry Main Directorate 11
'War Scare' 16
Warsaw Pact 164–5
White Motor Car Company 154–5
White Russians 9, 10, 15, 158
Winter offensive (1944) 162
Workers' amd Peasants' Red Army 9
World War I 13, 157
    Soviet analysis of battles 26–7
World War II 9, 43
    in 1943 127
    light tanks 52–8

Y
Yegorov, A., 'Provisional Instructions on the
    Organization of Deep Battle' 159

Z
Zhukov, Marshal G.K. **7**, 71, 142, 162, 163,
    164